Bee *that never leave a* Sting!

BY

DANIEL D. RODES

Bees That Never Leave a Sting

All Scripture references are from the
Authorized King James Version of the Bible.

All quotes and poems are written by Daniel D. Rodes

PUBLISHED BY:
Truth, Light & Life Ministries International
PO Box 70
Mount Crawford, VA 22841

ISBN 978-0-615-89013-5

Printed in the United States of America
for worldwide distribution

I lovingly dedicate this book:

In memory of my precious wife,
Esther Marie Hege Rodes (Wifie),
who faithfully stood by my side for over 50 years.
April 11, 1941-November 27, 2012

To all those who made this book possible.

Acknowledgements

I want to thank a special couple who has stood with my wife and I since the beginning of this ministry. They have been faithful through good times and hard times. I am forever grateful to Dale and Karen Burkholder for their help and support.

Thanks to those who have stood with me over the years and helped to make this ministry a success. We started as a small group reaching only a few people. Today, we are an international ministry reaching multitudes, even in the uttermost parts of the world.

I'm especially appreciative of Apostle Reuben Esh who works with me as overseer of our affiliate churches here in the USA.

I'd like to acknowledge my team of staff members who helped to compile this book. I want to thank each of them for what they contributed to it's completion.

Special thanks goes to Naomi Riehl and Cynthia Trissel for the many hours spent editing and designing this book. Also to Beth Martin for her help and support filling in wherever needed.

I have been publishing *Bees That Never Leave a Sting* in the Truth, Light & Life Quarterly for the past twelve years. When I completed 366, they were compiled into this devotional for you to experience every day throughout the year. The idea for these "bees" came from a book which was read to me as a child. In that book, the "bee" would buzz a warning when someone was tempted to do wrong. Those stories inspired me to write "bees" to encourage people to excel.

You have within you the power to be a burden or a burden bearer. You can make life bitter or sweet for yourselves and others. There are wonderful, exciting and pleasant things that can change a sad and unpleasant lifestyle. With the help of God, even marriages which seem to be hopeless, can be brought together.

In order to find the secret to a life of fulfillment and blessing, let's visit the hive of *Bees That Never Leave a Sting*. These wonderful bees can change a marriage, a family, a community, a church or even a nation; but best of all, You! Let's put these "bees" to practice. When you change, you can help change others.

As a pastor, church leader and church planter, I have learned if you do not experience daily moments with the Master—a devotion with your Maker—discouragement can weaken you and anxiety plague you. Without a lifestyle completely devoted to the Lord, your love will begin to languish. Your loyalty to the King of kings and Lord of lords will begin to diminish until you find yourself in the same condition as the Laodicean church: *"I know thy works, that thou art neither cold nor hot: I would thou wert cold or hot. So then because thou art lukewarm, and neither cold nor hot, I will spue thee out of my mouth. Because thou sayest, I am rich, and increased with goods, and have need of nothing; and knowest not that thou art wretched, and miserable, and poor, and blind, and naked"* (Revelation 3:15-17). When you have daily communion with your Heavenly Father—the Omnipotent, All-knowing, Almighty God—you will be strong in the Lord, regardless of the tests.

In this book, *Bees That Never Leave a Sting,* I want to encourage you to be more accountable to God, more loyal to His precepts and more enthused about serving Him. As you study this devotional each day, my prayer is that you will "bee" inspired to reach your highest potential and never be stung by the "bees" of failure, defeat and discouragement. If you heed to the warning of each of the "bees" in this book, they will never leave a painful sting!

Bee Able

How you analyze what you see sets the stage for victory or defeat. The Bible records a number of nations and kingdoms whom the Israelites were not able to drive out or destroy. Didn't the Lord promise them victory? Apparently, they did not listen to the buzz of "bee" able informing them they were capable of overthrowing the enemy. When Moses sent spies to search out the land, they returned with a negative report, *"And they told him, and said, We came unto the land whither thou sentest us, and surely it floweth with milk and honey, and this is the fruit of it. Nevertheless the people be strong that dwell in the land, and the cities are walled, and very great: and moreover we saw the children of Anak there"* (Numbers 13:27-28). Caleb's view of the enemy was different: *"And Caleb stilled the people before Moses, and said, Let us go up at once, and possess it; for we are well able to overcome it"* (Verse 30). He had confidence they would "bee" able to overcome the enemy. The other spies saw only defeat, *"But the men that went up with him said, We be not able to go up against the people; for they are stronger than we"* (Verse 31). If you see the giants, you will not have victory. But if you focus on the Lord, you will "bee" able to win.

You may hear someone say, "I was not able to resist temptation." As you read the following Bible verse, notice the conclusion: *"There hath no temptation taken you but such as is common to man: but God is faithful, who will not suffer you to be tempted above that ye are able; but will with the temptation also make a way to escape, that ye may be able to bear it"* (1Corinthians 10:13). You are promised an escape route that you may "bee" able to overcome all temptation. Temptation is real but so is victory.

Peter's faith was soaring high when he saw Jesus walking on the water: *"And in the fourth watch of the night Jesus went unto them, walking on the sea"* (Matthew 14:25). With great anticipation, he waited for the invitation, *"And he said, Come. And when Peter was come down out of the ship, he walked on the water, to go to Jesus"* (Matthew 14:29). That word *"come"* gave him courage to "bee" able to climb out of the boat onto the tempestuous waters. Peter confidently began walking toward Jesus until he focused on the boisterous wind surrounding him. His faith suddenly transformed to fear: *"But when he saw the wind boisterous, he was afraid"* (Matthew 14:30). What he saw at first, caused him to "bee" able to walk on water. What he saw next, caused him to sink. The wind was just as boisterous when he started to walk on water as it was when he began to sink. You will never "bee" able to reach your fullest potential when you're focused on fearful surroundings. If you keep your focus on Jesus, you will "bee" able to do *"...exceeding abundantly above all that we ask or think, according to the power that worketh in us"* (Ephesians 3:20).

"Faith is our ability to trust God with the unknown."

Bee Absolute

During my school days, the teaching was prevalent there is nothing absolute in education nor beliefs. However, as I studied the Bible, I found many things that were absolute. When something is absolute, it is not subject to change. It is not affected by conditions nor distorted by man's religious ideas, theology and traditions. Even in nature, some things are absolute such as gravity. If you were to doubt absolutes, you would be afraid to ride in an airplane.

Christianity is an absolute. In order to be a true child of God, there are certain absolutes you must know. The saving grace of the Lord Jesus Christ is the only way to receive redemption from your sins. The blood of Jesus is an absolute that will cleanse you from all sins, not 90% of them: *"If we confess our sins, he is faithful and just to forgive us our sins, and to cleanse us from all unrighteousness"* (I John 1:9).

God expects your marriage vows to "bee" absolute. Nothing should be able to separate you and your spouse. My wife and I had a joyful marriage which worked. We were married over 50 years before she passed away. Marriage can work day in and day out, every day. Chose to befriend this "bee." How wonderful it is to listen to "bee" absolute.

Bee Accountable

Accountability is integrity in action. It makes no excuses for missing the mark. When King David sinned, he was accountable for his behavior. He didn't blame anyone, but simply said, *"Against thee, thee only, have I sinned, and done this evil in thy sight"* (Psalm 51:4). This generation has lost the vision of "bee" accountable. Those who are accountable are not struggling with guilt and condemnation, nor are they blaming others for their problems. These people are valuable. They are dependable. They can be trusted. Those who choose to "bee" accountable are filled with expectation and great accomplishments.

You must "bee" accountable before God and man at home, in the work place, at church and among your friends. The Lord will hold you accountable for your behavior, decisions and failures. When you make a promise to someone, "bee" accountable to perform that promise. When you sign a contract, "bee" accountable to fulfill it. You are accountable to pay your rent and bills. Those who are accountable will have the blessing of the Lord resting upon them. Rise up and be what the Lord called you to be. "Bee" accountable.

"It is never wrong to do right and never right to do wrong."

Bee Accurate

Did you ever play the game of whispering in someone's ear and the next person repeated what they heard until it passed from one to the other around a circle? The original statement was usually distorted by the time it reached the last person. You should learn to "bee" accurate when quoting others. To "bee" accurate is to be honest and free from mistakes. When you speak, your words should "bee" accurate. When you repeat a story, there should be no shade of dishonesty or exaggeration. Sometimes, people think it is funny to speak an inaccurate statement, assuming others understand they are "just kidding." There have been times I was uncertain if they were telling the truth or not.

The Lord expects you to "bee" accurate in every area of your life. If you bought one dozen tomato plants from a greenhouse, how would you feel if you went home and found there were only ten? How do you think the Lord feels when you are not accurately quoting or interpreting His Word? II Peter 3:16 says that some people pervert the scriptures to their own destruction: *"They that are unlearned and unstable wrest, as they do also the other scriptures, unto their own destruction."* Christians should "bee" accurate. Christians must "bee" accurate. "Bee" accurate! This "bee" will never leave a painful sting.

Bee Acquainted

To "bee" acquainted with someone is to learn to know that person and become familiar with them. It is possible to be around a person for years and still not be fully acquainted with them. A husband and wife need to "bee" acquainted with each other. Your spouse may be suffering some kind of problem of which you are unaware. When you are acquainted with your spouse and have a close relationship, there is freedom to share frustrations, fears or temptations.

Parents need to learn to "bee" acquainted with their children. Many parents wish they had taken more time to become acquainted with their children after it was too late. A mother once spoke to me about her son who had committed suicide. She told me she had no knowledge that he had been suffering with depression. No doubt, if she would have had a closer mother-son relationship, she would have discerned something was wrong. You may not be aware of the struggles your children face unless you spend time with them and become acquainted with their needs.

You, also, need to "bee" acquainted with the Lord. You should know what He likes or dislikes in your life. A sincere love for the Lord is an asset in learning how to have *"the love of God...shed abroad in our hearts by the Holy Ghost which is given unto us"* (Romans 5:5). As you become more acquainted with the Lord, you will learn how to "bee" acquainted with those around you. This wonderful "bee" will help you avoid major problems you may face in the future. Let's "bee" acquainted. This "bee" will never leave a painful sting.

Bee Absolute

I t is important to "bee" active in the work of the Lord. People who choose to "bee" active greatly hinder the work of the ene-my. I believe people on the verge of a nervous breakdown could keep themselves from a lot of trouble if they would "bee" active in doing something for others. The Lord has pronounced a special blessing upon those in the ministry of helps. Notice the promise found in Mark 9:31: "*For whosoever shall give you a cup of water to drink in my name, because ye belong to Christ, verily I say unto you, he shall not lose his reward.*" Jesus promised that those who are actively serving others will not lose their reward.

You should "bee" active in praying for others and in reading the Word of God. In I Timothy 4:13, Paul writes to Timothy these words, "*Till I come, give attendance to reading, to exhortation, to doctrine.*" When you are active in reading, studying and meditating upon the Word of God, you will overcome many of the discourag-ing situations you face in life.

If you are struggling with a problem in your life, why not make a decision today to "bee" active? Learn to "bee" active in ministering to those in nursing homes or speaking uplifting words to those who have faced tragedy. You can "bee" active by giving a small gift or sending a letter of encouragement to cheer someone. Those who keep themselves busy are better able to come through hard times with a shout of victory. "Bee" active and notice how little time you have to think of your yourself and your problems. "Bee" active will never leave a painful sting.

Bee Addicted

M ost usually label addictions as harmful. They believe when a person is addicted to something, he has become a slave to it. But, there is one addiction mentioned in the Bible that everyone should desire: *"I beseech you, brethren, (ye know the house of Stephanas, that it is the firstfruits of Achaia, and that they have addicted themselves to the ministry of the saints)"* (I Corinthians 16:15). According to this verse, they chose to "bee" addicted to the ministry of the saints. Such an addiction to servanthood is indeed a lofty endeavor. It can change the way you think, the way you live and the way you treat others. If you were addicted to ministering to the needs of others, the world would indeed be a better place to live, wouldn't it?

You can become addicted to the ministry of the saints by looking for ways and means to help others. There are so many people in need. Elderly folks need someone to encourage them. The sick and afflicted often need someone to lift their spirits. People who are going through difficulties in life need someone to pray for them. As an overseer over a number of churches, I find people who seem to always be waiting for an opportunity to minister to my needs. Such people are very special to the Lord and to me. When you make a decision to minister to others, you will discover the work to be very rewarding and you will become addicted to the ministry of the saints. Then, "bee" addicted will not leave a painful sting.

Bee Adjusted

Over the years, I've discovered the need to "bee" adjusted in numerous areas of life. In travelling overseas and ministering to those from different cultures, I found the importance of learning to "bee" adjusted to their food, sleeping quarters and way of life. Whether you are moving into a new territory, making new friends or working for a new employer, you will need to make adjustments. If you learn to "bee" adjusted to your surroundings, you will soon find yourself cooperating peacefully with others. Paul said in Philippians 4:11 "*...I have learned, in whatsoever state I am, therewith to be content.*"

You must learn to "bee" adjusted in married life. Ephesians 5:21 instructs, "*Submitting yourselves one to another in the fear of God.*" Maybe you had different ideas before you were married, but if you choose to "bee" adjusted to the desires of your spouse, you can have a joyful and peaceful marriage.

Although the circumstances were far less than ideal, Joseph learned to "bee" adjusted when he was sold as a slave in Egypt. Because of his faithfulness, God rewarded him: "*And his master saw that the LORD was with him, and that the LORD made all that he did to prosper in his hand*" (Genesis 39:3). Learn to "bee" adjusted. In so doing, this "bee" will never leave a painful sting.

Bee Affectionate

To "bee" affectionate means to cherish, to be fond of, to be tender and loving. Life would be so different if everyone chose to "bee" affectionate. How beautiful marriages would be if husbands and wives would "bee" affectionate toward each other.

According to Romans 12:10, you are to *"be kindly affectioned one to another with brotherly love; in honour preferring one another."* You are to be gentle, kind and affectionate toward those with whom you live, work and attend church.

The Bible warns that some will be, *"...without natural affection, implacable, unmerciful"* (Romans 1:31). That is why you must listen to the buzz of "bee" affectionate. This "bee" is extremely important in the lives of true Believers. If this "bee" ever tires of reminding you to "bee" affectionate, you will suffer great loss.

"Love is not lust and lust is not love.
Love is of God; lust is of the devil."

Bee Afflicted

To "bee" afflicted is a painful experience not welcomed by the average person. Yet, in the moments of great affliction your faith can mount to new heights. The Psalmist understood the afflictions of the righteous, but he also knew the Lord was there to render aid in times of trouble. He said, *"Many are the afflictions of the righteous: but the LORD delivereth him out of them all"* (Psalm 34:19). In another Psalm, he explained how the Lord brought deliverance when the children of Israel were afflicted: *"Nevertheless he regarded their affliction, when he heard their cry"* (Psalm 106:44). The Lord heard their cry and led them through their afflictions. The Lord is always mindful of your afflictions and is ready to help you overcome. Take courage, my dear fellow Believer, His all-seeing eye is ever watching over His children.

Some teachers have explained that the Lord sends afflictions to draw you closer to Him. It is true, affliction may draw you closer to the Lord, but that is not the purpose for affliction. To "bee" afflicted proves who you are and what you are. It is normal for those who *"fight the good fight of faith..."* (I Timothy 6:12) to "bee" afflicted, but after the battle there is sweet peace and blessed assurance deep within the innermost being. You experience a realization of the promise found in Hebrews 13:5, *"I will never leave thee, nor forsake thee."* Consider Paul's testimony, *"I am exceeding joyful in all our tribulation"* (II Corinthians 7:4). Yes, afflictions will come, but if you are prepared to face them, they will be less difficult to overcome. Then, "bee" afflicted will not leave a painful sting.

Bee Aflame

To "bee" aflame is to be greatly excited. Keep that flame of hope burning within you, even when facing tests, temptations or difficulties. Paul was a prime example of what it means to "bee" aflame. That flame of zeal and power was burning brightly when he faced critical times in his life. He described all that happened to him as he sailed from nation to nation. He was faced with stormy seas and critical, false brethren. His enemies tried to stone him to death. He had many other hardships which tried to stop him, but that flame of zeal kept burning within him and he confidently declared, *"But none of these things move me, neither count I my life dear unto myself, so that I might finish my course with joy, and the ministry, which I have received of the Lord Jesus, to testify the gospel of the grace of God"* (Acts 20:24).

Abraham faced a time when his hope was tested to the limit. God had promised him a special son, yet years went by without a sign of this child who was to bring forth nations. Abraham was ninety-nine and his wife, Sarah, was nearly ninety, yet he remained aflame with the promise God had spoken to him. He refused to let fear and doubt rob him of the promised son. In Paul's epistle to the Romans, he explained Abraham's faith: *"Who against hope believed in hope, that he might become the father of many nations, according to that which was spoken. So shall thy seed be"* (Romans 4:18). Abraham kept that flame of hope burning day and night. He wouldn't let age nor time rob him of that hope. Because of his faith in God's promise, he was able to hold his beloved son in his arms.

You should "bee" aflame with the power of the Holy Spirit. There is work to be done that only the Holy Spirit can empower you to complete. You should be so aflame with soul winning enthusiasm that you are a witness of the saving grace of God to those around you at home, in the workplace and in the neighborhood. You should "bee" aflame with excitement about the life of Christ dwelling in you. "Bee" aflame because your name is written down in heaven. Children of God should "bee" aflame with the joy of the Lord and the leading of the Holy Spirit. Keep that which you hope to accomplish aflame within your very being. All of Heaven is on your side: "*Let the redeemed of the LORD say so, whom he hath redeemed from the hand of the enemy*" (Psalm 107:2). "Bee" aflame. This precious "bee" will do marvelous things for those who will listen to it's "get-with-it" buzz.

"It was only a little match that started the flame that kept the house warm all winter long."

Bee Afraid

It may seem strange to tell someone to "bee" afraid, but if Adam and Eve would have been afraid to disobey God in the Garden of Eden, Adam wouldn't have feared when the Lord called to him. Can't you see him trembling as he confessed, *"And he said, I heard thy voice in the garden, and I was afraid, because I was naked; and I hid myself"* (Genesis 3:10)? So many, today, seem to have lost the fear of God. If you were afraid to disobey God and His Word, you could be free from the wrong kind of fear that is unhealthy and dangerous.

You should "bee" afraid to violate the laws of the land. Romans 13:4 tells us, *"...But if thou do that which is evil, be afraid; for he beareth not the sword in vain: for he is the minister of God, a revenger to execute wrath upon him that doeth evil."* Husbands should "bee" afraid to mistreat their wives because the Bible says, *"Husbands, love your wives, and be not bitter against them"* (Colossians 3:19). Wives should "bee" afraid to disobey God's instructions: *"Wives, submit yourselves unto your own husbands, as unto the Lord"* (Ephesians 5:22). Children should "bee" afraid to disobey their parents because they are given both a command and a promise in Ephesians 6:1-3: *"Children, obey your parents in the Lord: for this is right. Honour thy father and mother; (which is the first commandment with promise;) That it may be well with thee, and thou mayest live long on the earth."* If you would learn to properly listen to "bee" afraid, this "bee" would not leave a painful sting.

"Bee afraid to bee afraid."

Bee Against

There are certain things you should "bee" against. Sometimes things happen or plans are made that you know would not please your Heavenly Father. You should "bee" against these plans. I once knew of a Christian school whose name referred to God. Some Christians moved to rename the school after an individual who had donated financial support. Although some were against it, the name was changed. Over the years, the school began to lose support and was closed.

You should "bee" against plans made in our nation knowing they are not in accordance with God's Word. Many years ago, this nation was founded on righteous principles and national leaders honored God. Today, however, God is often left out of the plans.

There are many beliefs taught in schools today that you should "bee" against. Students are being taught how to live immorally and to believe in Evolution. Teachers are leading them away from Scriptural knowledge. You should "bee" against allowing Atheists to teach your children in school.

Your heart should be so close to God, you are against anything that would grieve Him: *"The fear of the LORD is to hate evil: pride, and arrogancy, and the evil way, and the froward mouth, do I hate"* (Proverbs 8:13). When you choose to "bee" against things that are unscriptural, this "bee" will not leave a painful sting.

Bee Agreeable

S ome people become disturbed when things don't work out the way they planned. They blame and accuse others. If they would learn to "bee" agreeable, situations would appear different.

An agreeable person is pleasant, friendly and likeable. Amos 3:3 asks the question, *"Can two walk together, except they be agreed?"* You may not always understand what another person is pursuing, but that should not be a cause for strife. You can learn how to "bee" agreeable, even if you think they are wrong. If you work with others in an agreeable manner, they may even recognize their mistakes and make changes. Matthew 5:25 warns, *"Agree with thine adversary quickly, whiles thou art in the way with him; lest at any time the adversary deliver thee to the judge, and the judge deliver thee to the officer, and thou be cast into prison."*

Marriage is much more precious when a husband and wife learn to work together in an agreeable manner. Life becomes more pleasant. Esther and I were married for over 50 years. We both had to make adjustments, but through experience and correction, we learned to "bee" agreeable.

There is a promise given in Matthew 18:19 for those who choose to "bee" agreeable: *"Again I say unto you, That if two of you shall agree on earth as touching any thing that they shall ask, it shall be done for them of my Father which is in heaven."* This "bee" has been buzzing around for years, trying to advise people to agree. Surely, "bee" agreeable will never leave a painful sting.

Bee Alert

It is extremely important to "bee" alert. There are times when the Lord may warn you of impending danger that can be avoided if you are alert. Many years ago, I was walking on a path near the river, when I felt a signal to "bee" alert for danger. I stopped immediately and scanned the area ahead. Seeing nothing, I threw a stick in front of me. A very poisonous snake struck the stick. If I had not listened to "bee" alert, I could have been bitten.

We are now living in the time prophesied in the Scriptures: "*This know also, that in the last days perilous times shall come*" (II Timothy 3:1). These are days of great danger and deception. You need to "bee" alert to what is taking place. "*For there shall arise false Christs, and false prophets, and shall shew great signs and wonders; insomuch that, if it were possible, they shall deceive the very elect*" (Matthew 24:24). You need to "bee" alert to what spirit is motivating these so-called "moves of the spirit." Did not the apostle John warn us, "*Beloved, believe not every spirit, but try the spirits whether they are of God: because many false prophets are gone out into the world*" (I John 4:1)? You need to "bee" alert and careful not to believe everything watchdogs and critics say. They may warn of danger, but they also criticize true men of God who do not agree with their traditional teaching or doctrines of men. What you hear and believe must be in agreement with the Word of God. "Bee" alert. This "bee" will never leave a painful sting.

Bee Alive

A fter the death and resurrection of the Lord Jesus Christ, the proclamation went throughout the land, "*Saying, The Lord is risen indeed, and hath appeared to Simon*" (Luke 24:34). Today, the message that Jesus is alive is still being joyfully declared. Because He is alive, you, too, can "bee" alive in Christ as declared in I Corinthians 15:22: "*For as in Adam all die, even so in Christ shall all be made alive.*" When you choose to "bee" alive in Him, your works are no longer dead, "*How much more shall the blood of Christ, who through the eternal Spirit offered himself without spot to God, purge your conscience from dead works to serve the living God*" (Hebrews 9:14). The blood of Jesus cleanses your mind from dead works so you can "bee" alive.

You cannot fully "bee" alive unless you recognize the death and resurrection of Jesus brings eternal life. In Revelation 1:18, Jesus declares, "*I am he that liveth, and was dead; and, behold, I am alive for evermore, Amen; and have the keys of hell and of death.*" He burst through the bars of death and triumphed over hell and the grave. When He is alive in you, there is triumph. You can shout the victory. You are more than a conqueror: "*Nay, in all these things we are more than conquerors through him that loved us*" (Romans 8:37). "Bee" alive, today, in the power of the resurrection. This "bee" will never leave a painful sting.

Bee Altruistic

To "bee" altruistic is to be unselfish and to be concerned about the welfare of others. Wouldn't this earth be a wonderful place to live if everyone chose to "bee" altruistic? Ephesians 4:32 instructs us to have this characteristic, "*And be ye kind one to another, tenderhearted, forgiving one another, even as God for Christ's sake hath forgiven you.*"

Over the years, I have seen people whose life radiated such willingness to help others and displayed such an unselfish character that you couldn't help but love them. Altruistic individuals are a blessing and benefit to any nation or people. Blessings are promised to those who choose to "bee" altruistic. Proverbs 11:25 says, "*The liberal soul shall be made fat: and he that watereth shall be watered also himself.*" Also, we find another promise in Proverbs 22:9, "*He that hath a bountiful eye shall be blessed; for he giveth of his bread to the poor.*"

What a beautiful characteristic it is to "bee" altruistic, to be there when someone needs you, to be helpful and caring to both young and old. Truly, "bee" altruistic will never leave a painful sting.

Bee Amazed

W e were once a mighty nation greatly blessed because we feared Almighty God. It's amazing how much this nation has deteriorated over the years. Yet, there are still some who choose to separate themselves from the evil of this generation.

You should "bee" amazed by the courage of those who teach the truth of God's Word in the midst of adversity and hostility. Some have experienced much rejection because they were unafraid to speak out against apostasy in the churches. They were not satisfied with the average run of Christianity nor the modern day interpretation of Scripture. In the midst of rejection, they found victory and became giants in the faith. That's something that should cause you to "bee" amazed.

You should "bee" amazed at the Lord's mercy, gentleness and love toward His children. The book of Lamentations expresses the newness of God's mercy every day: *"It is of the LORD'S mercies that we are not consumed, because his compassions fail not. They are new every morning: great is thy faithfulness"* (Lamentations 3:22-23). You should "bee" amazed by how forgiving the Lord has been when you make mistakes. When used in this manner, "bee" amazed will never leave a painful sting.

Bee Anchored

S ometimes in life you may be tossed around with decisions and question which direction to follow. You can easily become confused in your spiritual life, as well, if you are not anchored properly. The Bible tells us, *"Which hope we have as an anchor of the soul, both sure and stedfast, and which entereth into that within the veil"* (Hebrews 6:19). You will notice in this verse, hope is the anchor to the soul. When you lose hope, you lose your anchor. You are unsure of yourself. When you choose to "bee" anchored in the Word, you will be established in hope, security and faith.

The reward for choosing to "bee" anchored is explained in Romans 5:5: *"And hope maketh not ashamed; because the love of God is shed abroad in our hearts by the Holy Ghost which is given unto us."* When you choose to "bee" anchored in hope, you will not be ashamed. "Bee" anchored will never leave a painful sting.

" Help us to be rock solid on the Solid Rock."

Bee Angry

The Bible does not forbid us to "bee" angry, but it does direct how to handle anger: *"Be ye angry, and sin not: let not the sun go down upon your wrath"* (Ephesians 4:26). Unchecked anger will turn into wrath and wrath uncontrolled will turn into rage. Rage is dangerous, damaging and harmful. The message is being declared, don't let your anger linger or it can cause you great trouble.

To "bee" angry may be acceptable in some situations, but if that anger isn't handled correctly, it can, and usually does, result in much damage. Many are the wounds caused by an out of control fit of anger from a person who must have forgotten the warning given in Proverbs 29:22, *"An angry man stirreth up strife, and a furious man aboundeth in transgression."* You are duty-bound to keep a check on your anger. Temper tantrums show weakness. Someone has said, "You cannot get rid of a temper by losing it." How true!

The Bible records the anger of Jesus in Mark 3:5: *"And when he had looked round about on them with anger, being grieved for the hardness of their hearts, he saith unto the man, Stretch forth thine hand. And he stretched it out: and his hand was restored whole as the other."* Jesus' anger was kindled because of the people's critical attitude toward Him. There is a time to "bee" angry when you see people coming against the works of God.

If you choose to control your anger, you will be safe. Don't let the "bee" of rage and anger sting you and those around you. There is a "bee" angry that does not leave a painful sting.

Bee Anointed

The Bible tells us that Jesus was anointed with great power. Acts 10:38 explains, *"How God anointed Jesus of Nazareth with the Holy Ghost and with power: who went about doing good, and healing all that were oppressed of the devil; for God was with him."* Notice that statement, *"God was with him."* Without God's help, it is impossible to "bee" anointed.

Thank God, you can also "bee" anointed. According to the Scriptures, you can have the same anointing as Jesus: *"Now he which stablisheth us with you in Christ, and hath anointed us, is God"* (II Corinthians 1:21). The anointing is the power of the Holy Spirit working within you. Choose to "bee" anointed and be mightily used of God. But remember, this anointing is not for your benefit nor to take you on an ego trip. This precious anointing is given to you by God to be used cautiously, carefully and reverently.

Every pastor must "bee" anointed to operate successfully in his God -given position. Missionaries must "bee" anointed to fulfill their God-given task. In fact, every person in the work of the Lord, whether leader or layman, needs a certain measure of God's anointing power upon them. The word "Christ" in "Christian" means to be an anointed person. God wants you to "bee" anointed; so you should desire to walk in that anointing.

People often ask me, "How can I receive the anointing?" You must be open to receive the anointing. Learn to relax and allow the anointing from the Lord to come upon you. If you are seeking the anointing to exalt yourself, the Lord will not give it to you. According to the Bible, the real purpose of the anointing is to destroy the yokes that keep people in bondage: *"The yoke shall be destroyed because of the anointing"* (Isaiah 10:27). To "bee" anointed is not determined by feeling. Sometimes you may not even notice the anointing power is upon you. Nevertheless, "bee" anointed. That is God's plan for His children.

- 23 -

Bee Appointed

How would you like to "bee" appointed to do something for the Lord? In his letter to Timothy, Paul said, "*Whereunto I am appointed a preacher, and an apostle, and a teacher of the Gentiles*" (II Timothy 1:11). The Lord needed a man so He appointed Paul to fulfill this assignment. The Lord is always looking for dedicated, committed, dependable people He can appoint to do a job for Him.

When Jesus was on the earth, He couldn't personally preach everywhere He was needed. He appointed others to help Him: "*After these things the Lord appointed other seventy also, and sent them two and two before his face into every city and place, whither he himself would come*" (Luke 10:1). Wouldn't that have been an honorable position to be chosen and used of the Lord to go in places where He himself would have gone?

Judas Iscariot was one of the men chosen to be a personal assistant and an apostle of the Lamb. There were only twelve people in the world throughout the ages who could have received such an honorable rank. Judas did not understand his position because his heart was not right with God. The Bible records the sad ending of this man after he betrayed the Lord, "*And he cast down the pieces of silver in the temple, and departed, and went and hanged himself*" (Matthew 27:5).

Not everyone is appointed to preach or travel over land and sea with the Gospel, but everyone is appointed to be a soul winner. If you keep yourself useable, you may someday "bee" appointed to do something great for God. "Bee" appointed will never leave a painful sting.

Bee Appreciative

To "bee" appreciative is to feel or show gratitude and thankfulness. Has something great ever happened to you? Have you learned to "bee" appreciative toward the ones who were responsible to make that great thing happen? Are you appreciative for what the Lord has done for you? Psalm 105:1 says, *"O give thanks unto the LORD; call upon his name: make known his deeds among the people."*

Years ago, I counseled a couple whose marriage was nearing disaster. I discovered they had not learned how to appreciate each other nor God's plan for leadership. After an hour of talking with them, joy arose in their hearts and they began to understand how to "bee" appreciative for each other. In that short time, their lives were transformed. They walked out of my prayer room holding hands with smiles on their faces. When I talked with them later, they confirmed their lives were completely changed.

You should learn to "bee" appreciative toward those around you. "Bee" appreciative for the victories others have won that benefit your life. Learn to "bee" appreciative in every circumstance: *"In every thing give thanks: for this is the will of God in Christ Jesus concerning you"* (I Thessalonians 5:18). "Bee" appreciative. This "bee" will never leave a painful sting.

" Don't get caught with a bad thought."

Bee Approved

Many people seek to "bee" approved by others, but never consider seeking the approval of the Most High God. In the book of Acts, Jesus was identified as a man approved of God: *"Ye men of Israel, hear these words; Jesus of Nazareth, a man approved of God among you by miracles and wonders and signs, which God did by him in the midst of you, as ye yourselves also know"* (Acts 2:22). Why was He approved of God? Because He was faithful and trustworthy in every area of life.

The apostles were approved by God to be sent out to preach the Gospel: *"Therefore they that were scattered abroad went every where preaching the word"* (Acts 8:4). There were also men, like Stephen, who was neither a pastor nor church leader, but was mightily used of God. He was simply a table waiter who went beyond the normal to "bee" approved of God. It is recorded in Acts that his face shown as an angel's. Even as he was dying, the approval of God was evident upon his life. Stephen cried out, *"Behold, I see the heavens opened, and the Son of man standing on the right hand of God"* (Acts 7:56). I like to think Jesus was giving him a standing ovation as he entered the realms of glory. How wonderful to "bee" approved of God so much that He would stand and welcome you home.

As a minister of the Gospel, I must study to "bee" approved of God in my conduct, behavior and handling of the Word: *"Study to shew thyself approved unto God, a workman that needeth not to be ashamed, rightly dividing the word of truth"* (II Timothy 2:15). My obedience in these areas will indicate whether or not I have the approval of God. Let's help each other "bee" approved of God. That "bee" is important in each of our lives and will never leave a painful sting.

Bee Armed

The flesh wants attention. It desires to have its own way. It seeks for something to satisfy its craving for sin. Peter understood the weakness of the flesh, therefore he proclaimed, *"Forasmuch then as Christ hath suffered for us in the flesh, arm yourselves likewise with the same mind: for he that hath suffered in the flesh hath ceased from sin"* (I Peter 4:1).

We will face temptations as long as we live. That is why we all need to "bee" armed. Jesus warned us, *"When a strong man armed keepeth his palace, his good are in peace: But when a stronger than he shall come upon him, and overcome him, he taketh from him all his armour wherein he trusted, and divideth his spoils"* (Luke 11:21-22). When we let down our guards, we can be robbed of our armor.

You need to "bee" armed with the Word of God as Jesus was in the wilderness. The devil tried to deceive the Lord, but Jesus quickly placed the Sword of the Spirit in the face of the devil by saying, "It is written." You need that same courage to always "bee" armed with the Word.

"Bee" armed to protect yourself against resentment, envy, unforgiveness, fear or any other enemy that tries to attack you. The Bible commands, *"Put on the whole armour of God, that ye may be able to stand against the wiles of the devil"* (Ephesians 6:11). When you are fully armed, you are fully protected. "Bee" armed and face the future in victory!

Bee Attentive

Have you ever tried to talk to someone when they were not attentive to what you were saying? It is rather frustrating, especially when what you are telling them is very important for them to hear. Once, when my wife and I were on a tour, our guide explained something to us while others in the group were engaged in conversation. After awhile, someone asked a question concerning the very thing that had just been explained. This brought a few chuckles from the rest of the group. Why weren't those individuals listening? They may not have realized the importance of the information that was being given. Sometimes, those who are giving instructions become discouraged because people are not paying attention to what they are saying.

You need to learn to "bee" attentive when someone is talking to you. To "bee" attentive shows respect. This is very important in marriage. You need to "bee" attentive to what your spouse is saying. At work, you need to "bee" attentive when your employer or foreman is giving orders. Children need to "bee" attentive to their school teacher. "Bee" attentive when someone is giving a lecture or preaching a sermon. "Bee" attentive when the Word of God is being spoken or read. "Bee" attentive to the Spirit of the Lord leading us, *"For as many as are led by the Spirit of God, they are the sons of God"* (Romans 8:14). "Bee" attentive! This "bee" will not leave a painful sting.

Bee Authorized

In Matthew 21:23, Jesus was confronted by His adversaries. They questioned him, "*...By what authority doest thou these things? and who gave thee this authority?*" Although He did not answer them directly, we know He was authorized by the Heavenly Father to cast out devils, heal the sick, raise the dead and preach the Gospel of truth to those around Him. Luke 4:18 confirms this, "*The Spirit of the Lord is upon me, because he hath anointed me to preach the gospel to the poor; he hath sent me to heal the broken-hearted, to preach deliverance to the captives, and recovering of sight to the blind, to set at liberty them that are bruised.*" Jesus authorized His followers to do the same works, "*And as ye go, preach, saying, The kingdom of heaven is at hand. Heal the sick, cleanse the lepers, raise the dead, cast out devils: freely ye have received, freely give*" (Matthew 10:7-8).

The way to "bee" authorized is to meet God's qualifications. You must believe you have the authority and exercise that authority boldly and confidently. The enemy of the soul understands when you are weak in faith or display the wrong behavior. When this happens, you lose the authority God has given you.

Instead of focusing on how to "bee" authorized, have faith in the authority God has given you. No one will "bee" authorized who is living in strife and debate, has a slandering, railing tongue or is operating contrary to the Word. "Bee" authorized. It is good to be acquainted with this "bee."

Bee Available

If you really want to be blessed, "bee" available. When you hear the buzz of "bee" available, you are needed. "Bee" available to encourage a neighbor, a friend, a minister or someone who is sick, elderly or shut in. "Bee" available when the Lord needs a peacemaker. Jesus said a peacemaker is a blessed person, *"Blessed are the peacemakers: for they shall be called the children of God"* (Matthew 5:9).

Throughout the Scriptures, there are times when the Lord needed an intercessor. Today, He is still looking for those who will intercede for the work of the Kingdom, cry out for revival, plead for the lost and pray for those on the mission field. You should "bee" available to fulfill this important need.

The Lord may be seeking for an ambassador. Would you "bee" available? II Corinthians 5:20 says, *"Now then we are ambassadors for Christ."* We should always "bee" available to be soul winners, *"The fruit of the righteous is a tree of life; and he that winneth souls is wise"* (Proverbs 11:30). We all need to "bee" available to spread the Good News to someone's prodigal son. Wherever you are needed, listen to the gentle buzz of "bee" available. Surely this bee will never leave a painful sting!

Bee Awake

M any are the "giants" in the churches who are sleeping. The church is a mighty giant, but she seems to be asleep. Paul cries out, *"It is time to awake out of sleep"* (Romans 13:11). The message is urgent. It is time for war, time to awaken the mighty men of valor. The prophet Joel sent out a proclamation across the ages of time, *"Prepare war; wake up the mighty men, let all the men of war draw near"* (Joel 3:9). We must "bee" awake and stay awake. The enemies are closing in on us. The devil knows his time is short. He is attacking our homes, churches, schools and seminaries. Do as the Bible says, *"Awake unto righteousness"* (I Corinthians 15:34).

General Christendom has successfully reasoned away the power the church should have. They say it passed away with other generations and other times, leaving the average church member weak and powerless. This is reason enough to "bee" awake and ready for war. The battle must be won. You must win it. You can win it. Pray that the sleeping giant will be awakened. Hear the buzzing of "bee" awake, *"Awake thou that sleepest"* (Ephesians 5:14). New opportunities await. The Lord is ready to help you. Wake up the mighty men. Let's fight until the battle is won.

"Wake up, get up, start up, speak up, keep up, shut up, look up, go up & stay up."

Bee Aware

Many times in life we suffer because we are not aware of the consequences of carelessness. This is especially true in the area of words. The book of Proverbs warns us, *"The words of a talebearer are as wounds, and they go down into the innermost parts of the belly"* (Proverbs 26:22). The same writer also says, *"Pleasant words are as an honeycomb, sweet to the soul, and health to the bones"* (Proverbs 16:24). You need to "bee" aware that your words and actions should be pleasant, agreeable and not cause unnecessary pain.

You need to "bee" aware of dangers that are around, but don't be fearful that something bad will happen to you. "Bee" aware that certain books, magazines, TV shows and a host of other things could be dangerous to your spiritual health.

"Bee" aware of the lure of temptation. James said, *"But every man is tempted, when he is drawn away of his own lust, and enticed"* (James 1:14). One day, Jesus cautioned Peter: *"...Simon, Simon, behold, Satan hath desired to have you, that he may sift you as wheat"* (Luke 22:31). He wanted Peter to "bee" aware that he was pending an attack from satan. The encouraging conclusion to that statement says, *"But I have prayed for thee, that thy faith fail not"* (Verse 32).

It is of utmost importance that you "bee" aware that someone will be influenced by what you say or do. You can leave either a good or a bad influence. You need to "bee" aware that angry and unsanctified words can do damage, not only to others, but to yourself as well. When you heed the warning of "bee" aware to be careful or cautious, it is then that "bee" aware will not leave a painful sting.

Bee Balanced

A well balanced person will not be swayed to the right or to the left but will be steadfast and firm in his everyday walk with God. He knows what he believes and will stand for the right.

To "bee" balanced does not mean partly hot and partly cold. God hates lukewarmness. He said in Revelation 3:15-16, "*I know thy works, that thou art neither cold nor hot: I would thou wert cold or hot. So then because thou art lukewarm, and neither cold nor hot, I will spue thee out of my mouth.*"

You need to "bee" balanced in every area of you life. You need to "bee" balanced between the positive and the negative, between low and high emotions, between the spiritual and the secular. You need to "bee" balanced in your work lest you become a workaholic or lazy. You need to "bee" balanced in your Bible study. You cannot study only negative or positive scriptures or you will not "bee" balanced. I have known people who sat around reading the Bible for hours or carried a Bible everywhere they went, but most of these were on the verge of mental disorders. "Bee" balanced. This "bee" will never leave a painful sting!

"When you are positive, you go forward;
When you are negative, you stand still or go backward."

Bee Baptized

After receiving the Lord Jesus Christ as Savior, your life is incomplete without baptism. To "bee" baptized is a very important part of your Christian life. I have met people who never felt it necessary to "bee" baptized. They reasoned that the man on the cross wasn't baptized. When Jesus gave instruction to His disciples before His ascension back to the Father, He said, "*Go ye therefore, and teach all nations, baptizing them in the name of the Father, and of the Son, and of the Holy Ghost*" (Matthew 28:19). He not only told them to baptize, but explained how to "bee" baptized in a way that even a child could understand. Jesus obviously considered baptism important for He gave us an example as He was baptized in the Jordan River by John the Baptist.

Peter says that baptism is "*...the answer of a good conscience toward* God..." (I Peter 3:21). To "bee" baptized is an important outward sign that you are no longer a part of the world, but have chosen the new way of life. It is a symbol of death and resurrection. Paul mentions this in Romans 6:4: "*Therefore we are buried with him by baptism into death: that like as Christ was raised up from the dead by the glory of the Father, even so we also should walk in newness of life.*" Christianity is not complete without water baptism, so it is important to "bee" baptized.

Bee Beautiful

Y ou can choose to "bee" beautiful, even if you are not physically attractive. When life has lost its luster and you are losing your youthful beauty, you can still "bee" beautiful. The Lord God is not as interested in preserving a beautiful face as He is in preserving a beautiful life. I have met people who would not be identified as beautiful outwardly, but their joyful personality and gentle spirit far outweighed the outward lack of beauty: "*A merry heart maketh a cheerful countenance...*" (Proverbs 15:13).

It was foretold of Jesus, "*...there is no beauty that we should desire him*" (Isaiah 53:2). However, Jesus had a beautiful personality. Many times throughout the Gospels, His words are expressed in a beautiful, kind and tender manner.

When you worship and praise the Lord from the depth of your heart, I believe the Lord sees a beautiful countenance that may be hidden from the eyes of man. The Bible records that the prophet Daniel had an excellent spirit. An excellent spirit is beautiful in the eyes of God. When you seek to "bee" beautiful in your character this "bee" will never leave a painful sting.

" Changing your mind is more important than changing your circumstances."

Bee Blameless

There was an elderly man and his wife who lived in Judea. They wanted a baby. They must have prayed a number of times for a child, but older and older they grew without any sign of their prayer being answered. One day, an angel appeared to this man and said, *"Fear not, Zacharias: for thy prayer is heard; and thy wife Elisabeth shall bear thee a son, and thou shalt call his name John"* (Luke 1:13). One of the things that impresses me about this couple is that the Bible says, *"And they were both righteous before God, walking in all the commandments and ordinances of the Lord blameless"* (Luke 1:6).

To "bee" blameless means to be irreproachable and faultless. That's an excellent characteristic for each of us to possess. Philippians 2:14-15 tells us how to "bee" blameless: *"Do all things without murmurings and disputings: That ye may be blameless and harmless, the sons of God, without rebuke, in the midst of a crooked and perverse nation, among whom ye shine as lights in the world."* Wouldn't it be great if everyone who called themselves Christians would "bee" blameless and walk in all the ways of the Lord daily? Truly, "bee" blameless would never leave a painful sting.

Bee Blessed

Are you ready to "bee" blessed? The Lord wants His children to prosper and "bee" blessed so we can be a blessing to others. After my wife, Esther, and I became aware of this fact, the blessing of the Lord increased in our lives. Proverbs 10:22 says, *"The blessing of the LORD, it maketh rich, and he addeth no sorrow with it."* When you are aware that the Lord wants to bless His children, you will adjust your life to receive those blessings. Psalm 32:2 reveals, *"Blessed is the man unto whom the LORD imputeth not iniquity, and in whose spirit there is no guile."* The Lord cannot fully bless those whose mouths are full of guile, slander or negative talking. Psalm 112:1 says, *"Blessed is the man that feareth the LORD, that delighteth greatly in his commandments."* If you expect to "bee" blessed, you must learn to be obedient. In Psalm 1:1, the Lord reminds us that we cannot "bee" blessed while sitting in the seat of the scornful: *"Blessed is the man that walketh not in the counsel of the ungodly, nor standeth in the way of sinners, nor sitteth in the seat of the scornful."* Sometimes, blessings are not lost because of major problems, but because you have not adjusted the small things in your life.

It matters how you respond to the blessings you receive. There should be a heart of gratitude. The song, "Count Your Many Blessings" is still good advice to remember if you want to "bee" blessed. There are so many blessings awaiting the people of God. Don't miss out on "bee" blessed!

Bee Bold

B oldness should be part of a Christian's character. According to the Bible, *"the righteous are bold as a lion"* (Proverbs 28:1). Bold Christians are not afraid to face challenges in life with a winning attitude. They expect to win every battle they face. Pastors, today, need to "bee" bold when they proclaim the gospel of good news to a lost and dying world.

The Bible tells us to "bee" bold when we pray. *"Let us therefore come boldly unto the throne of grace, that we may obtain mercy, and find grace to help in time of need"* (Hebrews 4:16). The apostles exercised that boldness in prayer during a time when they were threatened and warned not to preach in the name of Jesus. Acts 4:29 records their prayer, *"grant unto thy servants, that with all boldness they may speak thy word...."* When they chose to "bee" bold in their prayers, *"...the place was shaken where they were assembled together; and they were all filled with the Holy Ghost, and they spake the word of God with boldness"* (Acts 4:31). What a way to pray! What a great way to live!

David displayed boldness when he saw a lion taking one of his father's sheep. He boldly slew the lion. Another time, when a bear attacked his father's sheep, David boldly (and as far as we know, bare handedly) killed that bear. Later, when he was facing Goliath, he boldly referred to this giant as an uncircumcised Philistine without a covenant. David chose to "bee" bold because he knew he had a covenant with God. You and I, as Christians, are covenant people. We should exercise authority and boldness (but not arrogance) concerning the promises God made for us. I believe if Christians would exercise boldness, there would be a shout of victory in the camp of God. Wouldn't you really like to be as bold as the champions in the Bible? "Bee" bold, it is a "bee" that doesn't leave a painful sting.

Bee Brave

Throughout life, we face circumstances and situations that can cause us to become fearful. You can choose to be fearful, weak and fail or rise up and "bee" brave. To "bee" brave is a choice. To "bee" brave is to be courageous and to face difficulties in life with a determination to succeed through every trial; nothing will stop you from doing right, acting right and being right.

Brave men and women have risen throughout history who refused to become discouraged and quit when facing difficult circumstances. They chose rather to be courageous, valiant and bold concerning their problems. The apostles chose to "bee" brave and fear God instead of man when they were commanded to stop teaching and preaching about Jesus Christ. Paul, in writing to the Galatians, encouraged them, *"Stand fast therefore in the liberty wherewith Christ hath made us free, and be not entangled again with the yoke of bondage"* (Galatians 5:1). Once again, we need brave men and women to rise up in this generation and let the world know there are still those who have faith, confidence and trust in the Lord our God. These brave men and women will fearlessly stand up for the truth, even in the midst of apostasy. If you are not brave, why not choose to "bee" brave, starting today?

"Defeat is for the loser, victory for the chooser."

Bee Broken

To "bee" broken is a beautiful characteristic that God honors. To "bee" broken is to humble one's self in the presence of the Lord: *"And whosoever shall fall on this stone shall be broken: but on whomsoever it shall fall, it will grind him to powder"* (Matthew 21:44). There are two choices given in this verse. One is to "bee" broken concerning your sins and human failures. The other is to suffer the judgment of God. Brokenness shows the Lord you are at the end of yourself and need His help. He extends His mercy and lovingkindness to such individuals. The Psalmist wrote, *"The LORD is nigh unto them that are of a broken heart; and saveth such as be of a contrite spirit"* (Psalm 34:18).

To "bee" broken does not show weakness but strength. It shows total dependence upon your merciful, loving Heavenly Father. The broken heart is free from pride and arrogance. It is willing to fall into the arms of a loving God as King David did when he sinned with Bathsheba. David lamented over his sinful behavior and cried out to the Lord from a broken heart: *"Against thee, thee only, have I sinned, and done this evil in thy sight"* (Psalm 51:4). The guilt of immorality caused him to "bee" broken and humbled. He later penned these powerful words, *"The sacrifices of God are a broken spirit: a broken and a contrite heart, O God, thou wilt not despise"* (Verse 17).

A broken and contrite spirit keeps you from becoming hardhearted. This precious character keeps your relationships with others sweet and loving. When you are broken, you lose the drive to have your own way. It is no longer difficult to pray, "Thy will be done." What a wonderful "bee" is "bee" broken! This is a "bee" that never leaves a painful sting.

Bee Brotherly

There is a lovely portion of scripture that could change the atmosphere of multitudes of families and churches if you would heed its teaching. It is found in Hebrews 13:1: "*Let brotherly love continue.*" These four life-changing words could do wonders. Paul testified of the Thessalonians: "*But as touching brotherly love ye need not that I write unto you: for ye yourselves are taught of God to love one another*" (I Thessalonians 4:9).

The dictionary defines brotherly as having a trait typical of brothers who are friendly, kind and helpful to each other. To "bee" brotherly is very important among family members, but this trait should also be exercised with your church families, work places and in your general, overall friendships. To "bee" brotherly is very important in unifying Believers. If you would learn to "bee" brotherly, there would be less hurt feelings, less marriage problems and less division. Romans 12:10 instructs us to "*Be kindly affectioned one to another with brotherly love; in honour preferring one another.*" Learn to "bee" brotherly. Truly this "bee" will never leave a painful sting.

"Forgiveness is the best remedy for hurts caused by others."

Bee Busy

D o you remember the old proverb that says, "Idleness is the devil's workshop?" I believe there are many who can testify to the truth of that statement. Many a fallen brother has lamented the fact that when he was idle he yielded to the weakness of the flesh. Paul explained to us what can happen in idle moments: *"And withal they learn to be idle, wandering about from house to house; and not only idle, but tattlers also and busybodies, speaking things which they ought not"* (I Timothy 5:13). Most Christians can testify that when they are busy, they are not meditating upon all the evil that has befallen them or what someone has said against them. If you choose to "bee" busy, it will keep you from a lot of trouble.

Busy people tend to become successful in all areas of life. To "bee" busy in the work of the Lord is very important. Jesus kept Himself busy doing good to those around Him. Acts 10:38 tells us, *"How God anointed Jesus of Nazareth with the Holy Ghost and with power: who went about doing good, and healing all that were oppressed of the devil; for God was with him."* Jesus not only gave His time, He gave Himself to minister to others. Ephesians 5:1 reminds us, *"Be ye therefore followers of God, as dear children."* The Greek definition for follower means "to be an imitator." You need to imitate Jesus and "bee" busy doing good and helping others. The hymn writer asked, "This is the way the Master went, should not the servant tread it still?"

Bee Calm

This generation is plagued with frustration, tension and anxiety. When ministering to people, I often tell them to relax. "Bee" calm. Take it easy. Nothing good can be accomplished in a state of frustration. It is when you are calm and quiet that you find the peace and tranquility the Lord desires to give, "*...in quietness and in confidence shall be your strength...*" (Isaiah 30:15). You can enter into His rest when you are calm. In sweet confidence you can let the Lord help you through your problems and troubles.

When Jesus and His disciples were tossed about by a storm on the sea of Galilee, Jesus remained calm and took control of the circumstances. He spoke to the problem, "*Peace be still.*" The results were amazing: *"...and there was a great calm"* (Mark 4:39). In times of stress, you need to be calm. Instead of meditating upon your problems, meditate upon the Lord. You wouldn't be as troubled when facing difficulties if you kept "bee" calm operating in your life.

"Relax—it's the secret to tranquility."

Bee Capable

To "bee" capable is to be able, talented, skilled and qualified. There are many people who do not accomplish all they are capable of doing. They may not know what they have within them. Not knowing what you are capable of doing can shortchange you of success in life. Many times, I have heard statements such as, "I can't do that," or, "That's beyond my brain." Why can't you learn to "bee" capable? You may have to develop in an area or increase your knowledge, but you should learn to "bee" capable.

Often, if you focus on a task, you can "bee" capable of accomplishing more than you thought. Declare with Paul, "*I can do all things through Christ which strengtheneth me.*" Ask the Lord to help you "bee" capable. Ephesians 3:20 says, "*Now unto him that is able to do exceeding abundantly above all that we ask or think, according to the power that worketh in us.*" You have the power of the Lord within you to "bee" capable. This "bee" will never leave a painful sting.

"If you say you can, you probably can; if you say you can't, you probably can't."

Bee Careful

It pays to "bee" careful. You could avoid a lot of problems in life if you would learn to "bee" careful. Years ago, as I picked up my shotgun to go hunting, my mother said, "'Bee' careful. Guns are dangerous." Mother was right. One day, I wasn't as careful as I should have been. That day I understood the pain of a bullet as I was shot in the arm. After that, I learned to "bee" careful around loaded guns.

You need to "bee" careful in every area of life. "Bee" careful to fulfill the promises you make. You need to "bee" careful of who you choose to associate with as well as your children. You need to "bee" careful how you treat others. Jesus said, *"And as ye would that men should do to you, do ye also to them likewise"* (Luke 6:31). We should "bee" careful how we judge our fellowman. After all, Jesus said, *"Judge not, that ye be not judged. For with what judgment ye judge, ye shall be judged..."* (Matthew 7:1-2). You need to "bee" careful of the words you speak and how you say them. Sometimes a person may be hurt by careless words. Proverbs warns us, *"Death and life are in the power of the tongue: and they that love it shall eat the fruit thereof"* (Proverbs 18:21).

"Bee" careful not to let anything sidetrack you from doing the will of God in your life and blessing others. If you learn to "bee" careful in every area of life, this beneficial "bee" can protect you from failure. Remember, "bee" careful will never leave a painful sting.

Bee Cautious

Y ou will not find the word "cautious" in the Bible, but there is reference to the need of caution. For example, according to II Corinthians 6:14, you need to "bee" cautious with your associates or those who are a part of your life: "*Be ye not unequally yoked to-gether with unbelievers: for what fellowship hath righteousness with unrighteousness? and what communion hath light with dark-ness?*" Their influence could draw you back into darkness instead of you bringing them into the light. "*Ye therefore, beloved, seeing ye know these things before, beware lest ye also, being led away with the error of the wicked, fall from your own stedfastness*" (II Peter 3:17).

"Bee" cautious of sharing things with those who are known to gos-sip and slander. They may appear interested in what you are saying, but Proverbs 20:19 warns: "*He that goeth about as a talebearer re-vealeth secrets: therefore meddle not with him that flattereth with his lips.*" Not everyone can keep a secret or even repeat what you have said accurately. Some of these people tend to exaggerate what was said and may cause you great grief.

"Bee" cautious when others want to debate regarding their own opinions and ideas of the Scripture. They have no desire to change their beliefs to match the Word of God. Instead, they twist the Word to confirm their traditions. This would be a good time to step away from the conversation and heed the warning of Titus 3:9: "*But avoid foolish questions, and genealogies, and contentions, and strivings about the law; for they are unprofitable and vain.*"

Our Heavenly Father is beholding each step you take. You need to "bee" cautious because others are also watching you and following your steps. "Bee" cautious is a good "bee" who will never leave a painful sting.

Bee Certain

Many people are uncertain regarding their future. What will happen to them after death? What rewards will they receive for helping others in this world? Some people are not certain; others don't care.

My dear reader, you need to "bee" certain concerning things that are important: "Bee" certain that your name is written in the book of life. "Bee" certain you are in the will of God and fulfilling His plan for your life. "Bee" certain of your eternal well being, not only for yourself, but also for your family. "Bee" certain when training your children. "Bee" certain your marriage has a firm foundation.

There is nothing more important than being certain you are filled with love, both for our Heavenly Father and for others: "*And thou shalt love the Lord thy God with all thy heart, and with all thy soul, and with all thy mind, and with all thy strength: this is the first commandment. And the second is like, namely this, Thou shalt love thy neighbour as thyself. There is none other commandment greater than these*" (Mark 12:30-31). When you choose to "bee" certain, this "bee" will not leave a painful sting.

"It is better to seek wisdom before trying to give it to others."

Bee Challenged

We all need to "bee" challenged at times to improve in certain areas of our lives. If David had not been challenged by Goliath's proud words, *"I defy the armies of Israel this day; give me a man, that we may fight together"* (I Samuel 17:10), he may have never known that the Lord could deliver Israel by his hand.

Gideon tried to defend his weakness when the Lord chose him to lead the army of Israel: *"And he [Gideon] said unto him, Oh my Lord, wherewith shall I save Israel? behold, my family is poor in Manasseh, and I am the least in my father's house"* (Judges 6:15). He had plenty of excuses, but God wouldn't accept any of them. It was only after the angel challenged him that Gideon stepped out as a mighty man of valor to accomplish what God called him to do. This is another proof that God can override your weaknesses and do great things through those who are committed to him. When Gideon took the challenge set before him, Midian was defeated and Israel won a great victory. Go ahead and "bee" challenged to excel. Overcome your weaknesses and reach your highest potential.

Bee Changed

A s long as we live, we will face changes in life. Some changes we make are good. Others are not. The Bible tells us how to make the right kind of changes. It says we "*are changed into the same image from glory to glory, even as by the Spirit of the Lord*" (II Corinthians 3:18).

An important change to make is in your thinking. Some people believe they must accept whatever situation they are facing. That is not always true. In fact, it is seldom true. Through the Lord Jesus Christ, your circumstance can "bee" changed. A troubled marriage can "bee" changed to a joyful marriage. You can "bee" changed from a failure to a success. Instead of being down, discouraged and perplexed, your countenance can "bee" changed to cheerfulness.

You have the power within to change your destiny. Those who choose Jesus Christ as Savior and Lord are changed from the kingdom of this world to the kingdom of God. People who are in religious bondage can "bee" changed into the liberty that comes through the Lord Jesus Christ. Even the backslider can "bee" changed. Most changes come about through decision. Once you have learned to make quality decisions in areas that need to "bee" changed, you can become successful. Why not let "bee" changed work in your life? When you choose to "bee" changed in the right way, this "bee" will never leave a painful sting.

Bee Cheerful

People who choose to "bee" cheerful are a blessing. They often give uplifting words and do their work joyfully. Even their actions are encouraging. Cheerfulness is contagious. When answering the telephone, it is good to be courteous and give a clear, cheerful "Hello." Someone who may be in a grumpy mood needs to hear from a cheerful person. Once, I walked into a business place where a man behind the desk obviously was not in the best humor. I tried to cheer him up and suddenly the man burst out, "Most customers get mad at me, but you are helping to encourage me."

Not only can cheerfulness affect those around us for good, it can also affect personal physical health. According to Proverbs 17:22, *"A merry heart doeth good like a medicine: but a broken spirit drieth the bones."* It is good to start every day with a dose of this valuable medicine: *"A merry heart maketh a cheerful countenance"* (Proverbs 15:13).

Cheerfulness is a choice. Years ago, an elderly gentleman was asked why he was always joyful and had such a cheerful personality. He said, "Every morning, I have a choice to be cheerful or discouraged and I choose cheerfulness." Another man chose to always greet his wife and family with a cheery smile when he came home from work. He testified, "Even if my wife had a hard day, she and the children look forward to me coming home. They know I will cheer them up." When you focus on yourself and choose to ponder on problems, you are open to an attack. Cheer will disappear and all will be drear. Cheer up! It can't be that bad. It is time to "bee" cheerful!

Bee Chosen

The Bible says, *"For many are called, but few are chosen"* (Matthew 22:14). To be called means to be appointed, but to "bee" chosen is to be selected. Why are so many called and yet only a few chosen? It is not always the big things that hinder. It may be something that seems insignificant that needs to be cleansed. Maybe you are not fully committed or dedicated to the work assigned to you. Maybe you are satisfied to give less than your best. Whatever it is, change and "bee" chosen.

God changed Paul and chose him to be an apostle. Paul was a man devoted to destroying Christianity and stamping out any remembrance of the Lord Jesus Christ. When Annanias was sent to pray for Paul, he protested, *"Lord, I have heard by many of this man, how much evil he hath done to thy saints at Jerusalem"* (Acts 9:13). Paul had a bad reputation among the Christians, *"But the Lord said unto him, Go thy way: for he is a chosen vessel unto me, to bear my name before the Gentiles, and kings, and the children of Israel"* (Acts 9:15). Notice the statement, *"he is a chosen vessel unto me."* The Lord chose Paul—not for what he was, but for what he would become. God was seeking for someone with an honest heart and holy zeal to do His work and saw that potential within Paul.

People who please the Lord by obeying His Word and following His will are chosen. God chose Abraham because He knew Abraham would direct his family and household after him. He chose Moses because He saw a man with a meek spirit who would be a great leader. He chose Joshua who stood firm in faith when the other ten spies were against him. He chose Gideon because He saw great valor hidden within him. The Lord is still looking for those who will fulfill the call on their lives. To "bee" chosen by God is a wonderful privilege. Ask the Lord to help you "bee" chosen. "Bee" chosen will never leave a painful sting.

Bee Classified

W hen someone steps out to be a success in life, whether in winning souls, establishing a new business or excelling above the average, it is not unusual for them to "bee" classified as fanatics or troublemakers. This shouldn't disturb us. Didn't Jesus say, "*...If they have persecuted me, they will also persecute you; if they have kept my saying, they will keep yours also*" (John 15:20)?

The disciples of Christ were classified by the crowd as people who impacted others, "*These that have turned the world upside down are come hither also*" (Acts 17:6). That is an interesting statement because the book of Psalms says, "*...the way of the wicked he turneth upside down*" (Psalm 146:9). The fact is, the disciples were trying to turn the upside down city upright.

You often hear people classify others as good leaders, great pastors, excellent managers or successful businessmen. They classify some as notable people or great soul winners. Others are classified as outstanding mothers or fathers. Even if you are classified by negative statements, always remember to stand for the right. Always do the right thing and avoid becoming offended. Endeavor to "bee" classified as someone who is not satisfied being less than the best. "Bee" classified is a good "bee." Listen to his gentle buzzing and you will not become offended.

Bee Clean

To "bee" clean and remain clean is a lofty desire. Without a clean heart, you cannot reach God. The Psalmist asked a very important question: "*Who shall ascend into the hill of the LORD? Or who shall stand in his holy place?*" Then he answers his own question: "*He that hath clean hands, and a pure heart*" (Psalm 24:3 -4). The Lord expects His children to have a clean heart. Your actions and motives need to "bee" clean. You need to "bee" clean in your thinking. You need a continual cleansing in the same way your clothes need to be continually washed. It may not be that you are willfully sinning, but you need to be continually cleansed from any influence from mingling with the world in your everyday life and business.

King David experienced the shame of an unclean heart after he committed sin with Bathsheba. He pled with God: "*Create in me a clean heart, O God; and renew a right spirit within me*" (Psalm 51:10). Only after you have been cleansed can you experience the beautiful things that Heaven has to offer. The writer of Proverbs asked the question, "*Who can say, I have made my heart clean, I am pure from my sin?*" (Proverbs 20:9). Ask the Lord to cleanse you from all unrighteousness. Only He can truly make you clean.

When Jesus was healing the sick, He met a leper: "*And, behold, there came a leper and worshipped him, saying, Lord, if thou wilt, thou canst make me clean.*" How did Jesus respond to this request? "*And Jesus put forth his hand, and touched him, saying, I will; be thou clean. And immediately his leprosy was cleansed*" (Matthew 8:2-3). Leprosy is always associated with an unclean spirit. Jesus saw that the leper desired to "bee" clean and He granted that request. How do you think the leper felt after he was clean? His leprosy was gone! He was no longer separated from God! The unclean spirit was gone! How clean he felt! Surely, "bee" clean will never leave a painful sting!

Bee Comforted

W e all face circumstances in life when we need to "bee" comforted. It may be due to unexpected tragedy, disappointment or the loss of a loved one. The Bible promises us that we will "bee" comforted in times of mourning, *"Blessed are they that mourn: for they shall be comforted"* (Matthew 5:4).

I knew a woman who faced extreme disappointments, one right after the other—her newborn died; her husband died prematurely due to a disease; two of her daughters were killed in a car accident and another daughter suffered serious head injuries in a sledding accident. Through all of this, the woman refused to allow grief to overcome her. Instead, she found comfort from the Lord. Miraculously, one of the tragedies reversed. The daughter injured in the sledding accident recovered. Although the doctors reported her brain would be permanently damaged, she was fully restored and later became a school teacher, then married and had her own family. What great comfort this brought for the woman.

Our Heavenly Father often uses His precious Word to bring comfort in time of need. Romans 15:4 declares, *"Whatsoever things were written aforetime were written for our learning, that we through patience and comfort of the scriptures might have hope."* If you would cleave to the Word of God, it would give you hope and triumph even in the midst of difficulty and grief. It is marvelous how you can "bee" comforted by His Word. Stay in tune with "bee" comforted for surely this "bee" will never leave a painful sting.

Bee Committed

To "bee" committed means to fulfill your responsibility and to do your best at home or at work. To "bee" committed is not to be wish-washy; one time you feel one way, next time another. True commitment is essential in the life of a Christian.

To "bee" committed as a Christian means you act and live like a Christian every day. Temptations do not change your commitment. You should "bee" committed to read and study the Word of God daily: *"This book of the law shall not depart out of thy mouth; but thou shalt meditate therein day and night, that thou mayest observe to do according to all that is written therein: for then thou shalt make thy way prosperous, and then thou shalt have good success"* (Joshua 1:8). Let nothing stop you.

A husband and wife need to "bee" committed to their marriage. The Bible says, *"Wives, submit yourselves unto your own husbands"* (Colossians 3:18). When a wife is committed to obey this verse, she will fulfill her God-given role. The next verse says, *"Husbands, love your wives"* (Verse 19). When a husband is committed to love his wife, nothing can change that decision. It is a commitment.

Make up your mind to "bee" committed to what God has called you to do. Refuse to take an alternative route. "Bee" committed to holiness. "Bee" committed to integrity and honesty. If you are totally committed, you will not feel the sting of the "bee" that stings the unfaithful.

Bee Compassionate

J esus was compassionate when He saw the sick and suffering. Matthew 9:36 says, *"But when he saw the multitudes, he was moved with compassion on them..."* (Matthew 9:36). Because of His compassion, many of the sick were healed. Lives were changed. People who were in bondage were set free. This attribute would bring considerable healing to our world if people only knew how to "bee" compassionate. When compassion is manifested in our homes and churches, the whole community is affected.

You need to learn the value of compassion and, also, teach it to your children. Jesus told the story of a man who fell among thieves. He explained how the Samaritan chose to "bee" compassionate toward this man he did not know: *"But a certain Samaritan, as he journeyed, came where he was: and when he saw him, he had compassion on him, And went to him, and bound up his wounds, pouring in oil and wine, and set him on his own beast, and brought him to an inn, and took care of him"* (Luke 10:33-34). As a Christian, you should develop this characteristic. Million of souls are in need of a Savior. Some are dying; others need encouragement. If you show compassion to the suffering, the Lord will show compassion to you. "Bee" compassionate. It's God's way.

Bee Complete

E veryone is affected by things that are incomplete. A beautiful building may be ever so gorgeous, but if it is incomplete, it doesn't display its full beauty. Most people enjoy seeing things that are finished or complete.

You need to "bee" complete as a Believer. You need to act like a Christian. You need to understand what it means to "bee" complete and fulfill God's will for your life. Many people live and die and never complete their mission in life. Paul, in writing to the Colossians, said, *"And ye are complete in him, which is the head of all principality and power"* (Colossians 2:10). According to this verse, there is supernatural power available through the Lord Jesus Christ when you are complete in Him. It should be your utmost desire to "bee" complete in Christ Jesus. That completeness would mean that you are totally delivered from the powers of darkness (not infallible, but victorious). When someone makes a mistake or falls into some kind of sin, they can repent and still choose to "bee" complete in Him. If you choose to "bee" complete in Him, it will keep you from becoming a failure. "Bee" complete will never leave a painful sting.

"Failure says, 'quit,' motivation replies, 'not yet.'"

Bee Complimentary

Y ou should program yourself to see the good in others, to give a compliment to someone who did a notable deed. Ephesians 4:29 says, *"Let no corrupt communication proceed out of your mouth, but that which is good to the use of edifying, that it may minister grace unto the hearers."* Sometimes families have a tendency to point out faults instead of giving a compliment when a family member does a good job. One young man said he never heard a compliment from his parents. Even when he excelled in school, his dad would tell him he would never amount to anything. Every family member needs to hear a compliment when they have gone the extra mile or done more than what was required. However, caution should be used not to excessively emphasize a compliment which promotes ego.

As a pastor, I look for the little things our people do as well as the more notable achievements. I often open our services by complimenting the people for getting to church on time. It is not always the big things that are worthy of a compliment. Little things can make a big difference. "Bee" complimentary and find something good to say about someone today.

Bee Concerned

I come from a family with five brothers and nine sisters. Our mother would often "bee" concerned about us. Would we make the right choices in life? Would we choose the right kind of friends and associates? Would we have good marriages? Would we serve the Lord and be faithful to the end? These are all legitimate concerns. The future for ourselves and our children is unknown. We should "bee" concerned about the future, but not worried or overly anxious.

As an overseer of numerous churches across America and overseas, I believe I can understand Paul's remarks to the Galatian church. *"My little children,"* he writes, *"of whom I travail in birth again until Christ be formed in you"* (Galatians 4:19). Any qualified leader has a legitimate reason to "bee" concerned for his people. After all, God does hold us accountable to train and teach them in the ways of the Lord. You should "bee" concerned, but don't allow that concern to become worry. "Bee" concerned is a good "bee" to have in your life.

"You had better worry about worry;
that stuff will kill you."

Bee Confident

A confident person expects to be successful in all he does. Every great man and woman who became a success, whether in the physical or spiritual realm, was confident. They understood that unless they had confidence in what they proceeded to do, they would fail. To "bee" confident does not mean to be arrogant or overly sure of one's self. However, we all need a certain measure of self-confidence or we wouldn't be able to do all that the Lord has called us to do. I like what Paul has to say in Philippians 1:14: *"And many of the brethren in the Lord, waxing confident by my bonds, are much more bold to speak the word without fear."* Paul's bold preaching stirred up confidence in other ministers.

Prayer without confidence will bring few results. When you have confidence in your prayers, you can come boldly and without fear before the Lord. *"Let us therefore come boldly unto the throne of grace, that we may obtain mercy, and find grace to help in time of need"* (Hebrews 4:16).

Many Christians do not have enough confidence in themselves to be victorious Christians. They excuse themselves by saying they are weak and unworthy. This is unscriptural and has brought defeat to many. Our God is great enough to help you through every trial, temptation, obstacle, situation and circumstance you face in life; therefore, "bee" confident.

Bee Confidential

Most people, if not all, need someone in whom to confide. They need someone they can trust with whom to share their problems. When someone is willing to pour out their heart to a friend, they are seeking help, not exposure. They trust that person. They expect such information to be kept confidential. Some fear to expose their problems lest it should be advertised and published among the critics. People should be able to trust you to "bee" confidential when they need to talk about an embarrassing situation that is confronting them. Such information should never be exposed to others. It is not their business. *"A talebearer revealeth secrets: but he that is of a faithful spirit concealeth the matter"* (Proverbs 11:13). Keep to yourself what others share with you.

Some people are tempted to use prayer as a method of exposing someone's faults or problems. They explain the person's problem and add, "I want you to pray for them." Sometimes it is best not to give much information when requesting prayer for someone. Too often, when someone repeats a confidential conversation to others, it is blown out of proportion. We all need to "bee" confidential. Then, this "bee" will never leave a painful sting!

"You can trust a man who trusts God."

Bee Congenial

To "bee" congenial means to be good natured and hospitable; a person who is easy to work with. Congenial people are usually pleasant, peaceful and easily entreated. Those who choose to "bee" congenial leave a great impression on others. They are appreciated and can be trusted. We all enjoy being around those who are congenial.

I have the privilege of working with pastors and church leaders who choose to "bee" congenial. The Bible describes the qualifications for men who will be leaders: "*A bishop then must be blameless, the husband of one wife, vigilant, sober, of good behaviour, given to hospitality, apt to teach; Not given to wine, no striker, not greedy of filthy lucre; but patient, not a brawler, not covetous*" (I Timothy 3:1 -3). The pastors and leaders I work with are exactly as Paul described to Timothy. They are congenial men who refuse to argue about anything, but will stand with me when I need them. They understand my desire and vision for our churches and are willing to help me accomplish the tasks of the ministry. They are ready to do the work necessary to bring people closer to the Lord. Choose to "bee" congenial. This is a beautiful "bee" that will never leave a painful sting.

Bee Considerate

As long as you are in this world, you will find people who will not totally agree with you. It is here that you must learn to "bee" considerate. To "bee" considerate is to be thoughtful and show regard toward the opinions, desires and feelings of others. Instead of getting into strife and demanding to have things done your way, submit as Philippians 2:3 says, "*...In lowliness of mind let each esteem other better than themselves.*" If you would esteem others better than yourself, it wouldn't be so difficult to "bee" considerate.

If everyone chose to "bee" considerate, our world would be transformed. A selfish, self-centered person is unhappy. Such people have not found the blessings that come when you choose to "bee" considerate. You could save yourself a lot of trouble if you learn to "bee" considerate. When you make plans that involve others, "bee" considerate as to how it will affect them. You should "bee" considerate when speaking. Sometimes, you may be unaware that your words are harmful. You should "bee" considerate of the influence you are leaving at your workplace. When you learn to "bee" considerate of others, it can improve your relationships. "Bee" considerate. This "bee" will never leave a painful sting!

Bee Consistent

To "bee" consistent is an important part of Christian life. To "bee" consistent means to be firm and to be the same, day after day. Unless you are consistent, you will not be stable. "Bee" consistent in your faith as a Christian. "Bee" consistent in what you believe. "Bee" consistent in your Bible study and prayer life. "Bee" consistent as a witness of the saving grace of our Lord Jesus Christ. The world needs to see Christians act like Christians, all day, every day.

You need to "bee" consistent in your relationship with the Lord and fellowman. You should "bee" consistent in quality work. As a parent, you need to "bee" consistent in training and teaching your children.

I once spoke with the owner of a certain food processing operation. He told me that when he started the operation he had to work hard to keep the flavor of his products consistent. He said, "You can't sell something that one time tastes one way and the next time tastes different." If it is that important for food to "bee" consistent, wouldn't it be more important for your personal life to "bee" consistent? If you are one time up and another time down, who can trust you?

Although it is important to "bee" consistent, consistency in a negative way can be harmful and destructive to you and others. If you consistently think lack, poverty and defeat, that is what you will have. You need to "bee" consistent in the positive. If you would learn to "bee" consistent with goals, visions and plans, you could excel to greater heights. "Bee" consistent. This "bee" will never leave a painful sting when you use it carefully.

Bee Contagious

I once heard a young man deliver an enthusiastic speech. After he finished, an elderly man walked up to him and said, "Young man, your enthusiasm is contagious." What a compliment! We all need to "bee" contagious in encouraging others, don't we? When you meet people who are discouraged or perplexed, give them words of encouragement. When you feel discouraged yourself, just remember to encourage others and it will help to encourage you.

Paul wrote to Titus, "*In all things shewing thyself a pattern of good works: in doctrine shewing uncorruptness, gravity, sincerity*" (Titus 2:7). He wanted Titus to have a lifestyle that was contagious to others around him. "Bee" contagious. Surely this "bee" will never leave a painful sting.

*"If you can't inspire yourself,
you will not inspire others."*

Bee Content

T he Bible tells us, *"But godliness with contentment is great gain"* (I Timothy 6:6). Contentment is not governed by circumstances. It is not determined by what you have or don't have. Contentment is a choice. It's a decision. This doesn't mean you are to "bee" content with less than God has for you. I don't think Paul was suggesting you should "bee" content with poverty or lack when he wrote, *"...I have learned, in whatsoever state I am, therewith to be content"* (Philippians 4:11). He describes what he learned, *"I know both how to be abased, and I know how to abound: every where and in all things I am instructed both to be full and to be hungry, both to abound and to suffer need"* (Philippians 4:12).

The true servant of the Lord is content with what the Lord has called him to do, but not content where he is spiritually. Certainly, Paul wasn't content to be a mediocre Christian. No, he could do without food or comfort, if necessary, and still be content; but when it came to serving the Lord, he had a non-stop attitude. Whatever your lot in life, learn to "bee" content. It is not always easy, but it is something you can learn.

"Find a place serene, where God himself is seen."

Bee Converted

As Jesus was nearing the end of His earthly ministry and transferring it to his disciples, He said to Peter, "*When thou art converted, strengthen thy brethren*" (Luke 22:32). The Lord was saying, "Peter, when you are turned around, establish your brethren." Although Peter had followed the Lord for a number of years and was a member of Jesus' team, he was not converted. There are those who have considered themselves Christians for years who have never been converted. It seems that there are some who slip into the back door of a church and mingle themselves among the people but have never had a true conversion. This has caused much disappointment in churches scattered across the world.

The Bible gives us direction on what it means to "bee" converted: "*Repent ye therefore, and be converted, that your sins may be blotted out, when the times of refreshing shall come from the presence of the Lord*" (Acts 3:19). What a wonderful promise; our sins will be blotted out. But what is the requirement? Repentance. That means to think differently or to change directions. It is when you repent and "bee" converted that your sins are forgiven and blotted out by the merits of the precious blood of our Lord Jesus Christ. You are separated from the world and brought into a beautiful relationship with the Lord. Your will is broken and you seek to accomplish the will of God in your life.

The Psalmist had a desire in his heart to see others converted when he wrote, "*Then will I teach transgressors thy ways; and sinners shall be converted unto thee*" (Psalm 51:13). When you are converted, you will desire to see others converted. Everyone needs to "bee" converted and learn to know the ways of the Lord.
"Bee" converted will never leave a painful sting.

Bee Cool

I f you are around some young people very long, you may hear them say, "'Bee' cool." What they mean by "'bee' cool" is certainly not what I mean. To "bee" cool is to refrain from being "hot-tempered" or burning with anger.

Years ago, a father was outraged by something his son did wrong. His face was red with anger. An elderly man who was watching the scene said, "Sir, why don't you go down to the spring and get a drink of cool water before you discipline your son?" In other words, he meant, "'Bee' cool. Calm down before disciplining your son."

You need to learn to "bee" cool and keep your anger under control. This is especially important in the life of men. It seems like they have more of a tendency to become disturbed. You need to "bee" cool when you feel like becoming frustrated, irritable or impatient. When you become enraged, you can hurt both yourself and others.

If you have a problem with your temper, let me suggest that you learn to be strong in the Lord instead of becoming outraged when something doesn't go your way. Sometime in life, we all get into hot water or run into circumstances that are difficult to handle. Learn a lesson from a tea bag. The longer a tea bag is in hot water, the stronger the tea becomes. Afterward, when it is cool, that tea can make a refreshing drink on a hot day. When you are in hot water, "bee" cool. If you learn to "bee" cool, you can be a blessing to others.

Bee Correct

To "bee" correct is to be right, accurate and truthful. You may remember taking exams when you were in school. Before you could pass the test, the answers needed to "bee" correct. You should follow that same example in life. Learn to "bee" correct in every area. "Bee" correct before judging others. "Bee" correct before you repeat a story about someone. I believe many conversations would be ended shortly if everyone were conscious of that very wonderful "bee." To "bee" correct helped many average men and women to be greatly used by God. The Lord could trust them because they made a decision to "bee" correct in their manner of life, in their speech and in the way they treated others.

When husbands and wives make a decision to "bee" correct in the way they behave and communicate with each other, their homes will be transformed. You may need to ask yourself, "Am I correct in the way I respond to my spouse, parents or siblings? Am I correct in the way I minister to my neighbors?" These questions are very important. If you are a pastor or teacher, ask yourself, "Do I preach the Word correctly?" It is essential to "bee" correct in your interpretation of the Bible. Too many are destroyed by the doctrines of man. The Bible warns,"....*they that are unlearned and unstable wrest, as they do also the other scriptures, unto their own destruction*" (II Peter 3:16). When you read the Bible, do you hear that precious "bee" warning you to "bee" correct? You need to "bee" correct in what you believe.

You need to "bee" correct in your path of life, "*Because strait is the gate, and narrow is the way, which leadeth unto life, and few there be that find it*" (Matthew 7:14). You only have one opportunity to pass through this life. Make sure you are correct in the way you live. What matters is not what your past has been but what your future will hold. Will you "bee" correct when you stand before Almighty God and are examined for how you responded to others or how you served them? "Bee" correct. This "bee" will never leave a painful sting.

Bee Corrected

M ost people experience times in life when they need to "bee"
corrected. A child who is corrected learns valuable lessons in
life. The Bible says, *"Correct thy son, and he shall give thee rest;
yea, he shall give delight unto thy soul"* (Proverbs 29:17). Instead of
putting his parents to shame, he brings them delight, blessing and
joy because he was corrected when doing wrong.

You expect correction in childhood, but you also need to be familiar with Biblical correction: *"For whom the LORD loveth he cor-
recteth; even as a father the son in whom he delighteth"* (Proverbs
3:12). All of us need to "bee" corrected at certain times in our lives.
When we are willing to "bee" corrected, we can enjoy the Lord's
direction and His protection.

Correction is a very important part of a successful life. When you
can "bee" corrected, you are on your way to improvement. When
someone kindly and lovingly corrects you, it helps to develop your
inner man. It helps you to understand how much you need others. It
is a sign of maturity when you are willing to "bee" corrected.

A man and his wife were once traveling in an unfamiliar area.
When he turned on a wrong road, his wife tried to kindly tell him he
was going the wrong way. He reprimanded her and said, "I know
where I'm going." After traveling on the wrong road for an hour, he
had to admit that he was wrong. He later said, "I wish I had been
willing to be corrected. It would have saved us a lot of unnecessary
problems."

My wife, Esther, and I were to speak at a place. Someone accidentally gave us directions to travel west on a certain highway. My
wife said, "I am sure we are to go east."

I said, "Wifie, they should know where the meeting place is."

Again, she said, "I am sure we are to go east."

I said, "Well, let's check the map." Wifie was right. They made a mistake in telling us to go west.

I am not encouraging a wife to correct her husband in an unscriptural manner, but I have learned years ago to pay attention when my wife questions something. She just may be right. My advice to everyone is, "bee" corrected before you receive a painful sting.

*"I would rather change my mind
now than wish I had later."*

Bee Counted

I t is a valuable attribute to "bee" counted by the Lord as a useful vessel for His Kingdom. Abraham was a man God counted as righteous because of his faith: *"And he believed in the LORD; and he counted it to him for righteousness"* (Genesis 15:6). Phinehas was also counted as righteous because he was obedient to God's law: *"Then stood up Phinehas, and executed judgment: and so the plague was stayed. And that was counted unto him for righteousness unto all generations for evermore"* (Psalm 106:30-31). Because he could "bee" counted, many lives were saved.

I often think of the story of Gideon. This man was shy and timid, hiding from his enemy, yet God counted him as a useful man. The angel of the Lord found him threshing wheat where the enemy could not see him: *"And the angel of the LORD appeared unto him, and said unto him, The LORD is with thee, thou mighty man of valour"* (Judges 6:12). Gideon had no idea what was inside him, but he accepted the challenge to "bee" counted of God as a mighty man. Not only was Gideon chosen, but God gave him other men who were counted useful to help fight the battle. The fearful and shy warriors were sent home because they couldn't "bee" counted. God tried the remaining soldiers at the brook and instructed Gideon to take only the men who lapped water as a dog. Only three hundred remained who could "bee" counted. With this small army, God wrought a great victory.

The Heavenly Father is still looking for men and women, boys and girls who can "bee" counted faithful, reliable and dependable. Can the Lord count on you? Can you "bee" counted if the Almighty is looking for someone to send to a foreign country with the gospel or to the back streets of a city? Can you be trusted to go into the slums or dark alleys to rescue the people most of society rejects? Jesus reminded us through a parable that these people are important: *"Go ye therefore into the highways, and as many as ye shall find, bid to the marriage. So those servants went out into the highways, and gathered together all as many as they found, both bad and good: and the wedding was furnished with guests*" (Matthew 22:9-10). Can you "bee" counted with the number the Lord has chosen to go into these places to win the souls of men? I have been there; I have preached there. I love that work because the souls of men are precious to me. Jesus told us to work "*...while it is day: the night cometh, when no man can work*" (John 9:4). Choose to "bee" counted for the work of the Lord.

Jonah ran into a whale of a lot more trouble than he expected when he sailed away from God's command.

Bee Courageous

Courage has caused many average people to become mighty men. When a courageous person sees a job to be done, he sets out to accomplish it. He can't be stopped. Moses, Joshua, David and other great men of the Bible did not succeed because they didn't face opposition, conflicts and backsets. They won because they were courageous. When David was facing extreme circumstances, he chose to "bee" courageous, *"And David was greatly distressed; for the people spake of stoning him, because the soul of all the people was grieved, every man for his sons and for his daughters: but David encouraged himself in the LORD his God"* (I Samuel 30:6).

When Joshua was called to lead the children of Israel into the promised land, he was given some strong admonition, *"Only be thou strong and very courageous, that thou mayest observe to do according to all the law, which Moses my servant commanded thee: turn not from it to the right hand or to the left, that thou mayest prosper whithersoever thou goest"* (Joshua 1:7). It takes courage to stand against all the problems that leaders encounter. Joshua had a hard task ahead of him. God knew His people would murmur and complain. Joshua needed to be reminded to "bee" courageous and keep his eyes on the goal to bring these people into the land of promise.

To "bee" courageous is to step out in faith and exercise confidence in the Lord who called you to do the task. It takes courage to stand for the right when others around you are criticizing or finding fault with you. It takes courage to bring reconciliation between yourself and others. It takes courage to go all the way with the Lord when others think you are a fanatic. There will be times in life when you face situations that can cause you to become discouraged and want to quit. Make a decision now to "bee" courageous. Men and women of courage are strong. They are *"Stedfast, unmoveable, always abounding in the work of the Lord"* (I Corinthians 15:58). "Bee" courageous. It is God's way of true achievement.

Bee Courteous

The Bible instructs us to "*be courteous*" (I Peter 3:8). A courteous person is one who is warm and friendly toward others. They are often full of hospitality and kind deeds. They love to do nice things for others. They are polite to strangers, as well as their old familiar friends. A person who is courteous is often generous and helpful. Your home should radiate this glorious virtue.

I have travelled many miles by airplane and noticed the courtesy and helpfulness of the flight crew. They have been trained to serve their customers well. Businesses that train their employees to "bee" courteous toward each other and their customers are much more successful. Why can't we learn the value of courtesy, even if others don't return the same courtesy? "Bee" courteous. The world needs to see more courteous people.

" Give to life and life will give back to you."

Bee Creative

T he power to "bee" creative is within each of us. God has given you the power to change your negative, nonproductive thinking. When you think defeat, lack and failure, that is what will come your way. When this happens, you become frustrated and are unable to fully perform your God-given achievements. When you break away from a downcast, "born loser" mentality and set out to "bee" creative, life will take on new meaning. You don't have to be a genius with a brilliant mind to "bee" creative. Imagine yourself accomplishing something you never did before. Think of God using you in a way you thought was impossible. Didn't Jesus speak to us concerning the impossible? *"Nothing shall be impossible unto you"* (Matthew 17:20).

Many have never discovered their full potential. They have lost confidence to visualize the marvelous, creative power working in them. To them, to "bee" creative is mysterious and perhaps evil because tradition caused them to believe God wants them to be negative and willing to be a loser. This kind of belief has brought failure, heartache and loss to many Christians who have great, creative minds. The Lord gets little or no glory from a negative, nonproductive mind. As a Christians, you have a higher realm of responsibility than most realize. If there is any time you should fail, fail in failure.

Commit yourself to "bee" creative. Plan to succeed. God has given you a mind to "bee" creative. Start right now to develop your God-given mind to become all you can become. You and the Lord, together, can do great things that will bring glory to His name. Choose today to "bee" creative.

Bee Crucified

No one ever learns to truly live until they learn what it means to "bee" crucified. To "bee" crucified means that you are dead to sin. Romans 6:6 explains, *"Knowing this, that our old man is crucified with him, that the body of sin might be destroyed, that henceforth we should not serve sin."* After the old man has been crucified, you have a new, exciting, joyful life in Christ Jesus because your childishness, selfishness and desires to have your own will and way is dead. Now, you belong to the Lord and are willing to do what He asks without murmuring and complaining. Paul made a great discovery and wrote, *"I am crucified with Christ: nevertheless I live; yet not I, but Christ liveth in me: and the life which I now live in the flesh I live by the faith of the Son of God, who loved me, and gave himself for me"* (Galatians 2:20). He didn't stay dead. He became more alive than he had ever been because he learned what it meant to "bee" crucified.

You cannot crucify yourself. You must let the Lord crucify you. When Jesus went to the cross, there was no turning back. When you choose to "bee" crucified, there is no turning back. Go the whole way with the Lord. You will no longer be demanding your own will and way but will gladly submit to the will, plan and purpose of God. All Christians must learn this very valuable lesson—to "bee" crucified.

" Don't be cross when you're bearing your cross."

Bee Daring

There comes a time in each of our lives that we must "bee" daring. Daniel dared to pray at an open window knowing those who tricked the king to cast him into the den of lions were watching. Yes, he was cast into the den of lions, but what a shout of victory came when the Lord closed their mouths. Later, Daniel testified, *"My God hath sent his angel, and hath shut the lions' mouths, that they have not hurt me: forasmuch as before him innocency was found in me; and also before thee, O king, have I done no hurt"* (Daniel 6:22). Because Daniel dared to serve God faithfully, he was saved from the hungry lions.

Knowing the fiery furnace awaited them, Shadrach, Meshach and Abednego dared to refuse to worship any god other than the God of Abraham, Isaac and Jacob. They dared to say, *"...be it known unto thee, O king, that we will not serve thy gods, nor worship the golden image which thou hast set up"* (Daniel 3:18). These three Hebrews dared to stand for the right in the midst of a fiery trial because "bee" daring buzzed in their ears telling them to obey God. They were still thrown into the fiery furnace, but were delivered from the exceeding hot flames. Because three young men dared to stand true to the One they worshipped, King Nebuchadnezzar acknowledged their God was the one and only true God. He said, *"Blessed be the God of Shadrach, Meshach, and Abednego, who hath sent his angel, and delivered his servants that trusted in him, and have changed the king's word, and yielded their bodies, that they might not serve nor worship any god, except their own God"* (Daniel 3:28).

There is a vast difference between "bee" daring and being foolish. Dare to "bee" daring as the mighty men recorded in the Bible. As with Daniel, Shadrach, Meshach and Abednego, this "bee" will never leave a painful sting!

Bee Dead

R emember the hymn that says, "Dead to the world would I be, oh Father; dead unto sin, alive unto thee?" Many are the lips that have sung that precious hymn. Yet, how many of us have truly had this experience? To "bee" dead in a scriptural sense is not being without physical life. The fact is, those who have died to self and to a sinful way of life have more life, because the life of God now abides in them. Paul explained this in Romans 6:11, *"Likewise reckon ye also yourselves to be dead indeed unto sin, but alive unto God through Jesus Christ our Lord."* To be alive unto God is far greater than to be alive unto sin.

To "bee" dead means that the spiritual nature is in control instead of the carnal. We are no longer controlled by sin and all of its activities but are walking with the Lord in a holy manner. I Peter 2:11 explains: *"Dearly beloved, I beseech you as strangers and pilgrims, abstain from fleshly lusts, which war against the soul."* There is a war between the carnal and the spiritual, but the Lord has given us the victory through our Lord Jesus Christ. When the Holy Spirit reveals to you the difference, you can "bee" dead to the carnal and alive unto the spiritual. Surely, "bee" dead will not leave a painful sting.

"If we live prepared to die,
We will die prepared to live."

Bee Decided

There are areas in life you must "bee" decided. When you are decided, the issue is settled. When you say, "I have decided to be a Christian and follow Christ," there is no room for return. You have made a firm decision. It is fixed. You will not waver.

You should "bee" decided when making certain choices in life. You should "bee" decided that under no circumstances will you return to an unstable lifestyle. Indecision is sure to bring trouble. "Bee" decided to be a good husband or wife, father or mother. When someone says, "I have decided to do my best at my new job," they are expecting to be a successful employee. The reason some people succeed while others do not is found in their choice to "bee" decided. The buzzing of "bee" decided will remind you to stand firm. This "bee" will not leave a painful sting when used appropriately.

"Don't go too fast;
Don't go to slow;
Keep up a steady pace;
Keep on the go!"

Bee Defensive

In Apostle Paul's epistle to the Philippians, he reminded them: "*I am set for the defence of the gospel*" (Philippians 1:17). Like Paul, we need to "bee" defensive of the true Gospel when Bible scholars deny the virgin birth of our blessed Savior and boldly declare that parts of the Bible are fiction. It was the true Gospel that brought us to the Light. It was the Gospel that steered our feet away from the path of destruction. We must not allow a false gospel to sidetrack us.

A woman visited a church service where I was preaching and told me she was shocked that I preached a sermon based on the book of Esther. She was quick to inform me that her pastor had just taught them that the book of Esther was a fable. What an opportunity I had to defend the truth of the Bible. With a smile of satisfaction on her face, she remarked, "You are very convincing." She didn't understand it was the Holy Spirit convincing her, not my words. After all, it was the Holy Spirit who inspired the writers of the Holy Scriptures to record the words in this very important and valuable Book.

You need to "bee" defensive of your faith and walk with God. You need to "bee" defensive of your moral standards and holy living. Defend yourself against the forces that are trying to overthrow you. If you learn to "bee" defensive in the proper manner, this "bee" will never leave a painful sting.

Bee Deliberate

To "bee" deliberate can be a good quality. You can deliberately be kind to those who were unkind to you. You should deliberately choose to do right when you are tempted to do wrong. "Bee" deliberate in your Christian life. You need to deliberately love your enemies and pray for them that despitefully use you: "*But I say unto you, Love your enemies, bless them that curse you, do good to them that hate you, and pray for them which despitefully use you, and persecute you*" (Matthew 5:44). You should deliberately do good to those who are hostile toward you and return good for evil, "*Be not overcome of evil, but overcome evil with good*" (Romans 12:20). To "bee" deliberate in this way will never leave a painful sting.

"*Opportunities are everywhere if you dare to dare.*"

Bee Delighted

T here are certain things in life that bring us delight. It is good to "bee" delighted when great things happen. Many things throughout my life have caused me to "bee" delighted. Many years ago, due to health problems, I was unable to harvest my farm crops. I was delighted when a group of Believers and friends came together and brought in the harvest. Some of the women even came and helped my wife. They were so kind and gentle toward us. Although that was a long time ago, I am still delighted by the memory of their generosity.

Psalm 37:4 instructs us: "*Delight thyself also in the LORD; and he shall give thee the desires of thine heart.*" You should "bee" delighted to serve the Lord. You can learn to "bee" delighted by all the good things that He pours out upon you. This "bee" will never leave a painful sting.

"When the days are dreary, keep yourself cheery."

Bee Delivered

As children of God, we are never left to walk alone because the Lord is ever ready to deliver His people. When trouble seems to come on every side, the precious promise in Psalm 34:17 is still waiting for us to lay hold upon: *"The righteous cry, and the LORD heareth, and delivereth them out of all their troubles."* The Scriptures assure us of that wonderful deliverance. Heaven is never far away: *"The angel of the LORD encampeth round about them that fear him, and delivereth them"* (Psalm 34:7). The angels are not off in some yonder place, but around us who fear the Lord. What a peaceful and quiet assurance we can have knowing that Heaven is always ready to rescue us in times of trouble.

The Psalmist penned these comforting words years ago, but they are still fresh and meaningful today: *"Many are the afflictions of the righteous: but the LORD delivereth him out of them all"* (Psalm 34:19). He didn't promise to deliver us fifty percent of the time or even ninety-nine percent. Review those words again, *"but the LORD delivereth him out of them all."* We were never promised a life without troubles, afflictions and trying times, but the Lord has promised to deliver us out of them all the time. Seek the Lord in those hard times and choose to "bee" delivered.

It is good to reflect on the times the Lord delivered you in the past and thank Him for the deliverance. This will help encourage you to face the future in victory. There is no value in being bound with heartaches when the Lord is waiting and longing to set you free. If anything is tormenting or troubling you, choose today to "bee" delivered. This blessed "bee" will never leave a painful sting!

Bee Dependable

A businessman recently said, "It is very difficult to find dependable help in this generation." Why? Perhaps, our younger generation has not been taught how valuable and important it is to "bee" dependable. Many people fail in life, not because they lack opportunity, talent or the necessary funds to do the job, but because they are not dependable.

When Joseph was sold by the hands of his brothers and became a servant to Potiphar, he chose to always "bee" dependable, regardless of what had befallen him. Notice what the Bible says about his dependability: *"And Joseph found grace in his sight, and he served him: and he made him overseer over his house, and all that he had he put into his hand. And it came to pass from the time that he had made him overseer in his house, and over all that he had, that the LORD blessed the Egyptian's house for Joseph's sake; and the blessing of the LORD was upon all that he had in the house, and in the field"* (Genesis 39:4-5). Joseph refused to sit around pitying himself and nursing his hurts. As far as he was concerned, he would never again see his Dad who loved him. He was domed for failure, but he rose to the occasion and was determined to make the best out of what he had. No wonder the Lord lifted him out of the dungeon to a lofty position with the king. Not only did the king find Joseph to "bee" dependable, but the Lord found him faithful and was able to bless him greatly. It is written, *"A faithful man shall abound with blessings"* (Proverbs 28:20). "Bee" dependable; what a necessary "bee." He will never leave a painful sting!

Bee Determined

It is important to "bee" determined. Those who win in life are those who are determined to accomplish something. They set out to achieve success in both the spiritual and physical realm. They don't give up. They can't give up. Life is too important for them to waste. All the difficulties, backsets, failures and challenges of life cannot stop a man with determination, zeal and enthusiasm. He may fall. He may fail. He may stumble. But when determination grips him, he will arise and head for the top again: *"For a just man falleth seven times, and riseth up again..."* (Proverbs 24:16). People who choose to "bee" determined can come through trouble, sickness or hardship quicker and easier than others.

Some of the most influential people who ever lived have had times of defeat, but they were determined not to quit. Some of the most successful marriages didn't prosper because there were no difficulties or tests. They prospered because these couples had a determination to make their marriage work regardless of obstacles. People who have great ministries didn't become great because there were no problems or difficulties to stop them. It was because they had a determination to fulfill what God called them to do.

The Apostle Paul was determined to preach the gospel everywhere he went. He was imprisoned, stoned, rejected and suffered almost every imaginable backset, but in the midst of it all, he chose to "bee" determined so the world would hear the glorious gospel. "Bee" determined to serve the Lord and help others to find salvation through Jesus Christ. Then, this "bee" will never leave a painful sting!

Bee Different

When you choose to serve the Lord with your whole heart, you will "bee" different from the devil's crowd. The things of this world will no longer be a part of your life. Your thoughts, actions and lifestyle will "bee" different. Your goals will "bee" different. Your music, books and magazines will not carry the same message the world enjoys. Paul explained the miraculous difference in the life of a Believer, "*Therefore if any man be in Christ, he is a new creature: old things are passed away; behold, all things are become new*" (II Corinthians 5:17).

Jesus used sheep and goats to illustrate how the people of God differ from the world: "*And before him shall be gathered all nations: and he shall separate them one from another, as a shepherd divideth his sheep from the goats*" (Matthew 25:32). There is a vast difference between sheep and goats. Their behavior, their eating habits and their overall character is very different. You are to "bee" different than the world because you belong to a different kingdom. Jesus told us, "*My kingdom is not of this world*" (John 18:36). If the Lord is walking in you, you should be in agreement with His kingdom.

It is important to "bee" different and separate yourself from the confusion of the doctrines of man. Hebrews 13:9 warns us: "*Be not carried about with divers and strange doctrines. For it is a good thing that the heart be established with grace.*" You should "bee" different by allowing grace to teach you how to interpret the Word of God correctly. Paul warns: "*For the time will come when they will not endure sound doctrine; but after their own lusts shall they heap to themselves teachers, having itching ears*" (II Timothy 4:3). He was prophesying of this generation. If you are not careful, you will heed to those who only teach part of the gospel. Choose to "bee" different. God will direct those who have an honest heart and desire to obey His Word. Listen to "bee" different when you feel like following the wrong crowd for this "bee" will surely never leave a painful sting.

Bee Diligent

A diligent person is persistent, hard-working and careful. It is very important to "bee" diligent, especially if you are a leader. Romans 12:8 declares: *"...he that giveth, let him do it with simplicity; he that ruleth, with diligence; he that sheweth mercy, with cheerfulness."* According to this verse, the choice to "bee" diligent is a very powerful decision. You must choose to rule well in the position you are called to serve, whether as a king, national leader, church leader or the leader in your home.

"Bee" diligent when training your children so they will grow up correctly and follow the right pathway in life. Teach them to earnestly contend for the faith. Train them to "bee" diligent at home, at church and in the work place.

Paul instructed us to "bee" diligent in spiritual matters in II Peter 1:10: *"Wherefore the rather, brethren, give diligence to make your calling and election sure: for if ye do these things, ye shall never fall."* You must "bee" diligent to have the seal of the Holy Spirit upon your life. "Bee" diligent to serve the Lord from the depth of your heart. "Bee" diligent to accomplish everything the Lord has called you to do. Truly, "bee" diligent will never leave a painful sting.

Bee Disappointed

All of us face disappointment at times when things don't go as we had planned. Go ahead, "bee" disappointed; it's alright, but don't become discouraged. "Bee" disappointed when you tried hard but failed, but then get up and go again. The Bible tells us, "*a just man falleth seven times, and riseth up again*" (Proverbs 24:16). Sure, he was disappointed he fell, but he didn't stay in that fallen position. You may, at times, "bee" disappointed because you made the wrong decision or agreed to something that didn't work out as you had planned. It is proper to "bee" disappointed, but you should not let that cause you to become depressed nor to quit.

To "bee" disappointed can be a benefit because you learn from experience. This is part of the maturing process of life. Some people, like Peter, have made major mistakes. Peter was disappointed that he denied the Lord. He went out and wept bitter tears of repentance. We have all made mistakes and were disappointed by them, but thanks be to God, we can be forgiven and go forth in victory. Paul said, "*Brethren, I count not myself to have apprehended: but this one thing I do, forgetting those things which are behind and reaching forth unto those things which are before, I press toward the mark for the prize of the high calling of God in Christ Jesus*" (Philippians 3:12-14). Paul wasn't sitting around grieving over his past. He left the past behind him and went forward into victory. Like Paul, forget the past, press forward and learn from "bee" disappointed lest this "bee" should leave a painful sting.

Bee Discerning

A postle Paul, in his writings to the Corinthians, mentions a gift of the Spirit that is especially necessary in our day—the discerning of spirits (I Corinthians 12:10). If there ever was a time to "bee" discerning, it is today. Many people proclaim they are anointed of God or have a "thus saith the Lord" message, but are living contrary to sound, Biblical teaching from the Word of God. Beware! The true word of the Lord will never be unscriptural nor exalt the flesh. Thank God, there are still God-fearing, holy messengers of God with a true "thus saith the Lord" who have a Biblical lifestyle.

Many have been confused, brokenhearted and brought into delusion because they didn't heed the warning buzz of "bee" discerning. You can, and should, develop in this gift of discernment. Beloved, you need to have the discerning of spirits operating in you at all times.

"Whoever God is for, you dare not be against;
Whatever God is for, you dare not be against."

Bee Disciplined

To "bee" disciplined is very important in a Believer's life. To "bee" disciplined is to act upon knowledge or learning. Those who are well disciplined learn to develop in self-control. They develop a characteristic of order and efficiency. They learn to submit to authority. They have chosen to "bee" disciplined in word and deed. Their mind, will and emotions are well disciplined.

A child who is disciplined according to the Biblical child training learns the value of conducting his life in a proper manner: "*The rod and reproof give wisdom: but a child left to himself bringeth his mother to shame*" (Proverbs 29:15). Many parents have been put to shame because they neglected to properly discipline their children. If your children have gone astray, repent of your neglect and pray earnestly for the Lord to help discipline them and turn them around. Over the years, I have seen glorious changes take place through prayer. People who were once of out control were marvelously changed.

It is not unusual for the Lord to discipline His children. According to Hebrews 12:5-6, we are not to despise such chastisement, "*My son, despise not thou the chastening of the Lord, nor faint when thou art rebuked of him: For whom the Lord loveth he chasteneth, and scourgeth every son whom he receiveth.*" Verse 8 explains, "*If ye be without chastisement, whereof all are partakers, then are ye bastards, and not sons.*" "Bee" disciplined if you need it. Praise the Lord, you are a Son of God. Hallelujah!!!

Bee Dissatisfied

T here are times when it is good to be satisfied, but there also comes a time to "bee" dissatisfied. You should "bee" dissatisfied with fruitless Christianity. I am very dissatisfied with a fruitless ministry, whether it be my own or that of others. I am dissatisfied that we, as Believers, have allowed multitudes to go to Hell. This dissatisfaction has caused earnestness in my heart to pray for lost souls and to spread the gospel message. I have been preaching on the radio since 1988 and I am more excited today about reaching the world than ever before.

You should "bee" dissatisfied with your lack of achievements, but to remain dissatisfied is not productive. You must do more than "bee" dissatisfied with past failures. You must increase your fruitfulness and become successful concerning spiritual things. Jesus said, *"Herein is my Father glorified, that ye bear much fruit; so shall ye be my disciples"* (John 15:8). "Bee" dissatisfied will not leave a painful sting when it inspires you to excel.

"More people say a prayer than pray a prayer."

Bee Disturbed

We are living in a time when we should "bee" disturbed by the things we see happening around us on every hand. You should "bee" disturbed because the Bible is being mocked, ridiculed and rejected. The moral decline and loss of truth in our land should greatly disturb you. Jesus was disturbed when He saw how the people defiled the temple: "*And Jesus went into the temple of God, and cast out all them that sold and bought in the temple, and overthrew the tables of the moneychangers, and the seats of them that sold doves, And said unto them, It is written, My house shall be called the house of prayer; but ye have made it a den of thieves*" (Matthew 21:12-13). You should "bee" disturbed because there are puppets in the pulpit instead of honest and courageous leaders. Pastors are more interested in entertaining the people than bringing them to a decision for Christ. We need men behind the pulpit who call for dedication, commitment and courage to live above the world's system.

Allow yourself to "bee" disturbed by the multitudes of unsaved people who are heading for a Christ-less grave. I met a man while handing out tracts one day. He was very disturbed because someone was interrupting his life and trying to direct him toward the Lord. He wanted to live his own life without anyone's assistance. Weeks later, I was prompted to return to his house and talk with him again about accepting the Lord. During the conversation, I learned he had been brought up in a Christian home. Because he became very disturbed and was rather hostile toward me, I never revisited. Several weeks later, I heard he had been killed. His father asked me, "Aren't you the one who kept talking to my son about the Lord? Unknown to you, after you talked with him the last time, he made a change and began attending church regularly." The first visit, he was disturbed in a wrong manner. The last visit caused him to "bee" disturbed in a good way. If you learn to "bee" disturbed for the lost souls around you, this "bee" will never leave a painful sting.

Bee Done

S ome people make the comment, "I'm done with sin. I'm not going to do that anymore." However, it isn't long until they are doing the same thing again. I've heard people say they were done with Christianity because they couldn't live in victory. They were fed up with falling back into their past lifestyle. God desires to set you free from sin and failure. When you are done with your way of doing things, God will be able to operate in you and perfect those things that have been holding you back. He will, "*Make you perfect in every good work to do his will, working in you that which is well-pleasing in his sight, through Jesus Christ; to whom be glory for ever and ever. Amen*" (Hebrews 13:21).

Maybe, you feel like you're done. You're ready to give up. Things are always going wrong in your life and you have completely lost hope. There is good news. God is not done with you. He wants to restore and help you. We need to listen to the buzz of "bee" done when we feel like quitting. Instead of giving up, it will declare, "I'm done with failure. I'm done with quitting. I'm done getting angry. I'm done making mistakes." When you choose to "bee" done with your way and surrender to God's way, "bee" done will never leave a painful sting.

Bee Dynamite

When dynamite is ignited, an explosion results. When you allow the Holy Spirit to arise within you, He gives you the power to "bee" dynamite. I remember as a young boy, we had a huge rock near our house that needed to be removed. The equipment we had could not move it so we decided to use dynamite. That is how you need to remove hindrances, obstacles, backsets and discouragements from your life. The ignition of the Holy Spirit exploding within you will burst asunder the barriers which are holding back victory. You will be empowered to do what normally would have been impossible. Remember, Jesus said, "*...If ye have faith as a grain of mustard seed, ye shall say unto this mountain, Remove hence to yonder place; and it shall remove; and nothing shall be impossible unto you*" (Matthew 17:20).

When the disciples chose to "bee" dynamite, they raised the dead, cast out devils and reigned with authority. When you choose to "bee" dynamite, your life will be completely revolutionized. You will live a joyful, victorious life full of meaning. Then, you will have dynamite power to help others out of their troubles. "Bee" dynamite will never leave a painful sting.

Bee Eager

To "bee" eager is to have great enthusiasm and zeal in pursuit of something. It causes you to win in the face of opposition. To "bee" eager helps to build faith when making your requests to the Lord. It increases your expectation to receive. You expect good things to happen. You expect to have a good day. You expect the Lord to bless you. You expect His favor to rest upon you.

Some of our grandsons wanted to take me fishing on Lake Huron. They hired a professional fishing guide for the day. To say we were eager to get on with fishing would be a mild statement. What a day! Not only did we get our limit, but we caught big fish.

"Bee" eager to obey the will, purpose and plan of God for your life. "Bee" eager to win more souls for the Lord and tell others what the Lord has done for you. "Bee" eager to accomplish something in life that you have never accomplished. The next time you are asked to do something new or to do a favor for someone, "bee" eager to do it!

When you get up in the morning, think of how many opportunities are before you. This may be your day to minister to someone who is facing a problem. When you choose to "bee" eager, life can be a tremendous blessing.

Bee Early

I n Psalm 63:1, the Psalmist recognized how important it is to "bee" early, *"O God, thou art my God; early will I seek thee: my soul thirsteth for thee, my flesh longeth for thee in a dry and thirsty land, where no water is."* Those who seek the Lord early will find Him. Many people wait to seek the Lord until they are older or more mature. The Lord is looking for people to serve Him at an early age. Ecclesiastes 12:1 states, *"Remember now thy Creator in the days of thy youth, while the evil days come not, nor the years draw nigh, when thou shalt say, I have no pleasure in them."*

Wisdom is one of the greatest desires that a human can have. The book of Proverbs tells us that wisdom must be sought early: *"I love them that love me; and those that seek me early shall find me"* (Proverbs 8:17). If you choose to "bee" early in searching for wisdom, it will result in great reward. So, choose to "bee" early. This "bee" will never leave a painful sting.

"To get a head start, start using your head."

Bee Eligible

To "bee" eligible is to say, "I am qualified," or, "I am fit to be chosen." Some may be called to be missionaries or to do some other important work for the Lord, but they don't meet the standards set forth by our Heavenly Father. You must come to the place in life where you are eligible to step into the calling the Lord has for you. Our Heavenly Father has given you the opportunity to excel, yet you may have to make changes in your life to "bee" eligible for such promotion.

Esau was the firstborn son of Isaac. This qualified him to receive the birthright, but his fleshly appetites got in the way and made him no longer eligible to receive the birthright or the blessing from his father. Because of this, his twin brother, Jacob, was able to deceive their father and steal the blessing. The Lord couldn't protect the blessing from being taken.

Many of God's children will never receive all the Lord has for them because they haven't prepared themselves to "bee" eligible. Ask yourself the question: "Would I 'bee' eligible to receive all the blessings the Lord has for me?"

Bee Emotional

To "bee" emotional is a God-given trait, but caution must be used not to become excessively emotional. Our Heavenly Father understands your emotions when you face great disappointment and sorrow or when you have been betrayed by someone you dearly loved.

In the prophetic words of the Psalmist, you can hear an emotional disturbance taking place: *"Yea, mine own familiar friend, in whom I trusted, which did eat of my bread, hath lifted up his heel against me"* (Psalm 41:9). This perhaps is a prophecy concerning Jesus who would be betrayed by Judas, one of His beloved disciples. What a good reason to "bee" emotional. A friend He trusted betrayed Him. A friend He ate with had turned against Him.

You may "bee" emotional when your friends suffer the loss of a loved one or when tragedy visits someone dear to you. When Jesus was approaching the tomb of Lazarus, we see how He was moved by his death. The following two words write volumes: *"Jesus wept"* (John 11:35).

Heed the words of Solomon. There is *"a time to weep, and a time to laugh; a time to mourn..."* (Ecclesiastes 3:4). There is a time to "bee" emotional. When you are balanced in emotions, you will not have an emotional breakdown. Emotions are in order, so weep when you need to weep and laugh when you need to laugh, but keep your emotions in balance.

Bee Empowered

Why are so many Believers weak and powerless? Too many cannot withstand the hardships that come their way from day to day. The Lord God planned for His children to "bee" empowered and strong in Him. People who seek to "bee" empowered are those who rise above others in accomplishments. They excel in life because they are weaned from mediocrity. Troubles and hardships cannot stop them.

Many people never receive all the power of God available to them. The Lord desires for us to "bee" empowered in every area of life. A pastor, teacher or evangelist who is empowered to preach is anointed with the power of God to bring souls to the Lord. In fact, the Lord has given every one of us power to win souls, *"But ye shall receive power, after that the Holy Ghost is come upon you: and ye shall be witnesses unto me both in Jerusalem, and in all Judaea, and in Samaria, and unto the uttermost part of the earth"* (Acts 1:8). According to Deuteronomy 8:18, God has empowered us to get wealth: *"But thou shalt remember the LORD thy God: for it is he that giveth thee power to get wealth, that he may establish his covenant which he sware unto thy fathers, as it is this day."* Why be powerless when you can "bee" empowered?

Anyone can choose to "bee" empowered by the Holy Spirit to do the work the Lord has called them to do. To "bee" empowered is to be stronger than your weakness. To "bee" empowered removes the limitations that keep you from doing the impossible. To "bee" empowered is to have mountain moving faith and the ability to remove obstacles and hindrances. To "bee" empowered is to defeat the work of the devil and win every battle in life.

Bee Encouraged

Has something gone wrong in your life? Have you been misunderstood or misjudged? "Bee" encouraged. When David was accused of not being a good leader in I Samuel 30:6, the Bible says, *"but David encouraged himself in the LORD his God."*

Mistakes and failures should not keep a person from reaching their highest achievement. Make any necessary changes, but "bee" encouraged to rise to the top. Some of the greatest men and women in the world have failed and failed, but in the end came through victorious. They learned to "bee" encouraged. They refused to sit around pitying themselves. They refused to make excuses for their failures.

A number of years ago, there was a man who was sure he could never accomplish anything in life. Everything he set his hand to do failed. According to his own testimony, he said, "I had to change my way of thinking. I had to think differently about myself. When I did, the whole world changed around me." Later, this man became a successful businessman.

"Bee" encouraged to minister to the needs of others. Encourage yourself to be a blessing to those around you. "Bee encouraged" never leaves a painful sting.

Bee Endued

T he disciples were instructed to wait in Jerusalem until they were endued with power from on high: "*And, behold, I send the promise of my Father upon you: but tarry ye in the city of Jerusalem, until ye be endued with power from on high*" (Luke 24:49). What does it mean to "bee" endued? They were to be clothed and empowered with the Holy Ghost. When the disciples were endued with the power of the Holy Ghost, they were able to work miracles, signs and wonders. Although some tell us the power passed away with the apostles, they cannot support this belief with the Bible.

I believe we have lost a lot of power today and adjusted to a weaker Christianity which lacks the ability to heal and deliver those in need. We need to "bee" endued with the power of the Holy Ghost. The Holy Ghost will give us the strength to overcome all temptations, trials and tests. As we press forward to "bee" endued with power from on High, may God visit his people with the same Holy Ghost power that was poured out on the early church. This "bee" will never leave a painful sting.

" The difference between possible and impossible is
IM (I am) in the way.
When IM is removed, impossible becomes possible."

Bee Energetic

I like to think of being energetic as having the energy to do something with zeal and determination. An energetic person is vigorous and full of ideas. He has a force to get a job done. He can do that job in record time and do it well. He has energy to get up in the morning with a dare to win. He has energy to accomplish something others are afraid to do. I am not suggesting foolishness, but rather breaking free from the norm. The kind of energetic person I am thinking of makes no excuses for not achieving his goal. If he fails at one thing, he does another. If he falls, he won't stay down, *"For a just man falleth seven times, and riseth up again"* (Proverbs 24:16). Troubles and backsets won't keep him down. He'll get up and try, try again. When his energy level is low, his enthusiasm shouts, "GO"!

I enjoy being around people who are energetic, don't you? I knew a man, years ago, who was illiterate, yet he was a foreman in a big company with many people working under his command. How did he get to this place? He was an energetic young man who wanted to accomplish something in life despite his limitations. This man became a great success—not because of his limitations, but because he was energetic.

The energetic person energizes himself. When he is discouraged, he encourages himself. When he wants to quit, the flame of hope causes him to strive for the top again. What a way to go! "Bee" energetic.

Bee Energized

W e all face times in life when we need to "bee" energized. *"Even the youths shall faint and be weary, and the young men shall utterly fall"* (Isaiah 40:30). These are the words of Isaiah the prophet. In verse 31, he adds this marvelous promise: *"But they that wait upon the LORD shall renew their strength; they shall mount up with wings as eagles; they shall run, and not be weary; and they shall walk, and not faint."* Things may happen in life that have a tendency to drag you down or cause you to lose your energy. You may face disappointment or backset that can affect you in a negative way, but the promise remains, *"they that wait upon the Lord shall renew their strength."* This promise has helped many people. Its lifting words can help you to overcome and encourage you to lift others who may need to "bee" energized.

You can "bee" energized by daily reading Bible verses that encourage, strengthen and motivate. Fill your mind, mouth and heart with powerful Bible verses like Philippians 3:13: *"Brethren, I count not myself to have apprehended: but this one thing I do, forgetting those things which are behind, and reaching forth unto those things which are before."* Pondering past failures can drag you down, but Scriptures like this can help you "bee" energized.

Another thing that can help you "bee" energized is by reading sound books by those who learned how to "bee" energized. You can also "bee" energized by associating with people who have a positive outlook in life. It is essential to learn how to "bee" energized so you can respond enthusiastically to difficult situations in life. "Bee" energized. This "bee" is very essential in your daily life.

Bee Enriched

T he church at Corinth was not without problems as we observe by reading Paul's letter to them. But in the beginning of his letter to the Corinthians, he mentioned they were enriched by Jesus Christ, "*That in every thing ye are enriched by him, in all utterance, and in all knowledge*" (I Corinthians 1:5). What a compliment! In his second epistle, he writes, "*Being enriched in every thing to all bountifulness, which causeth through us thanksgiving to God*" (II Corinthians 9:11). Here, we see a glimpse of the riches of God's grace. It's amazing how this church, with its weaknesses, could draw from the rich streams of Heaven. Paul saw something in these people that caused them to enjoy the riches of the kingdom of God. They were coming out of their weaknesses into the strength of the Lord and were being enriched by Him.

How would you like to "bee" enriched in everything? Wouldn't it be great to have the abundant blessings of the Lord resting upon you? You should desire to "bee" enriched, not only for your own benefit, but also for the good of others. This is a quality everyone should pursue.

" At the darkest times in life, God is still light."

Bee Enthusiastic

Enthusiasm is contagious. When you are enthusiastic, not only will you motivate others, but will boost yourself as well. To "bee" enthusiastic is a choice. When you choose to "bee" enthusiastic, you will have a greater outlook in life. The troubles you face will look smaller and less impossible to overcome when you remind yourself to "bee" enthusiastic. If you desire to "bee" enthusiastic, you need to think differently than the looser. You need to talk differently than those who are defeated. Winners like to be around winners because they enthuse each other.

"Bee" enthusiastic about getting up in the morning and facing a new day. "Bee" enthusiastic about the things you hope to accomplish today. "Bee" enthusiastic about what the Lord is doing in your life and in the lives of your family and friends.

Apostle Paul had this testimony, "*I therefore so run, not as uncertainly; so fight I, not as one that beateth the air*" (I Corinthians 9:26). He wasn't wasting his energy. He had set out to win over all the obstacles, hindrances and backsets in life. He had chosen to "bee" enthusiastic. He overcame extremely difficult situations. If Paul could do it, we can do it. "Bee" enthusiastic! This "bee" will never leave a painful sting.

Bee Epistles

Have you ever considered how many people may be watching you—your manner of life, your speech, the way you dress, the things you read and your overall characteristics? Whether you are aware of it or not, you are a type of epistle being read by others. Paul mentioned this in his letter to the Corinthians: "*Ye are our epistle written in our hearts, known and read of all men*" (II Corinthians 3:2).

To "bee" epistles is to live so Scripturally correct that people will recognize you are living according to the Bible. The Lord expects you to be an example for others to follow. Your manner of life should display no hypocrisy or falsehood. If you need to make correction, do it today. It is important to "bee" epistles for the kingdom of Heaven.

"The can't-ers can't, but the can-ers can."

Bee Equipped

Many people have traveled to the mission field unequipped. They were not prepared for the situations they faced. They were not trained how to use proper equipment. Training is important before you can fully learn to "bee" equipped. You need to learn how to face difficult situations, how to operate in different cultures and how to work with people who have different beliefs. This will help you to be better equipped when going forth to do the work of the kingdom.

Many are not using the full equipment the Lord has given them. Ephesians 6:11 describes why you should "bee" equipped: *"Put on the whole armour of God, that ye may be able to stand against the wiles of the devil."* The Lord has equipped His servants with the mighty power of the Holy Ghost to fulfill the calling He placed upon them. He has equipped you with angelic hosts to minister to you and establish you. The more you learn to cooperate with these Spirits, the better you will "bee" equipped to serve the Lord to the fullest. "Bee" equipped. This "bee" will never leave a painful sting.

" *God has something I don't have.*
I have something God doesn't have.
I have a problem.
God has the solution."

Bee Established

The book of Hebrews reminds us, *"Be not carried about with divers and strange doctrines. For it is a good thing that the heart be established with grace"* (Hebrews 13:9). When you choose to "bee" established in grace, you will "bee" established in other areas of life. To "bee" established is to be steadfast, to be fixed, not wishy-washy, not one time up and another time down. Successful teachers must "bee" established in the subjects they plan to teach. Good businessmen must "bee" established in their line of business or they will fail. A Christian must "bee" established in sound doctrine or he will be carried about by every wind of doctrine.

As a pastor, I think I can understand Paul's concern when he instructed the Romans. *"I long to see you,"* he says, *"that I may impart unto you some spiritual gift, to the end ye may be established"* (Romans 1:11). Every true pastor desires to see his people established in the Spirit and in the Word of Truth. Christians who are established in spiritual things are led by the Spirit of God. They know where they are going and are not easily discouraged. They are a great asset to a confused and disturbed world.

To "bee" established in the negative sense can bring people to defeat. A person who is established in sorrow, grief or depression will suffer with negative thoughts and actions. A person who is established in his mind that he is a born loser will be a loser until he chooses to "bee" established in right thinking. No one is born to be a loser. You can choose to "bee" established in becoming a success.

Years ago, a young man failed in everything he set his hands to do. He told me, "I'm a born loser." I tried to encourage him otherwise, but he remained negative. He was sure his family line was born to fail. One day, he went to work for a businessman. He loved his job and worked hard. He began to see that he had talent to do a job well. A few years later, his boss retired and this same man, who had thought he was a "born loser," purchased the business and became a great success. He chose to "bee" established in the positive instead of the negative.

Set a goal to "bee" established in your personal life, in your marriage, in your work place and in your relationships with others, at home and abroad. When you are well established, you become stable, *"steadfast, unmovable, always abounding in the work of the Lord"* (I Corinthians 15:58). It is important to "bee" established.

"If you look up, you stay up;
if you look down, you stay down."

Bee Eternal

Nothing in this life is as important as knowing you have eternal life. In I John 5:13 we read, *"that ye may know that ye have eternal life."* What is more comforting or assuring than that verse? To "bee" eternal is a decision you alone can make. The Bible instructs, *"...lay hold on eternal life"* (I Timothy 6:12). You need to lay hold on it while you are here on earth. Eternal life is only promised to those who receive Jesus Christ as their personal Lord and Savior. Paul explains what happens to a person after they receive Jesus as Savior: *"Therefore if any man be in Christ, he is a new creature: old things are passed away; behold, all things are become new"* (II Corinthians 5:17). According to this verse, those who have eternal life no longer have the old lifestyle. Old things are passed away. They are gone. They don't control you anymore. Jesus taught, *"And I give unto them eternal life; and they shall never perish, neither shall any man pluck them out of my hand"* (John 10:28). That does not give you license to sin nor become careless in your Christian life. Those with eternal life will live in accordance to the will, plan and purpose of God and be backed by the Word of God. They will live like they have eternal life.

I have witnessed the change in people whose lives had been very wicked until they were transformed into the Kingdom of Light. Their countenance, attitudes and habits were dramatically changed. What happened in the internal began to show on the external.

On the day of judgment, you will not be asked what denomination you joined nor the name of the church you attended, but rather, if you have received eternal life through our Lord Jesus Christ. Surely, "bee" eternal will never leave a painful sting.

Bee Evangelistic

So many churches have lost their evangelistic outreach. Some people feel they are too busy to evangelize. Others feel that they cannot "bee" evangelistic because they are timid, backward, uneducated, too young or too old. We have had enough excuses over the years why Christians are losing their evangelistic outreach. I believe it is time to prepare ourselves to "bee" evangelistic.

No matter who you are or where you live, you can "bee" evangelistic. To "bee" evangelistic is to help win people to the Lord and Savior, Jesus Christ. Whether you are at home, traveling or on a vacation, learn to "bee" evangelistic. To "bee" evangelistic does not necessarily require a person to do some major thing, such as hold a revival meeting or crusade or conduct a street meeting. For some people, to "bee" evangelistic may be to just share the good things of the Lord with others and to encourage people to give their lives to the Lord Jesus Christ on a one to one basis. When you get up in the morning, ask the Lord if there is someone He would like you to witness to today. Ask Him to lead you to that person. You may be surprised by how many doors of opportunity are opened.

A number of years ago, as I was entering a place of business, I saw a woman painting a sign. She was doing an excellent job. I said to her, "You must be an expert, painting signs of that caliber." To my surprise, she turned and faced me with an outburst. I knew something dramatic had happened in her life by her response. I asked, "Is there something I could do to help you?" With that invitation, she poured out her tale of woe and the Lord used me at that very unexpected place to minister to someone who was hurting.

Someone may be waiting for you to give them a word of courage before they accept Jesus Christ as their Savior and Lord. What an opportunity! What a privilege! How rewarding it is to "bee" evangelistic!

Bee Exact

To "bee" exact, you must have integrity. You do exactly what you said you would do. The generation around us is not always exact. They don't fulfill their commitments. A carpenter may not finish his job exactly as promised. I spoke with a contractor who builds large buildings. He said, "We are living in such a dishonest world, I have to charge extra on my contracts to pay for lawyer fees to sue big companies who will not fulfill their part of the contract."

I have met people, over the years, who priced a job and honored their contract even if they had underestimated their price. I have also dealt with contractors who promised to build for an exact amount of money, but in the end charged thousands of dollars more. If you have a problem in this area, you can change by choosing to "bee" exact. We need to listen to the buzz of "bee" exact when we feel like compromising. Surely, this "bee" will never leave a painful sting.

"To misquote a person is a major insult to integrity."

Bee Exalted

You sometimes hear people say it is wrong to "bee" exalted. Not according to Scripture. As surprising as it may appear, the Lord is not opposed to a person being exalted. He is against someone exalting himself. Jesus said, *"Whosoever shall exalt himself shall be abased; and he that shall humble himself shall be exalted"* (Matthew 23:12). Who will exalt the humble? The Lord will see to it that the humble are exalted. Peter writes, *"Humble yourselves therefore under the mighty hand of God, that he may exalt you in due time"* (I Peter 5:6). Go ahead and "bee" exalted, but never exalt yourself or you will surely be abased.

I have known people who were embarrassed when someone exalted them. They acted as if they had committed a major sin. Let me say again, it is not wrong to "bee" exalted, but it is wrong to exalt one's self. Self exaltation is fostered with pride, which the Lord hates. If you seek to "bee" exalted, you are satisfying your own ego. If you daily walk in sincere humility, sooner or later, the Lord will exalt you. The Lord greatly exalted King David. He exalted Daniel, Job, Noah, Mordecai, Abraham and many others and He will exalt you in due time if you humble yourself. Remember, don't seek to "bee" exalted, but allow the Lord to honor you.

Bee Excellent

The Bible says, *"The righteous is more excellent than his neighbour"* (Proverbs 12:26). This verse tells us that righteousness causes a person to "bee" excellent. Daniel was a man with an excellent spirit. Note what the people saw in this righteous man, *"Then this Daniel was preferred above the presidents and princes, because an excellent spirit was in him; and the king thought to set him over the whole realm"* (Daniel 6:3). Not only did people see the excellent spirit of Daniel, but God also recognized it. When the messenger of Heaven appeared to this righteous man, he said: *"O man greatly beloved, fear not: peace be unto thee, be strong, yea, be strong"* (Daniel 10:19).

In the gospel of Luke, Theophilus was referred to as an excellent man, *"It seemed good to me also, having had perfect understanding of all things from the very first, to write unto thee in order, most excellent Theophilus"* (Luke 1:3). Proverbs 17:27 says, *"...A man of understanding is of an excellent spirit."* What a goal—to "bee" excellent. If everyone chose to have an excellent spirit, how much difference it would make in our work place, in our homes, and in our churches. Surely, this is a "bee" that will never leave a painful sting!

Bee Excited

S omeone said excitement is shallow. I believe it is time for us to "bee" excited. In spite of all the uncertainties, fears and doubts, I'm excited when I think about the future. We should "bee" excited that the Lord is still leading us day by day, *"The steps of a good man are ordered by the LORD: and he delighteth in his way"* (Psalms 37:23). What an exciting thought!

The angels get excited when someone is redeemed: *"I say unto you, that likewise joy shall be in heaven over one sinner that repenteth, more than over ninety and nine just persons, which need no repentance... Likewise, I say unto you, there is joy in the presence of the angels of God over one sinner that repenteth"* (Luke 15:7, 10). In the same way, we should "bee" excited when someone gives their heart to the Lord Jesus.

We should "bee" excited when the Lord answers our prayers in a supernatural way. On one of our travels, we had an unusual experience. As our airplane was landing, it began to shake and parts were strewn on the runway. In the midst of all the delays and hindrances, the Lord answered our prayers, keeping us safe and helping us reach our destination on time. I was excited when we safely reached our final destination. What a mighty God we serve! Listen to the buzzing of "bee" excited and respond to that precious "bee" which will never leave a painful sting.

Bee Excused

There are times in life you may need to "bee" excused. Unexpected situations may arise, causing the need for you to "bee" excused from plans that were previously made.

I knew a man who had made arrangements to travel somewhere with a friend. On the appointed day, this man received a phone call that unexpectedly changed his plans. Immediately, he telephoned his friend to let him know he would be unable to make the trip. It was too late; there was no answer. He had already left for the meeting place. This man jumped into his car and drove the distance to where he had promised to meet his friend. There, he explained the situation and asked to "bee" excused from their plans. His friend willingly consented to his legitimate request.

Sometimes people ask to "bee" excused without a legitimate reason. Jesus explained the danger of these excuses through a parable: *"And they all with one consent began to make excuse. The first said unto him, I have bought a piece of ground, and I must needs go and see it: I pray thee have me excused. And another said, I have bought five yoke of oxen, and I go to prove them: I pray thee have me excused"* (Luke 14:18-19). These people felt their plans were more important than the plans of God. Their excuses prevented them from receiving a tremendous blessing from the Lord. Be cautious. Make sure your excuses are justifiable.

The Bible records the story of a man who owed a large sum of money to his master, but was unable to repay him. He pled with him to "bee" excused from this terrible debt: *"The servant therefore fell down, and worshipped him, saying, Lord, have patience with me, and I will pay thee all. Then the lord of that servant was moved with compassion, and loosed him, and forgave him the debt"* (Matthew 18:26-27). Because of this man's humility, His master had mercy and excused him. "Bee" excused can be very helpful when used correctly.

Bee Expedient

To "bee" expedient is to do things that are beneficial and useful to obtain the desired results or that are suitable to the circumstance or occasion. Paul writes in I Corinthians 10:23 *"All things are lawful for me, but all things are not expedient: all things are lawful for me, but all things edify not."*

There are some things in life that are permissible, but are not expedient for a winner. A winner will not flee from hard work. He will persist in labor until the job is completed. An athlete will not allow distractions to deter him from the goal. It may be lawful for him to eat certain things or do things that others allow, but it would not "bee" expedient if he desires to excel beyond the average. You should apply the same perspective in your Christian life. Although recreation and entertainment is not wrong, it may not "bee" expedient on a regular basis if you desire to be spiritually minded. The distractions of the world should not hinder you from serving the Lord wholeheartedly.

"Bee" expedient in every area of life and the Lord will show you ways of reaching out into new territory and attaining a new level of success. "Bee" expedient is still a very valuable "bee" that will never leave a painful sting.

Bee Extraordinary

B reak away from the norm. Why not? The world has seen enough failure, sadness and discouragement. They need to see someone rise on the scene who can shout the victory every day. You can be that person. Start each day out right. Expect to accomplish something worthwhile. Make a firm, quality decision that you will not be satisfied until you have done your best. "Bee" extraordinary and make a big difference in this world. Many are defeated, but you can be a winner.

"Whatsoever thy hand findeth to do, do it with thy might" (Ecclesiastes 9:10). If there is a job to do, do it, but do it with all your might. If you are willing to step out beyond many of the mediocre Christians and "bee" extraordinary, the Lord will help you to accomplish much more than you ever dreamed possible.

There are people who made a decision to do everything with their might and the Lord blessed them abundantly. Many of the conveniences we enjoy came because someone chose to "bee" extraordinary, to invent something no one else thought of, to accomplish something few thought could be accomplished. They were not born with a winner's heart. They became winners because they chose to "bee" extraordinary. People often think those who accomplish the greatest things in life are great intellectual giants or that God gave them supernatural talent to accomplish what they did. Who knows the giant within you? Only you can determine the limitations in your life. Past failures cannot keep you from becoming extraordinary. To "bee" extraordinary is a decision that you can make today. If you have failed, start over again. Jesus said, *"Nothing shall be impossible unto you"* (Matthew 17:20). Who is He talking to? He is talking to you. This promise is not to just a few people, it is for those who have made a decision to "bee" extraordinary. Such people can be a blessing to multitudes. Are you willing to have this "bee" operating in your life? Make up your mind to "bee" extraordinary.

Bee Factual

A s Christians, the Lord should be able to trust us to "bee" factual. The words you speak should contain no exaggeration, no partial truth. The Bible instructs, *"Provide things honest in the sight of all men"* (Romans 12:17). It is not easy to find a person you can trust to "bee" factual. Much of what you hear is only partial truth. Anything from the speech of a politician running for office to the propaganda of the news media may only be part truth.

Rumors are usually not factual. They may contain a few facts, but in general, they are exaggerated. I wrote a little verse that warns us to beware of rumors:

> *A rumor's like a snowball,*
> *You roll it in the snow*
> *And it isn't very long*
> *And it will really grow.*
> *Someone starts a rumor,*
> *Then adds a thing or two;*
> *It's a different story*
> *By the time it gets to you.*
> *So when you hear a rumor,*
> *Search it through and through;*
> *It may be just a rumor,*
> *That isn't even true.*

It may be good to analyze what you hear. Is it fact or is it someone's opinion? Is it fact or is it what someone imagined? It is our responsibility, as Believers, to "bee" factual. This "bee" will never leave a painful sting.

Bee Faithful

J esus said, *"Be thou faithful unto death, and I will give thee a crown of life"* (Revelation 2:10). You should strive to receive that crown, but before you can obtain it, you must choose to "bee" faithful. Paul admonished the church of Corinth: *"Moreover it is required in stewards, that a man be found faithful"* (I Corinthians 4:2). Many people have calls on their lives to do something for the Lord, but they have not been found faithful. When you choose to "bee" faithful, you will be able to withstand every trial and test in life. Your goal is not to please yourself, but to please the Lord. You must choose to "bee" faithful to fulfill the work God has called you to do.

An employer seeks for people who choose to "bee" faithful to the work assigned to them and do their job well without murmuring and disputing. Pastors are looking for people in the church whom they can trust to fill certain positions. It is only those who choose to "bee" faithful who are trustworthy.

A faithful person is a valuable person. It's all in your choice. You can either choose to "bee" faithful or choose not to "bee" faithful. One carries a great reward; the other does not. Choose, today, to "bee" faithful.

Bee Fascinated

There are so many things in life that should cause you to "bee" fascinated. Who can help but "bee" fascinated when looking at the Rocky Mountains soaring into the heavens or seeing the beauty of Lake Louise? Most are fascinated when watching Niagara Falls pour her millions of gallons of water over the cliff. Life, in itself, is fascinating but it is even more fascinating for those who have accepted Jesus Christ as Savior and Lord and are walking in the will, plan and purpose of God. The flowers seem to be brighter, the sky a deeper blue and the sunshine more brilliant when you are led by the Spirit of the Lord. Think of that—being led by the Spirit of the Lord. God said, *"The steps of a good man are ordered by the LORD: and he delighteth in his way"* (Psalm 37:23). Doesn't that fascinate you?

The disciples couldn't help but "bee" fascinated when they saw Jesus heal the sick, raise the dead and cast out demons. You should also "bee" fascinated when you see all the great things that the Lord is doing in this day. I can't help but "bee" fascinated when I think of Jesus, hanging on the cross to die for my sins and the sins of the whole world. Yet I am more fascinated when remembering that Jesus didn't stay on the cross, He didn't stay in the grave, but has ascended to the Heavens and is seated on the right hand of the throne of God. What a wonderful reason to "bee" fascinated! This "bee" will never leave a painful sting.

Bee Favored

W hen the cruel hands of Joseph's brothers sold him to the Egyptians, "bee" favored was there with him. The Lord was with Joseph and he soon found great favor in the eyes of Potiphar. When Potiphar saw the favor of the Lord resting upon this blameless young man, he gave him the authority over all his house. In fact, *"he left all that he had in Joseph's hand; and he knew not ought he had, save the bread which he did eat. And Joseph was a goodly person, and well favoured"* (Genesis 39:6). Such favor was upon Joseph because of choice. He met the conditions for the favor of the Lord to rest upon him.

The same favor of the Lord rested upon Daniel [Belteshazzar], Hananiah [Shadrach], Mishael [Meshach], and Azariah [Abednego]. The king had assigned Ashpenaz to search his kingdom for *"Children in whom was no blemish, but well favoured, and skilful in all wisdom, and cunning in knowledge, and understanding science, and such as had ability in them to stand in the king's palace, and whom they might teach the learning and the tongue of the Chaldeans"* (Daniel 1:4). Why did these young men meet those high qualifications? What made them shine out above others even though they were carried away from their home into the land of captivity? They chose to be different than other young people of their day. Even in captivity, the favor of God was upon them.

Esther was another young person upon whom the Lord could place His favor and blessing: *"And the king loved Esther above all the women, and she obtained grace and favour in his sight more than all the virgins; so that he set the royal crown upon her head, and made her queen instead of Vashti"* (Esther 2:17).

When the angel Gabriel appeared to the young virgin, Mary, he proclaimed, *"Hail, thou that art highly favored, the Lord is with thee:*

blessed art thou among women" (Luke 1:28). Not just favored—highly favored. This young girl walked in the favor of the Lord because she chose to live a life that was well-pleasing in the sight of the Lord. Choose to "bee" favored. Surely, this "bee" will never leave a painful sting!

GOD SEES IT ALL

How sweet it is to trust
In confidence and love
That God sees down below
As well as up above.

And every storm that comes
Shall not escape His eyes
In sorrow, pain or death
He hears His children's cries.

Bee Fearless

A person may be ever so intelligent, educated and sophisticated but still struggle with fear. Most deal with fear some time in life. Job (whom God called a perfect and upright man in his generation) cried out in anguish, *"For the thing which I greatly feared is come upon me, and that which I was afraid of is come unto me"* (Job 3:25). This should be a warning not to keep company with fear.

For you to "bee" fearless, you must first understand that God did not give you the spirit of fear: *"For God hath not given us the spirit of fear; but of power, and of love, and of a sound mind"* (II Timothy 1:7). This kind of fear is negative. Since God gave you a sound mind instead of fear, you must change your thinking. Instead of meditating upon fearful thoughts, choose to "bee" fearless. The Bible tells us not to be afraid, even in troubled times, *"He shall not be afraid of evil tidings: his heart is fixed, trusting in the LORD"* (Psalm 112:7). To "bee" fearless is to be fixed, trusting in the Lord.

The Psalmist gives a clear and encouraging testimony of what happens when a person is fearless: *"The LORD is on my side; I will not fear: what can man do unto me?"* (Psalm 118:6). Again, Psalm 3:6 has this powerful testimony, *"I will not be afraid of ten thousands of people, that have set themselves against me round about."* Isaiah also gave a marvelous testimony when he said, *"Behold, God is my salvation; I will trust, and not be afraid: for the LORD JEHOVAH is my strength and my song; he also is become my salvation"* (Isaiah 12:2). As these patriarchs were successful in overcoming the spirit of fear, you can do the same. The Bible gives you the key how to overcome in I John 4:18. *"There is no fear in love,"* he says, *"but perfect love casteth out fear: because fear hath torment."* He then gives the reason why many are struggling with fear: *"He that feareth is not made perfect in love."* If you are plagued with fear, examine your love toward God and man.

Although the Bible warns, *"The fear of man bringeth a snare"* (Proverbs 29:25), it also commands us to have the fear of God. Ecclesiastes 12:13 explains why you are to fear the Lord: *"Let us hear the conclusion of the whole matter."* What is the conclusion? *"Fear God, and keep his commandments: for this is the whole duty of man."* You are to fear God but not man. You are to fear God but not troubles. The fear of God is not a tormenting spirit. Rather, the fear of the Lord brings confidence and trust. When you fear the Lord, you will not live in sin. Therefore, "bee" fearless toward man, but be filled with the fear of the Lord.

*"Fear is negative faith and faith is positive faith.
Frighten fear with cheer."*

Bee Fed

Wouldn't it have been a delight to "bee" fed by the loaves and fishes Jesus multiplied? Yet, Jesus rebuked those who followed Him only for the loaves and fishes: "*Verily, verily, I say unto you, Ye seek me, not because ye saw the miracles, but because ye did eat of the loaves, and were filled*" (John 6:26). How disappointing it must have been to the Lord to realize that some of His followers were more interested in natural food than spiritual. Natural food is good and necessary, but Matthew 4:4 says, "*...Man shall not live by bread alone, but by every word that proceedeth out of the mouth of God.*"

What a difference it would make if all Believers had a longing for the deeper things of God. The Lord desires for us to "bee" fed strong meat, but few can enjoy such a spiritual diet. Why? "*But strong meat belongeth to them that are of full age, even those who by reason of use have their senses exercised to discern both good and evil*" (Hebrews 5:14). Paul challenged the church at Corinth because he was unable to feed them the meat of the Word. I can almost hear his lamenting words, "*I have fed you with milk, and not with meat: for hitherto ye were not able to bear it, neither yet now are ye able*" (I Corinthians 3:2). Faithful church leaders want to see their people grow up so they can be partakers of the deeper things of Heaven. Too many are satisfied with less than the best Heaven has to offer.

You need to "bee" fed so you can feed others. You need to "bee" fed Heavenly manna so you can reach a world that has lost the way. When you choose to "bee" fed with spiritual things, this "bee" will not leave a painful sting.

Bee Fertile

Y ears ago, my wife and I bought a farm. After unsuccessful attempts to produce crops in one of the fields, we were told someone had removed topsoil from the land. All that remained was unproductive subsoil. Even attempting to plant grass for pasture was futile. We concluded the field would never produce anything because it was not fertile.

Some people are as infertile as our land. They try to do things to please God, but their heart is not fertile soil for the Word of God to take root. They read the Bible and try to live a fruit bearing life, but have an unproductive heart, filled with carnality, animosity, greed or an angry disposition toward others. When their faith is tested, they have nothing to help them overcome because their heart is not established on a firm foundation.

The Heavenly Father expects you to "bee" fertile and productive in all that you do. Ecclesiastes 9:10 explains one way to "bee" fertile: "*Whatsoever thy hand findeth to do, do it with thy might....*" You must put forth an effort to "bee" fertile. Help encourage those around you to "bee" fertile and fruit bearing in the things of God: "*But he that received seed into the good ground is he that heareth the word, and understandeth it; which also beareth fruit, and bringeth forth, some an hundredfold, some sixty, some thirty*" (Matthew 13:23). "Bee" fertile in the Word of God. This "bee" will never leave a painful sting.

Bee Fervent

T he Bible instructs to "bee" *"fervent in spirit"* (Romans 12:11). When you are fervent in spirit, you have the zeal and enthusiasm to accomplish that which would otherwise be left undone. When you choose to "bee" fervent, your prayer life takes on new meaning. James reminds us, *"The effectual fervent prayer of a righteous man availeth much"* (James 5:16). To "bee" fervent means to be earnest. When you are fervent, you will not give up when the way is hard nor quit when under test.

In Peter's writings to the church, he penned some powerful words, *"And above all things have fervent charity* [love] *among yourselves: for charity shall cover the multitude of sins"* (I Peter 4:8). Wouldn't our relationships with others be so much better if we chose to "bee" fervent in the area of charity? Marriages would become a blessing instead of a war zone. Our work place would be more pleasant. To "bee" fervent in charity is a "bee" that would never leave a painful sting.

" Enthusiasm hates laziness;
laziness hates enthusiasm."

Bee Filled

T he Bible admonishes you to "bee" filled with God. What a marvelous possibility! Think of this, *"And to know the love of Christ, which passeth knowledge, that ye might be filled with all the fullness of God"* (Ephesians 3:19). To "bee" filled with God is to "bee" filled with His love because *"God is love"* (I John 4:8). You can "bee" filled with His joy because He has given you His joy, *"These things have I spoken unto you, that my joy might remain in you, and that your joy might be full"*(John 15:11). You can "bee" filled with His peace for He said, *"Peace I leave with you, my peace I give unto you"* (John 14:27). He wants you to "bee" filled with His holiness *"Because it is written, Be ye holy; for I am holy"* (I Peter 1:16). To "bee" filled with God removes the limitations that would hinder you. Jesus said, *"nothing shall be impossible unto you"*(Matthew 17:20).

To "bee" filled with God is to "bee" filled with the Holy Spirit. To "bee" filled with the Spirit is to "bee" filled with the fruit of the Spirit, for it is written, *"But the fruit of the Spirit is love, joy, peace, longsuffering, gentleness, goodness, faith, Meekness, temperance: against such there is no law"* (Galatians 5:22-23). What a marvelous list of Heavenly qualities! What would this world be like if we were all filled with the fruit of the Spirit? Even our marriages would be filled with love and romance.

If you are filled with the fullness of God, you will "bee" filled with hope, enthusiasm, zeal and blessed expectation instead of fear and worry. You will "bee" filled with joy, praise and thanksgiving every day. Listen to these words once again, *"be filled with all the fullness of God"* (Ephesians 3:19). When you are filled with His fullness, this "bee" will never leave a painful sting.

Bee Finished

It may be easy to start something, but hard to finish what was started. King Saul started out right. He had the right motives. He purposed to be a good king of Israel, but when he lost sight of the Lord, his life ended in disaster. You need not be a failure in what the Lord calls you to do. Jesus is *"the author and finisher of our faith"* (Hebrews 12:2). What He authors, He will help you finish if you put forth an effort to do your part.

To "bee" finished is a choice. Paul made that choice. In his letter to Timothy, he testified, *"I have finished my course, I have kept the faith"* (II Timothy 4:7). It is after the finish line that the rewards are given. To "bee" finished at the end of life is a great accomplishment. Jesus told His followers, *"My meat is to do the will of him that sent me, and to finish his work"* (John 4:34). Later, in His High Priestly prayer, He testified, *"I have finished the work which thou gavest me to do"* (John 17:4). What a goal—to "bee" finished. Surely, this "bee" will never leave a painful sting!

"You need to quit quitting."

Bee Firm

There are times in life when you must "bee" firm. You need to "bee" firm in your commitments to the Lord and others. You need to "bee" firm in standing for the right. You need to "bee" firm in integrity. You need to "bee" firm in your relationship with Christ. There should be no possibility of turning back, no half-hearted Christianity. Hebrews 3:6 says, *"...hold fast the confidence and the rejoicing of the hope firm unto the end."* If you are firm in what you believe, you will not be easily sidetracked. Ephesians 4:14 states, *"That we henceforth be no more children, tossed to and fro, and carried about with every wind of doctrine."* If you don't make a decision to "bee" firm, you may be led astray by deceivers. "Bee" firm is a very important "bee" to follow, so "bee" firm in your commitments and decisions.

"Backsets are less painful and discouraging when you remain motivated."

Bee Fixed

To "bee" fixed on the Lord is a safe and secure place. The Psalmist knew what it meant to "bee" fixed. In Psalm 57:7 he testified, *"My heart is fixed, O God, my heart is fixed: I will sing and give praise."* When your heart is fixed on the Lord, you need not be afraid but can trust in Him. Listen to these comforting words from Psalm 112:7, *"He shall not be afraid of evil tidings: his heart is fixed, trusting in the LORD."* It is your only secure resting place. In troubled times, you can rest in the shelter of the Almighty. It is a place where you can be free from the fears that surround you on every side. You can have a calm resting place near to the heart of God.

How often we bear unnecessary concerns and worries because we have not learned to "bee" fixed on the Lord. The Lord desires to protect and care for you. There is victory in, *"Casting all your care upon him; for he careth for you"* (I Peter 5:7). To "bee" fixed is a choice. If you choose to "bee" fixed on the Lord, you won't "bee" fixed on things that rob you of a beautiful day.

Bee Flawless

Y ou hear people say, "No one can 'bee' flawless; we all make mistakes and we all fail." The Bible does say in Romans 3:23, *"For all have sinned, and come short of the glory of God,"* but it doesn't tell you to stay in that condition. Daniel was a man in whom no fault was found. His enemies searched for any weakness: *"Then said these men, We shall not find any occasion against this Daniel, except we find it against him concerning the law of his God"* (Daniel 6:5). In other words, Daniel was flawless. How did he become that way? He made a choice. You will never become flawless without a desire and a quality decision to strive for perfection.

David was another patriarch who had a testimony of being flawless. This is recorded in I Samuel 29:3: *"Achish said unto the princes of the Philistines, Is not this David, the servant of Saul the king of Israel, which hath been with me these days, or these years, and I have found no fault in him since he fell unto me unto this day?"* That sounds like David had become flawless. I am not suggesting that he reached a place of sinless perfection. He was still dwelling in flesh and blood, but he appeared flawless to Achish. Let's take the challenge; strive to "bee" flawless. "Bee" flawless will never leave a painful sting! Amen?

Bee Flexible

Y ou will face times in your life when you need to "bee" flexible. To "bee" flexible sometimes means to submit to another
person's ideas. Ephesians 5:21 says, "*Submitting yourselves one to
another in the fear of God.*" You may need to change your way of
doing something because someone else has a better plan. There may
be times when you feel your way is best, but you can adjust your
ways to please others if their way is not wrong. Being flexible does
not mean giving in to wrong or allowing someone to unduly take
advantage of you.

When a person is flexible, they can adjust to circumstances and situations that may not be favorable. A flexible person can move into
another area or find a different occupation and still be content.
Learn to be like a plant. If it is not flexible on a windy day, it will
break. We would have a lot less trouble in our churches if we could
all learn to cooperate with this very important "bee"—"bee" flexible.

"*They say the wise man changes his mind, but the
man who doesn't have to change his mind is wiser still.*"

Bee Flowing

Jesus made a remarkable statement that should affect everyone, *"He that believeth on me, as the scripture hath said, out of his belly* [heart] *shall flow rivers of living water"* (John 7:38). Out of your innermost being should flow rivers of living water. Not one river; not a mere creek—rivers. Those rivers should "bee" flowing out of you at all times. It will give you the ability to help those who need encouragement and guidance.

The fruit of the Spirit should also "bee" flowing out of you, *"The fruit of the Spirit is love, joy, peace, longsuffering, gentleness, goodness, faith Meekness, temperance"* (Galatians 5:22-23). What a difference you could make in your lifetime with the fruit of the Spirit manifesting in you day by day, week by week, year by year.

You should "bee" flowing in daily worship, praise and thanksgiving to your Heavenly Father for all the precious things you enjoy in life. Ephesians 5:19 instructs, *"Speaking to yourselves in psalms and hymns and spiritual songs, singing and making melody in your heart to the Lord."* When that sweet and heartfelt melody flows toward the throne room, the Lord will bless you abundantly. So, "bee" flowing! This "bee" will never leave a painful sting.

Bee Focused

It is important to "bee" focused on right things. If you focus your attention on the negative, your response will be negative. If you choose to "bee" focused on positive things, you will have more positive possibilities. The Scriptures instruct, *"Looking unto Jesus the author and finisher of our faith"* (Hebrews 12:2). Your daily life should always "bee" focused upon your Savior and the things He has done for you. If you are facing depressing circumstances, focus instead on Jesus. He will help you win great victories.

"Bee" focused on what you want to accomplish in life. The apostle Paul mentioned in Philippians 3:13-14 that he needed to "bee" focused on the future. He said, *"But this one thing I do, forgetting those things which are behind, and reaching forth unto those things which are before, I press toward the mark for the prize of the high calling of God in Christ Jesus."* The book of Hebrews describes how the patriarchs of old focused on the future. They understood their stay on earth was only temporary, *"But now they desire a better country, that is, an heavenly"* (Hebrews 11:16). When you are focused on Heavenly things instead of what you see around you in the natural, "bee" focused will never leave a painful sting.

Bee Followed

People are always looking for someone to follow. Jesus was a man who could "bee" followed. I Peter 2:21 says, *"For even hereunto were ye called: because Christ also suffered for us, leaving us an example, that ye should follow his steps."* Apostle Paul was confident he could safely "bee" followed. He told the Corinthians, *"Wherefore I beseech you, be ye followers of me"* (I Corinthians 4:16). This verse reveals Paul's unwavering walk with the Lord. In II Thessalonians 3:7, we see why he could so boldly encourage his churches to follow him. *"For yourselves know,"* he reminded them, *"how ye ought to follow us: for we behaved not ourselves disorderly among you."*

All leaders should be safe to follow. This is especially true of a father in the home or a leader in the church. A good father considers it his God-given responsibility to make sure his children can safely follow him. A church leader should be able to instruct his people, *"Be ye followers of me, even as I also am of Christ"* (I Corinthians 11:1). Hebrews 13:7 tells us, *"Remember them which have the rule over you, who have spoken unto you the word of God: whose faith follow, considering the end of their conversation."* This verse is describing leaders whose faith can "bee" followed. Such examples are greatly needed in this generation. You should be the kind of living epistle that can always "bee" followed.

Bee Forbearing

Y ou need to "bee" forbearing, understanding and considerate of those around you. Colossians 3:13 instructs, "....*Forbearing one another, and forgiving one another, if any man have a quarrel against any: even as Christ forgave you, so also do ye.*" You may not always understand others. There may be times you silently question their actions or decisions because of your own ideas of how things should be done. Ephesians 4:2 counsels us how to work together: "*With all lowliness and meekness, with longsuffering, forbearing one another in love.*" Sometimes, you need to admit that you are wrong and another person's way is better. It may not be easy, but in the end, it is very rewarding. There were times I couldn't understand another person's actions, but I chose to "bee" forbearing and didn't respond. The more I associated with that person, the more I understood their decisions. When you learn to "bee" forbearing with others, your differences can be settled peaceably. "Bee" forbearing is a precious "bee" that will never leave a painful sting.

" Put other's failures on the shelf;
Point the finger at yourself."

Bee Forceful

S ome things require a forceful mentality instead of a "hope-so" mentality. To "bee" forceful is not to be domineering, controlling or obnoxious but to courageously fight the battles of life. You should "bee" forceful when you are ready to quit, give up or conclude that you are defeated. Jesus told us that the kingdom of Heaven would suffer violence. He speaks of a group of enforcers that would change defeat to victory: *"And from the days of John the Baptist until now the kingdom of heaven suffereth violence, and the violent take it by force"* (Matthew 11:12). You should "bee" forceful when breaking down those barriers that are holding you back. Don't let anything stop you. "Bee" forceful is a very important "bee." This "bee," when used correctly, will help you win great victories.

" Never shirk from hard work."

Bee Forewarned

While traveling through one of the mid-western states, we passed a flashing sign advising travelers to tune in to the weather station for an urgent message. We were warned that severe storms and tornadoes were active to the north. To "bee" forewarned gave us an alertness to be careful as we headed in the direction of possible danger.

There are many areas in life where we need to "bee" forewarned. We need to "bee" forewarned that sin is dangerous and will separate us from God. We also need to "bee" forewarned that certain things are an abomination to the Lord. Among those abominations is *"he that soweth discord among brethren"* (Proverbs 6:19). To sow discord means to stir up strife or contention among brethren. This is a problem in some areas, so we need to "bee" forewarned to avoid becoming involved in this wrong. We are called to live in peace. The God of peace will help us avoid any kind of strife in our homes, churches or workplaces. The Bible also forewarns us that, *"Perilous times shall come"* (II Timothy 3:1). Here, we are forewarned that a time is coming that can be deceptive and harmful to us. We must take heed to this warning to avoid being snared.

The Holy Spirit will often forewarn us of danger or trouble. Many have testified, over the years, how the Spirit forewarned them of something. By heeding that warning, they were delivered from a major disaster. Once, while walking with our sons along a path near a lake, I picked up in my spirit that something was wrong. I stopped and told them a poisonous snake was lying somewhere near. We found the snake lying right along the path we were walking on. Thank God, we can "bee" forewarned. This "bee" will never leave a painful sting.

Bee Forgetful

Memory can be a precious thing, but memory can also be very destructive and harmful. Learn to "bee" forgetful of those things which stir bad memories. "Bee" forgetful of the injuries caused by careless words or thoughtless acts. "Bee" forgetful of the loss of dreams which caused you discouragement and perplexity. "Bee" forgetful of your failures in pursuing accomplishments. Life can be full of trials and tests, but if you major on them, you will be greatly hindered. Life can also be filled with expectation, joy and marvelous hope because we serve a miracle working God. "Bee" forgetful of the failures of the past. Rise up and face the future with expectation, faith and confidence in your Heavenly Father.

If you choose to "bee" forgetful of all the bad memories of the past, your future can radiate with the beauty of the Lord and you can go forth in constant victory. Paul said in Philippians 3:13-14, *"Brethren, I count not myself to have apprehended: but this one thing I do, forgetting those things which are behind, and reaching forth unto those things which are before, I press toward the mark for the prize of the high calling of God in Christ Jesus."* Take his advice and "bee" forgetful of things that you should not store in your memory. When you learn to "bee" forgetful, you can set your face like flint to the future and become a true winner.

Bee Forgiving

S ome Christians are in confusion and turmoil because they have never learned to "bee" forgiving. Colossians 3:13 says, *"Forbearing one another, and forgiving one another, if any man have a quarrel against any: even as Christ forgave you, so also do ye."* To "bee" forgiving is Christ-like. You do not forgive others because they deserve it; you forgive others because Christ has forgiven you. When you learn to forgive those who injured you, it releases you from the pain of that experience. Peace and joy follow such forgiveness.

Those who do not forgive until asked suffer many painful hours of unnecessary torment. Jesus spoke some very strong words in Matthew 18:35, *"So likewise shall my heavenly Father do also unto you, if ye from your hearts forgive not every one his brother their trespasses."* In the verses prior to this, Jesus spoke about the tormentors who harassed those who refused to forgive. "Bee" forgiving at all times. This will help you to live free from the agony of an unforgiving spirit.

A lady once told me she couldn't forgive a person who injured her. I said, "Oh, yes, you can. It is God's way. You can do anything God tells you to do." When she finally chose to forgive, she began to rejoice because she was free at last. Jesus said, *"For if ye forgive men their trespasses, your heavenly Father will also forgive you: But if ye forgive not men their trespasses, neither will your Father forgive your trespasses"* (Matthew 6:14-15). Unforgiveness brings people into bondage. "Bee" forgiving and be free. "Bee" forgiving is a wonderful "bee" which never leaves a painful sting.

Bee Fortified

To "bee" fortified is to be strengthened against attack. If there ever was a time for the people of God to "bee" fortified against the enemies of the cross, it is now. Job met the qualifications to "bee" fortified by the Lord. The devil recognized this protection and questioned God, *"Hast not thou made an hedge about him, and about his house, and about all that he hath on every side"* (Job 1:10). Yes, God had set a hedge (fort) around Job. Because of his decision to be righteous, the Lord was protecting him.

You should also choose to "bee" fortified. Your home should "bee" fortified to protect yourself and your children from invasion. Unless you choose to "bee" fortified, you could easily fall into the hands of your enemies. Our churches should "bee" fortified to avoid the entrance of wolves that would destroy the sheep. Therefore, "bee" fortified. This "bee" will never leave a painful sting.

Bee Free

What is a greater blessing than to know you are free? Jesus said it is the knowledge of the truth that makes man free, *"And ye shall know the truth, and the truth shall make you free"* (John 8:32). Then, a few verses later, He spoke that precious promise, *"If the Son therefore shall make you free, ye shall be free indeed"* (Verse 36). The Son makes you free from anything that has you bound. For some, it may be a bad habit, a marriage problem, a bad temper, a swearing problem or an addiction. For others, it may be a dishonest heart, a slandering or lying tongue, guilt and condemnation, evil thought patterns or anything that is keeping someone bound. If you want to "bee" free, you can. Ask the Lord to help you "bee" free. What a joy to "bee" free at last!

"Speak to the mountain about God instead of speaking to God about the mountain."

Bee Friendly

I like to associate with friendly people, don't you? The Bible explains, *"A man that hath friends must show himself friendly: and there is a friend that sticketh closer than a brother"* (Proverbs 18:24). To "bee" friendly is a choice. To "bee" friendly is to be kind, helpful, sympathetic, supportive and ready to be a friend to others. You should "bee" friendly toward your neighbors, co-laborers, family members and everyone you meet. I have personally met people who had a notable, friendly character. To "bee" friendly comes naturally to some, while others must put forth more effort to "bee" friendly; but everyone can choose to "bee" friendly. Start today. You may meet someone who needs a friendly touch. "Bee" friendly will never leave a painful sting!

A FRIEND

I always like a fellow
That's a friendly sort of guy;
Who can still shake hands and love you
When you don't see wye to eye:
You can talk the matter over,
Disagree—he's still a friend;
We just smile and change the subject
With no bruises left to mend.

Published in Creative Review 1977
© Copyright Daniel D. Rodes

Bee Friends

Friendship is precious. Working together with friendly, honest, loving people can be rewarding and pleasant. What a blessing to have a good, faithful, understanding friend!

Marriage is a place where friendship is important. My wife, Esther, and I were married for over fifty years. Not only were we a husband and wife team, we were the best of friends. That loving friendship became more meaningful each year. Proverbs 17:17 tells us, "*A friend loveth at all times.*" How beautiful it is to "bee" friends.

Did you know you are to even treat your enemies as if they were your friends? Matthew 5:44 instructs: "*But I say unto you, Love your enemies, bless them that curse you, do good to them that hate you, and pray for them which despitefully use you, and persecute you.*" As you follow the guidelines of this verse, you may find your enemies becoming your friends. There are some persecuted Christians who chose to show forgiveness and kindness toward their enemies. Later, those enemies became their friends instead of foes. To "bee" friends is surely a "bee" that will never leave a painful sting.

"Love will keep a multitude of friends."

Bee Fruit Bearing

The Lord expects you to be a fruit bearing Christian: *"Every branch in me that beareth not fruit he taketh away: and every branch that beareth fruit, he purgeth it, that it may bring forth more fruit"* (John 15:2). He removes those things in your life that are nonproductive so you will "bee" fruit bearing. A gardener will do everything in his power to cause his fruit trees to produce. He prunes, purges and fertilizes them. Imagine the gardener walking through his orchard. What joy he experiences as he sees every tree bearing fruit. Suppose one of the trees doesn't produce. Can you feel his disappointment? Jesus tells a parable: *"A certain man had a fig tree planted in his vineyard; and he came and sought fruit thereon, and found none. Then said he unto the dresser of his vineyard, Behold, these three years I come seeking fruit on this fig tree, and find none: cut it down; why cumbereth it the ground?"* (Luke 13:6-7). Notice how the vinedresser responded, *"...let it alone this year also, till I shall dig about it, and dung it: And if it bear fruit, well: and if not, then after that thou shalt cut it down"* (Verses 8-9). Many people are like this parable. God is giving them another chance to "bee" fruit bearing before He cuts them off. As a Believer, you must "bee" fruit bearing; it's God's way!

Bee Fruitful

Your fruit reveals the type of person you are. Jesus said, *"Wherefore by their fruits ye shall know them."* (Matthew 7:20). People should be able to recognize that you are a Christian by your fruit. There are a number of ways that you, as a Christian, can "bee" fruitful. One is mentioned in II Peter 1:8, *"For if these things be in you, and abound, they make you that ye shall neither be barren nor unfruitful in the knowledge of our Lord Jesus Christ."* Another way to "bee" fruitful is to have the fruit of the Spirit manifesting in every area of life. You also should "bee" fruitful in soul winning and ministering to the needs of others. To be a fruitful Christian is to be holy, righteous and doing the works of the kingdom: *"That ye might walk worthy of the Lord unto all pleasing, being fruitful in every good work, and increasing in the knowledge of God"* (Colossians 1:10). When you are fruitful in the things of God, "bee" fruitful will never leave a painful sting.

*"I'll try is not enough;
I will is better still."*

Bee Full

Our Heavenly Father desires and plans for His people to experience the fullness of God, the fullness of Christ Jesus and the fullness of the Holy Spirit. Ponder this promise from Ephesians 3:19: *"...that ye might be filled with all the fulness of God."* In chapter four of the same book, there is another challenging scripture: *"Till we all come in the unity of the faith, and of the knowledge of the Son of God, unto a perfect man, unto the measure of the stature of the fulness of Christ"* (Ephesians 4:13). These marvelous promises are not just for a few chosen people. The words, *"we all,"* include all of God's faithful children. Now, turn the page in your Bible to chapter five and seize this promise: *"And be not drunk with wine, wherein is excess; but be filled with the Spirit"* (Ephesians 5:18). If you are part of the body of Christ, you should enjoy the fullness of all He offers, *"Which is his body, the fulness of him that filleth all in all"* (Ephesians 1:23). What a gracious church we would have if all people chose to "bee" full!

We should seek to "bee" full of the joy of the Lord. Not just the temporal joy that floats up and down like a see-saw, but the kind of joy Jesus said would remain. John 15:11 tells us, *"These things have I spoken unto you, that my joy might remain in you, and that your joy might be full."* This is more than fantasy; it is an actual possibility. In fact, this God-given joy should become a way of life: *"Thou hast made known to me the ways of life; thou shalt make me full of joy with thy countenance"* (Acts 2:28).

The ability to "bee" full of Heaven is waiting for you. When you are full of God and His Word, it is like sweet honey to your soul, *"More to be desired are they than gold, yea, than much fine gold: sweeter also than honey and the honeycomb"* (Psalm 19:10). The honey made by "bee" full is sweet. This "bee" will never leave a painful sting.

Bee Fun

L ife can "bee" fun and is fun to those who refuse to be discouraged and perplexed about the uncertainty of tomorrow. This fun is not some shallow emotional experience, but rather a mature fun that comes from walking in the ways of the Lord. If you are discouraged, perplexed and downcast, maybe you should ask the question found in Psalm 42:5, *"Why art thou cast down, O my soul? and why art thou disquieted in me? hope thou in God: for I shall yet praise him for the help of his countenance."*

Life is meant to "bee" fun. Parents should establish an atmosphere of fun in their homes. A place where their children can enjoy life. This does not mean engaging in foolishness or always playing games, but creating a cheerful, pleasant environment.

I have friends who are fun. They have pleasant, encouraging characteristics that fill the whole atmosphere with joy. If you choose to "bee" fun, life will be more pleasant for those around you. Obviously, "bee" fun will never leave a painful sting.

*" Enjoy at least one good laugh a day
to remain emotionally stable."*

Bee Generous

To "bee" generous is to be willing to give and forgive. Generous people are unselfish. In Paul's address to the Corinthians, he wrote, *"How that in a great trial of affliction the abundance of their joy and their deep poverty abounded unto the riches of their liberality* [generosity]" (II Corinthians 8:2). Here, Paul is expressing his gratitude to those who chose to "bee" generous during difficult times.

The Lord sees your generosity and notes the condition of your heart as well as the circumstances. Notice what He saw in the woman who gave two mites: *"For all these have of their abundance cast in unto the offerings of God: but she of her penury hath cast in all the living that she had"* (Luke 21:4). Two mites doesn't appear to be generous giving, does it? No one knew she had given all she had. The Lord expects you to "bee" generous without sounding a trumpet to let everyone know how much you sacrificed. Such giving would rob you of your blessings and be displeasing to the Lord: *"But when thou doest alms, let not thy left hand know what thy right hand doeth"* (Matthew 6:3). What a lovely "bee" is "bee" generous! To truly "bee" generous with a good attitude is a "bee" that will never leave a painful sting.

Bee Gentle

K ing David made a great discovery which he revealed in Psalm 18:35: "*...thy gentleness hath made me great.*" Gentleness is one of the keys to gaining greatness. To "bee" gentle is a choice which fills you with the lovely characteristics of meekness and tenderness toward others.

A woman who was married to a harsh, demanding man told her pastor, "If I argue with him when he is angry, he gets furious. If I don't say anything, he accuses me of being stubborn." But then she received an idea to practice Proverbs 15:1: "*A soft answer turneth away wrath: but grievous words stir up anger.*" The next time her husband went through his daily rage of lashing out at her, she spoke softly and kindly, "I really don't want to hurt you. I want to have a pleasant marriage." He reacted with harsh words and slammed the door on his way out to work. She was disappointed, but during the next few days she began to observe a remarkable change.

A few months later, he told her, "Your gentle words tore me up, but thank God, they helped change me."

She smiled and said, "*A soft answer turneth away wrath.*"

Gentle people seem to have the favor of the Lord resting upon them. A father who is gentle toward his wife and children brings heaven to earth. That family may not be wealthy or live in a mansion, but the atmosphere in that home is of a heavenly nature. If gentleness is not a virtue in your life, you can change. You can choose to "bee" gentle. Then, you can say with David, "*thy gentleness hath made me great.*" Gentleness—the "Bee" which never leaves a sting! So start to chart your way to greatness!

Bee Genuine

Have you ever trusted someone to "bee" genuine only to find out later they were not who they claimed to be? How disappointing! How would you feel if you found out your dearest friend was not a genuine friend? What if he only pretended to be your friend, but behind your back he was slandering you? How would you feel if your secrets were exposed? Would you be ashamed or would you feel good about yourself? If you had taken a large amount of money to the bank only to discover it was counterfeit, how would you feel? There are so many counterfeit people, some even seem to be sincere Christians. Jesus saw the hypocrisy of the Pharisees and said, *"This people draweth nigh unto me with their mouth, and honoureth me with their lips; but their heart is far from me"* (Matthew 15:8). He must have been greatly disappointed to see people who only pretended to love God. When someone wears a mask to hide their true identity, they are a misery to themselves and others.

We can "bee" genuine. I heard an elderly gentleman say, "I want my friends to know what I am inside. I have nothing to hide." We must "bee" genuine every day with our friends, family and God. Only then can we have the peace of mind that genuine Christians enjoy.

Bee Gifted

Have you ever considered what would happen if you used all your gifts and talents to the glory of God? In Luke 19:12-27, Jesus spoke a parable concerning servants who received talents from their master. One multiplied his talent ten times, another five. But one hid his talent instead of allowing it to be useful. Therefore, it was taken away from him: "*For I say unto you, That unto every one which hath shall be given; and from him that hath not, even that he hath shall be taken away from him*" (Luke 19:26). Some people have unused gifts and talents. If they would use what they have been given, God could increase those gifts.

It is possible to "bee" gifted in more areas than you are aware. When I was in school, some of my classmates were exceptionally talented. They had many gifts and abilities. Years later, I noticed that some of the ones who appeared less gifted soared above the gifted ones. Why? They chose to go beyond the normal. They chose to accomplish. They chose to "bee" gifted. They became worthwhile, useful and helpful because they used their gifts correctly. I don't know what happened to the ones who were once talented, but those who were less gifted became quality men and women. Another boy I knew, who sat beside me in church, later achieved a major position in government. Only because he chose to use his gifts to the fullest did he reach that high position.

I still admire those who use their talents, gifts and abilities in the work of the kingdom of God. Oh, how we need to "bee" gifted! This "bee" will never leave a painful sting.

Bee Glad

W hy are some people so full of gladness while others are in despair? To "bee" glad is a choice and a privilege. The Scripture declares, *"Be glad in the LORD, and rejoice, ye right-eous: and shout for joy, all ye that are upright in heart"* (Psalm 32:11). Although the Lord will help you, the fact still remains, those who choose to "bee" glad will find reasons to "bee" glad. The Psalmist made a firm, quality decision. *"I will be glad...,"* He says in Psalm 9:2. What joy fills you when your heart is glad!

It is not always easy to "bee" glad, but it is extremely rewarding! Do you want to be glad? You can be. Make a decision right now that regardless of your circumstances you will "bee" glad. *"Let them shout for joy, and be glad, that favour my righteous cause: yea, let them say continually, Let the LORD be magnified, which hath pleasure in the prosperity of his servant"* (Psalm 35:27). You will "bee" glad you chose to "bee" glad.

"I'm excited about getting excited."

Bee Godly

To "bee" godly is to be devout and have a special reverence for God. You are a holy, righteous person not living in open rebellion nor justifying the sin nature but reaching out to the holy God who has created you in His own image. II Peter 2:9 says, *"The Lord knoweth how to deliver the godly out of temptations, and to reserve the unjust unto the day of judgment to be punished."* What a promise! The Lord will deliver the godly out of temptations.

To "bee" godly is to be right. It doesn't mean you become infallible, but it does mean you do not willfully sin against God or others. You will refrain from anything that could defile you by what you read, hear or see. I am sure that would eliminate a lot of videos, DVD's, CD's, TV shows, books and magazines. To simplify, to "bee" godly means you have nothing to do with the devil and his operation. You are a separated, chosen, called out, Heaven bound person.

To "bee" godly is a choice; you can either leave it or receive it, but there are consequences if you choose not to "bee" godly. The Bible says godliness has great value: *"Godliness is profitable unto all things, having promise of the life that now is, and of that which is to come"* (I Timothy 4:8). Without godliness, it is impossible to please God. Jesus said, *"I do always those things that please him"* (John 8:29). If you have that same desire in your heart, then you have a desire to "bee" godly. That "bee," my friends, will never leave a painful sting.

Bee Going

When you are around people with a slandering tongue, it is a good time to "bee" going. It is time to "bee" going when someone tries to discourage you from doing the will of God for your life. You should "bee" going if you are part of a church that doesn't teach the whole truth. You need to get away from anything that would harm your relationship with God. "Bee" going when sin is tempting you. II Timothy 2:22 tells us to *"Flee also youthful lusts: but follow righteousness, faith, charity, peace, with them that call on the Lord out of a pure heart."*

Millions are headed for Hell and we need to "bee" going to reach them. Jesus commanded in Mark 16:15, *"...Go ye into all the world, and preach the gospel to every creature."* You should "bee" going in the right direction so others can safely follow. The Apostle Paul said, *"Brethren, be followers together of me, and mark them which walk so as ye have us for an ensample"* (Philippians 3:17). He was going in a way that would lead others correctly. "Bee" going is a very important "bee" to remember. Listen to its buzzing when you need a little prodding to do what is right. It will never leave a painful sting.

Bee Graceful

O ver the years, I have met numerous people who were well acquainted with "bee" graceful. They had a pleasant way of expressing themselves. Their personality was beautiful and attractive. Their whole composition appeared graceful. People like this are a blessing.

"Bee" graceful has qualities everyone should desire. I met a man who had just started working at a certain business. It wasn't long until the flow of customers increased. One day, I heard him gently encourage his superior to deal kindly with one of the customers. His employer followed his advice. I was impressed to see an employee and employer working together because "bee" graceful was on the scene.

Esther had "bee" graceful operating in her life. Esther 2:17 records, *"And the king loved Esther above all the women, and she obtained grace and favour in his sight more than all the virgins; so that he set the royal crown upon her head, and made her queen instead of Vashti."* Why did she receive such favor? I believe she had befriended "bee" graceful. Surely this blessed "bee" will never leave a painful sting!

Bee Grafted

S ome nurseries who supply fruit trees graft different types into one tree. In our back yard, we had a tree that yielded five different kinds of fruit from the same trunk. Branches from other trees had been grafted onto the main vine. You need to "bee" grafted into the Vine in order to be productive and successful in your Christian life. Jesus said in John 15:5, "*I am the vine, ye are the branches: He that abideth in me, and I in him, the same bringeth forth much fruit: for without me ye can do nothing.*" You need to "bee" grafted into the Master's vine to be productive in your love, joy, and peace. The fruit of the Spirit becomes a part of you when you have been grafted into the main Vine.

After you have been grafted, you must beware that you can be cut off if you do not bear good fruit. Paul warns against pride in Romans 11:18-21, "*Boast not against the branches. But if thou boast, thou bearest not the root, but the root thee. Thou wilt say then, The branches were broken off, that I might be graffed in. Well; because of unbelief they were broken off, and thou standest by faith. Be not highminded, but fear: For if God spared not the natural branches, take heed lest he also spare not thee.*"

When you choose to "bee" grafted, you choose to be productive in every area of life. Those who have been grafted can become successful soul winners. They can be successful in their marriage. They can be successful in their church relationships. They can be successful in their workplace because they are drawing from the true Vine. Obviously, when you choose to "bee" grafted to the Vine, it will never leave a painful sting.

Bee Grateful

To "bee" grateful is to be appreciative. This "bee" is of utmost importance. It conveys the need to be thankful and express gratitude toward those who have done something for you. According to I Thessalonians 5:18, we are instructed to "bee" grateful at all times: "*In every thing give thanks: for this is the will of God in Christ Jesus concerning you.*" II Timothy 3:2 warns that in the last days many would become unthankful, "*For men shall be lovers of their own selves, covetous, boasters, proud, blasphemers, disobedient to parents, unthankful, unholy.*"

It is especially important to "bee" grateful to the Lord. Think often of what the Lord has done for you. He gave His life as a ransom that all might be saved. You should "bee" grateful, giving thanks daily for your salvation. To "bee" grateful is such an important "bee" in the lives of all God's children. Do you suppose such a precious "bee" would ever leave a painful sting?

"*It is hard for trouble to prevail*
when enthusiasm is active."

Bee Great

T he Bible records John the Baptist as a great man, *"For he shall be great in the sight of the Lord"* (Luke 1:15). What made him great? Was it because he had great parents? The Bible records that his parents *"were both righteous before God, walking in all the cammandments and ordinances of the Lord blameless"* (Luke 1:6). I believe he was great because he chose to allow God to mightily use him. He preached in the wilderness without compromise and fearlessly confronted the king concerning his unscriptural lifestyle. John wasn't great in his own eyes, but God saw him as a man who was great—a man suitable for the task.

Great men choose to "bee" great. It is a decision. If you become great in the eyes of man, you may never "bee" great in the eyes of God. Choose to "bee" great by accomplishing noble work for Lord. Then, "bee" great will never leave a painful sting.

"You get nowhere until you dare to dare."

Bee Guarded

Ⅰt is important to "bee" guarded. This "bee" is very valuable in any church, workplace or family. Proverbs 4:23 says, "*Keep thy heart with all diligence; for out of it are the issues of life.*" It is important to guard your heart and not allow evil thoughts or sin to penetrate you. A true pastor will guard his flock and not allow wolves to enter. Parents must guard their children. Some children are offended or grieved because their parents want to know where they are, where they were or what they were doing. Parents know that children need to "bee" guarded. They need to "bee" guarded in their choice of friends. They need to "bee" guarded in making the proper choices in life. They need to "bee" guarded in the area of courtship for their future wellbeing. Many people have broken hearts and wrecked lives because they refused to heed "bee" guarded. Some lamented years later they wished they had heeded the buzzing of "bee" guarded. Don't be offended by "bee" guarded. Surely this bee will never leave a painful sting.

"Keep on guard when it's hard."

Bee Habitual

M any people think of a habit as something bad, but there are good habits you should embrace. Daniel was habitual in kneeling before the Lord three times a day as recorded in Daniel 6:10: "*Now when Daniel knew that the writing was signed, he went into his house; and his windows being open in his chamber toward Jerusalem, he kneeled upon his knees three times a day, and prayed, and gave thanks before his God, as he did aforetime.*" Paul also chose to "bee" habitual in prayer. In II Timothy 1:3, he said, "*I thank God, whom I serve from my forefathers with pure conscience, that without ceasing I have remembrance of thee in my prayers night and day.*" David lived a life of habitual praise. He said, "*Seven times a day do I praise thee because of thy righteous judgments*" (Psalm 119:164).

If you want to "bee" habitual in praising the Lord or earnestly praying, begin now. Set aside a time every day to focus on the greatness of God. Thank Him for the wonderful gift of salvation through His son, Jesus. Make a habit of studying the Word daily. Let it become a necessary part of your lifestyle. Then, "bee" habitual will never leave a painful sting.

Bee Handy

I once read of a man who lived in a very untamed area. There were many dangerous animals, as well as snakes and other harmful creatures. This man always kept his gun or some other kind of weapon handy in case he needed it.

A handy person is ready to be used when someone has a need. Many opportunities arise every day in which you can accomplish something to benefit others. "Bee" handy when you are needed to help to feed the poor, minister to those who have lost a loved one or comfort those who are grieving because of a disaster or tragedy.

I had a stroke which placed my body out of commission. I needed to have people surrounding me who could "bee" handy. While learning to walk again, there were several handy people who were willing to help me any time I needed them.

We should "bee" handy when the Lord needs us. Surely, this "bee" will never leave a painful sting.

Bee Happy

To "bee" happy is to be glad and content, knowing you are making the right choices and serving the Lord without guilt and condemnation. In Psalm 146:5 we read, *"Happy is he that hath the God of Jacob for his help, whose hope is in the LORD his God."* Occasionally, you hear someone object to the word "happy" being used in reference to a Christian. They claim happiness is a very shallow emotional expression. Since the word "happy" is used in both the Old and New Testament, I believe it should be considered a valuable expression among Believers.

You should "bee" happy when serving the Lord and your fellow-man. This kind of happiness endures hardship and rejection. Peter wrote in his epistle to the church: *"If ye be reproached for the name of Christ, happy are ye; for the spirit of glory and of God resteth upon you: on their part he is evil spoken of, but on your part he is glorified"* (I Peter 4:14). A lifestyle of this nature is precious in the sight of the Lord. The apostle James penned a similar statement in James 5:11, *"Behold, we count them happy which endure."* To "bee" happy day in and day out should be a normal for those who love and serve the Lord. Hallelujah!!! Be supremely happy. This "bee" will never leave a painful sting!

Bee Harmless

To "bee" harmless means not to cause harm or inflict pain on someone. The human race seems to have a way of hurting each other. Jesus instructed His disciples to "bee" harmless as they went out to preach the gospel of the kingdom. "*Be ye therefore wise as serpents,*" He told them, "*and harmless as doves*" (Matthew 10:16). We, as fathers, mothers, sons or daughters, should choose to "bee" harmless. Wouldn't that make our homes a lovely place? Wouldn't it be great if every employer, leader, pastor, school teacher and person in authority would choose to "bee" harmless? What about all those under authority? Wouldn't it be wonderful if they would also choose to "bee" harmless? Look at these precious words from Philippians 2:15: "*That ye may be blameless and harmless, the sons of God, without rebuke, in the midst of a crooked and perverse nation, among whom ye shine as lights in the world.*" The book of Hebrews tells us that Jesus was harmless (Hebrews 7:26). This should be a characteristic of the children of God. You should and can "bee" harmless. Put forth every effort to "bee" harmless and avoid injuring friend or foe. "Bee" harmless is truly a "bee" that will never leave a painful sting.

Bee Healed

Y ou would think everyone who is sick would want to be healed but, surprisingly, some enjoy the attention they receive from being ill. Others want to "bee" healed but don't know how to receive their healing. The first step to receive healing of any kind is a desire to "bee" healed. Do you remember the man who was sick for 38 years in John 5:6? Jesus asked him a strange question, *"Wilt thou be made whole?"* The man needed to have a desperate desire to "bee" healed. I am sure there were many who desired to "bee" healed but were not. Who is to judge why they were not healed? I have known people who were wounded because they were blamed for not having faith to "bee" healed. Learn to be kind and compassionate to those who are suffering on the bed of affliction: *"...pray one for another, that ye may be healed"* (James 5:16).

In Hebrews chapter 12 we read, *"Wherefore lift up the hands which hang down, and the feeble knees; And make straight paths for your feet, lest that which is lame be turned out of the way; but let it rather be healed"* (Hebrews 12:12-13). It is hard to receive healing when you are discouraged, drooped over and sad. According to studies made by some physicians, a large number of people are sick as a result of fear, guilt, worry and a melancholy emotional lifestyle but those who are enthusiastic, joyful and full of hope usually recover much more quickly.

People who have love have greater faith to "bee" healed. According to Galatians 5:6, faith and love work together: *"...faith which worketh by love."* One man told me he loved his wife back to health. Isn't that a marvelous testimony?

I have seen many people healed from emotional illness, diseases and afflictions of every kind. Maybe you need healing. If you do, why don't you arise and "bee" healed? "Bee" healed is a wonderful bee that will never leave a painful sting.

Bee Heavenly Minded

There is an old saying, "Don't be so Heavenly minded that you are no earthly good." That statement sounds like good advice, but it isn't true. It is impossible for someone to be so Heavenly minded that he is no earthly good. Jesus was the most Heavenly minded person who ever walked the earth and He did more good for the human race than any other person in the world. Let's look at this another way: instead of being so Heavenly minded that you are no earthly good (as the old saying goes), be so Heavenly minded that you can be of much earthly good and supersede the earthbound mentality.

If you would choose to "bee" Heavenly minded, your decisions would be made more carefully. You would not be selfish or self centered because a Heavenly minded individual thinks God's way. The Bible tells us we have the mind of Christ. "*For who hath known the mind of the Lord, that he may instruct him? But we have the mind of Christ*" (I Corinthians 2:16). In order to increase your Heavenly-mindedness, study and meditate upon the Word of God until you become Christ-like in all your activities and responsibilities. To "bee" Heavenly minded is indeed of great earthly value. This "bee" will never leave a painful sting.

"A good psychology is to start each day with a Bible verse to ponder all day long."

Bee Helpful

This "bee" is a precious "bee" that has been a benefit to the human race for centuries. Even in the beginning of creation, God knew man needed someone to "bee" helpful to him: "*And the LORD God said, It is not good that the man should be alone; I will make him an help meet for him*" (Genesis 2:18). When a wife functions as a helpmeet according to the Bible, she is indeed a blessing.

A helpful person sees ways to help others. Most helpful people are not downhearted, discouraged, perplexed or suffering from depression. Their focus is not on themselves but on how they can benefit others. We need each other. We need to learn to help each other. People who choose to "bee" helpful are very valuable. In the book of Exodus, we find how Moses helped to water the flock for the daughters of Reuel: "*And the shepherds came and drove them away: but Moses stood up and helped them, and watered their flock*" (Exodus 2:17). Surely, "bee" helpful will never leave a painful sting.

Bee Heroic

A hero is full of faith, confidence and trust. A hero cannot be stopped. He is not focused on himself but on the will, purpose and plan of God for his life. Peter, Paul and some of the other apostles were obviously heroic. David was also a hero. In I Samuel 17:36, he boldly declared: *"Thy servant slew both the lion and the bear: and this uncircumcised Philistine shall be as one of them, seeing he hath defied the armies of the living God."* This hero was named a man after God's own heart.

Hebrews 11 records the honor roll of heroic Believers. These superseded the average faithful person. They were not only ready to live a quality life for the Lord, they were ready to die shouting the victory.

"Bee" heroic. In so doing, you may persuade someone else to take the challenge to "bee" heroic. Maybe they will even supersede what you have done. Truly, this "bee" will never leave a painful sting.

"Why waste today on yesterday's failures?"

Bee Hid

The prophet Zephaniah made an extremely important statement in the Book that bears his name, *"Seek ye the LORD, all ye meek of the earth, which have wrought his judgment; seek righteousness, seek meekness: it may be ye shall be hid in the day of the LORD'S anger"* (Zephaniah 2:3). What a wonderful promise—to "bee" hid in the time of judgment. In the book of Colossians we read, *"...your life is hid with Christ in God"* (Colossians 3:3). What a blessed place to be when all around you is uncertain!

"Bee" hid may be buzzing around the head of someone tempted with pride. Listen to his gentle buzz advising you to "bee" hid! You need to "bee" hid from the evil around you. The Psalmist writes, *"Hide me from the secret counsel of the wicked; from the insurrection of the workers of iniquity"* (Psalm 64:2). You need to be protected from the temptation to follow the workers of iniquity. As the eagle is hid in the cleft of the rock so shall you "bee" hid when you heed to the warning buzz of "bee" hid—the "bee" that never leaves a painful sting!

*" Satan may set up a plan to destroy you,
but you can up set his plan."*

Bee Holy

The Lord requires you to "bee" holy. I Peter 1:16 says, "*Because it is written, Be ye holy; for I am holy.*" A life without holiness is a life without the true blessings of God. To "bee" holy means to be blameless and consecrated to the Lord. You take on the nature of God. You are separated from the evil, corrupt and Christ-rejecting world. You become spiritually minded instead of carnally minded. You do things God's way instead of your way. You live according to the Bible and not according to the world's standard. You are free from sin and evil. You do not become infallible, but are victorious over sin: "*But as he which hath called you is holy, so be ye holy in all manner of conversation*" (I Peter 1:15).

Over the years, there has been emphasis placed on holiness in outward appearance instead of the condition of the heart; however, true holiness starts within. It is the spiritual condition of the heart. If you have true holiness, it will be noticeable on the outside. Even your countenance will display holy living. The Bible says that holiness is beautiful, "*O worship the LORD in the beauty of holiness*" (Psalm 96:9). Holiness is not a suggestion, it is a commandment. It is a way of life. "Bee" holy. This "bee" will never leave a painful sting.

Bee Honest

We are living in a world where dishonesty seems to be a way of life for many. When I was a young boy, a neighbor told me, "It used to be that most people were honest and a handshake could seal any contract." What happened to honesty? Some people cannot trust others because they are dishonest themselves. If you have a problem with dishonesty in your life, it will affect others around you. The Bible says, *"Wherefore putting away lying, speak every man truth with his neighbour..."* (Ephesians 4:25).When you speak the truth, you will never become dishonest. Be an example to those around you. Teach your children the value of honesty. An honest person is a valuable person.

In a home where husbands and wives are honest with each other, there is trust. They can honestly work out their differences. Instead of quarreling, they are honest enough to see their own weaknesses. Such homes can become a blessed sanctuary.

Honesty is a virtue that should be cultivated in every Christian's life. The Bible tells us to *"...Provide things honest in the sight of all men"* (Romans 12:17). This would be a better world if everyone would choose to "bee" honest. This "bee" will never leave a painful sting.

Bee Honorable

T he Bible tells us in I Chronicles 4:9, *"And Jabez was more honourable than his brethren: and his mother called his name Jabez, saying, Because I bare him with sorrow."* Why was Jabez more honorable than his brethren? Was it not because of his choice? You must choose to "bee" honorable. You should "bee" honorable in your home life, in the work place, in the church where you serve and in the neighborhood and community. You need to "bee" honorable in the ministry to which you are called.

To "bee" honorable is to be noble. An honorable person is an honest, dependable, reliable, trustworthy person. Such are not just honorable in the sight of others, but also in the sight of the Lord. "Bee" honorable. This bee will never leave a painful sting!

*"You cannot pray, 'Thy will be done,'
until your will is broken."*

Bee Hopeful

T he Bible tells us, "*That at that time ye were without Christ, be-ing aliens from the commonwealth of Israel, and strangers from the covenants of promise, having no hope, and without God in the world*" (Ephesians 2:12). To be without hope is indeed a desperate situation. Thanks be to God who delivered us from the bondage of sin and darkness that we can "bee" hopeful of a glorious future.

Throughout life, we face circumstances where we must choose to "bee" hopeful. Abraham faced a very trying time in his life after he was promised a son. He was getting older by the day without seeing the manifestation of the promise God had made to him. That didn't make him lose hope in God nor in the promise. Romans 4:18 tells us, "*Who against hope believed in hope, that he might become the father of many nations, according to that which was spoken, So shall thy seed be.*" It was that hope that caused Abraham and Sarah to be able to hold a baby in their arms when physically speaking it was impossible. Hope can help to bring into reality what seems to be impossible. The Bible says, "*Hope maketh not ashamed...*" (Romans 5:5). This promise tells us that hope keeps us from suffering shame. If Abraham would have lost hope, he would have lost his expectation of receiving the promised son. When hope is lost, you may not receive the manifestation of what you desired. It was not because the Lord didn't want you to have it, but rather, you lost your faith in reaching for it.

The Bible tells us that the Scripture can give us hope: "*For whatsoever things were written aforetime were written for our learning, that we through patience and comfort of the scriptures might have hope*" (Romans 15:4). When you are faced with circumstances in life that seem to have no answer, listen to the encouraging sound of "bee" hopeful and rise up with new expectation to face an uncertain future. Indeed, "bee" hopeful will never leave a painful sting.

Bee Humble

The humble find favor with the Lord and are blessed. Throughout the Scriptures, if someone humbled themselves after they sinned, the Lord would forgive them and extend grace and favor. The Lord is affected by humility, *"...God resisteth the proud, but giveth grace unto the humble"* (James 4:6). You will notice the statement in this verse, *"God resisteth the proud."* A proud person is self centered and doesn't realize how his behavior affects others. Humble people have an unselfish attitude. They are easy to be entreated and pleasant to live with.

Be careful not to judge those you believe to be proud. I have known people who appeared on the surface to be rather arrogant, but after learning to know them, I discovered humility in their characteristics. Humility is of great value. It is a virtue all Christians should possess. Some people fear to exercise humility because someone may take advantage of them. This is not true. God will help those who are humble in spirit. A humble spirit is a lovely spirit. Humility should be a top priority in your life, in your relationships at home, at work, at church and every other area.

A humble wife is a blessing to her husband. A woman with a humble spirit is of great value; *"...even the ornament of a meek and quiet spirit, which is in the sight of God of great price"* (I Peter 3:4). The Lord also places a great value on a humble man. God mightily used Moses who was the meekest (most humble) man on earth. He was given the privilege of speaking face to face with the Lord (Exodus 33:11). Therefore, "bee" humble, the world has had enough of pride.

Bee Humorous

I believe there would be much less stress, tension and anxiety if we had a little humor in the home, the work place and the church. I'm not talking about foolish talking or jesting that the Bible condemns (Ephesians 5:4). Hurtful remarks toward a wife or another person are not the kind of humor I am referring to. That is not humorous. That is far from humor.

I once knew a pastor who spoke against humor, but before he finished his sermon he gave a humorous illustration. Humor isn't wrong, in itself. Most people possess some humor. Jesus even gave illustrations that were rather humorous. Notice His response to the Pharisees who warned that Herod desired to kill Him: "*Go ye, and tell that fox, Behold, I cast out devils, and I do cures to day and to morrow, and the third day I shall be perfected*" (Luke 13:32). To me, that is a rather humorous statement. Another time, Jesus rebuked the Pharisees. "*Ye blind guides,*" He explained, "*which strain at a gnat, and swallow a camel*" (Matthew 23:24). I think that is somewhat humorous, don't you?

I have cautioned people to be careful their humor doesn't turn into lies. There is a difference between being somewhat humorous or presenting a lie in the form of a joke. We can choose to "bee" humorous and be an encouragement to others.

Bee Hungry

D id you ever try to eat when you weren't hungry? What happened? Regardless of how good food smelled or how tasty it was, you could not enjoy it until you were hungry. This same thing happens in the spiritual realm. Only hungry people desire to be fed from Heavenly manna. Only hungry people can enjoy the precious promises of God's eternal Word. Only hungry people can feed upon the Lord.

You will never be hungry for the things of God until you begin to ponder and meditate upon the Word of God. Jesus said in John 6:53, *"Verily, verily, I say unto you, Except ye eat the flesh of the Son of man, and drink his blood, ye have no life in you."* To "bee" hungry is a decision. It is a choice that carries great reward because the Lord said such people are blessed. Jesus said, *"Blessed are they which do hunger and thirst after righteousness: for they shall be filled"* (Matthew 5:6). People who are hungry after God are blessed. So, "bee" hungry.

"Without God, you can do nothing."

Bee Hurt

Whether you like it or not, you will suffer hurt sometime in life. Jesus was not exempt from such injury. Many were the painful remarks made against this perfect Son of God. You don't read that Jesus went off somewhere to meditate on His hurts. Instead, He gave a precious solution to avoid being hurt more than necessary. Closely observe His instructions. First, He explained the problem, *"Blessed are ye, when men shall revile you, and persecute you, and shall say all manner of evil against you falsely, for my sake."* Second, He gave a very effective solution, *"Rejoice, and be exceeding glad: for great is your reward in heaven"* (Matthew 5:11 -12). You must learn to take the mastery over your hurts. Remember, the Lord has given you charge over your life. If you follow the instructions Jesus gave and chose to rejoice, you could eliminate many of wounds inflicted by others.

When you are hurt by some unkind word or deed, make a firm decision, "I will not ponder on this hurt." Incidentally, this is how you keep the spirit of unforgiveness and bitterness from lodging in your human spirit. Jesus gave you the solution; now, put it to practice. It's okay to "bee" hurt temporarily, but refuse to let it take the mastery over your life. If you do this, "bee" hurt will never leave a painful sting.

Bee Important

S ome people are afraid to "bee" important because churches have taught false humility. I am not promoting pride, arrogance or inflated ego, but rather the fact that it is not wrong to "bee" important. It is when someone feels superior to others that a problem with self is revealed.

How many men would still make good dads if they didn't feel they were important? How many pastors honestly feel they are not important? If you are not important at your work place, then why are you there? You may be working along with hundreds of other employees, but you are important as you fill your place. Whether you are a father, mother, son or daughter, you are important in the home. The Lord made you to be an important person—act like it!!!

" You must believe you can achieve."

Bee Included

W e all should desire to "bee" included in what God is doing for His people. The Bible records many great champions of the faith. How would you like to "bee" included in the genealogies of the Biblical champions? "Bee" included with men and women of faith. "Bee" included with those who fought the battles of life and won. "Bee" included with those who finish their time on earth with a shout of victory. "Bee" included with those who stand for the right in this wicked and adulterous generation.

You should "bee" included with those whose names are in the Book of Life. In his letter to the Philippians, Paul recognized some who were recorded in this precious Book: "*And I intreat thee also, true yokefellow, help those women which labored with me in the gospel, with Clement also, and with other my fellowlabourers, whose names are in the book of life*" (Philippians 4:3). We all need to "bee" included in that wonderful Book. You also should desire to "bee" included in the Book of remembrance: "*Then they that feared the LORD spake often one to another: and the LORD hearkened, and heard it, and a book of remembrance was written before him for them that feared the LORD, and that thought upon his name*" (Malachi 3:16). When you choose to "bee" included with those who fear the Lord this "bee" will never leave a painful sting.

Bee Influenced

Y ou will "bee" influenced by others all your life, but you
should be aware of who is influencing you. It is beneficial to
"bee" influenced by others if they leave a good influence upon you.
An optimist will influence you to be positive and enthusiastic. A
pessimist will influence you to think negatively. A politician will
try to influence you to vote for him; his opponent will try to influence you to see the negative side. You will "bee" influenced by
your associates on the job, in your home and in your church. Most
have been influenced by friends and leaders from childhood. Children influence each other. You are influenced by attitudes. Consider
how you influence others and what influence they leave on you.

You should desire to "bee" influenced by those who have set a
good example of holy and righteous living. You should "bee" influenced by those who have accomplished something in life. Paul left
a powerful influence on other ministers during his prison experience. He explained to the Philippians. *"And many of the brethren in
the Lord, waxing confident by my bonds,"* he writes, *"are much
more bold to speak the word without fear"* (Philippians 1:14).
When these ministers saw the boldness of Paul they were inspired
to preach fearlessly. "Bee" influenced is a wonderful "bee," but be
careful who is influencing you.

Bee Influential

E veryone should "bee" influential if they leave the right kind of influence. When Paul instructed Timothy to be an example, he was instructing him to "bee" influential toward others, "*Let no man despise thy youth; but be thou an example of the believers, in word, in conversation, in charity, in spirit, in faith, in purity*" (I Timothy 4:12).

Charles Darwin was influential in leading multitudes to believe the theory of evolution. How much better it would have been if he had been influential in leading people toward faith in God instead of a "big bang" theory. His writings are still leaving a bad influence in many of our universities. Those professors have been "monkeying" with the minds of people for years teaching that we sprang from monkeys. That is to "bee" influential in the wrong way.

We can "bee" influential toward our family members, as well as our friends, neighbors and our nation in general. The Lord has given each of us an opportunity to be a witness of His saving grace and to give a testimony of what the Lord has done for us. This will help us to "bee" influential in a good way that will lead people to the Lord Jesus Christ. Let us remember that others are affected by our life and conduct and we must be careful what kind of influence we leave behind us.

Bee Inspirational

A ll Christians should "bee" inspirational since we are filled with inspiration from the Word of God. To "bee" inspirational is to be positive even in a negative situation. Wouldn't life take on a new, refreshing atmosphere if everyone would "bee" inspirational?

You should "bee" inspirational to those who may be weary of the way. Encourage the faint hearted with lifting words. Inspire those who have experienced failure to rise up with new hope. "Bee" inspirational to those who may be suffering from tragedy. A few words of inspiration could transform a dreary day into pleasantness for some person, "*Pleasant words are as an honeycomb, sweet to the soul, and health to the bones*" (Proverbs 16:24). You can choose to "bee" inspirational. Why not start today? This "bee" will never leave a painful sting.

TAKE A WALK SOME SUNNY MORNING

*Take a walk some sunny morning
In among the blooming flowers,
As you go back to life's duties
See how bright it made your hours.*

*There are words of lifting beauty
Like the beauty of those flowers,
That may help some lonely person
To enjoy some cloudy hours.*

*Rod and Staff Publishers
© Copyright Daniel D. Rodes*

Bee Inspired

There are times in life when the way may become difficult. It is during these times you need to "bee" inspired. One way to "bee" inspired is by reading books and articles from successful people. Such words of encouragement may inspire you to press forward. Moses inspired Joshua with these encouraging words, *"And Moses called unto Joshua, and said unto him in the sight of all Israel, Be strong and of a good courage: for thou must go with this people unto the land which the LORD hath sworn unto their fathers to give them; and thou shalt cause them to inherit it"* (Deuteronomy 31:7).

One author wrote of a man who chose to live by faith many years ago and operate an orphanage without soliciting any funds. What inspired him to live by faith? He had a knowledge of the Word and a zeal to please God and help those in need. To remain inspired, he would not allow himself to be sidetracked by negative voices.

In our endeavors to "bee" inspired, we need to set a goal to listen to God's Word and learn from successful people—not only Biblical characters, but people in our day. Then, "bee" inspired will not leave a painful sting.

Bee Instant

To "bee" instant has a mentality of readiness and alertness. To "bee" instant is to be ready for whatever you face. That is why Paul admonished Timothy, "*Preach the word; be instant in season, out of season; reprove, rebuke, exhort with all longsuffering and doctrine*" (II Timothy 4:2). Pastors may be called upon to serve at a moment's notice. I tell the ministers who serve with me to be ready to preach, pray or die in an instant. Not only church leaders, but everyone can learn from this precious "bee."

You need to "bee" instant in your prayer life—ready to pray at a moment's notice. I often receive calls from those who needs prayer NOW! That is why Romans 12:12 instructs us to be instant in prayer, "*Rejoicing in hope; patient in tribulation; continuing instant in prayer.*" Learn to "bee" instant, to act upon any situation at any time. We all need to learn from this "bee," therefore, "bee" instant!

"You will never get the job done until you start the job."

Bee Joined

T he Bible instructs us to "bee" joined together as Believers. Paul, in writing to the church of Corinth, said, *"Now I beseech you, brethren, by the name of our Lord Jesus Christ, that ye all speak the same thing, and that there be no divisions among you; but that ye be perfectly joined together in the same mind and in the same judgment"* (I Corinthians 1:10). Being joined together with perfect unity is essential in a body of Believers. This is especially expressed in Ephesians 4:16 where we read, *"From whom the whole body fitly joined together and compacted by that which every joint supplieth, according to the effectual working in the measure of every part, maketh increase of the body unto the edifying of itself in love."* To "bee" joined with the right kind of people for the right reason can be very beneficial.

When Believers are all working toward the same goal and following the Scriptural pattern, there will be unity and a beautiful harmonizing relationship. This same relationship is important in marriage. What a blessing marriage can be when a man chooses to "bee" joined to his wife. Genesis 2:24 tells us, *"Therefore shall a man leave his father and his mother, and shall cleave unto his wife."* This same expression is repeated in Ephesians 5:31: *"For this cause shall a man leave his father and mother, and shall be joined unto his wife, and they two shall be one flesh."* Notice the phrase, *"shall be joined unto his wife."* When we choose to "bee" joined, there is no more separation or difference. It is a cooperation between two parties.

Any relationship that is joined together without Christ will not be successful under pressure. Let us not just "bee" joined to one another, but "bee" joined together with the Lord. Surely, to "bee" joined together with Christ will never leave a painful sting.

Bee Joyful

Y ou would think everyone would like to be around people who are joyful, wouldn't you? Well, that's not always the case. I have met people who complained because a joyful person disturbed their complacency and "pity party" mentality. They concluded that everyone should be "down" at least part of the time. No wonder people are so tired, weary and downtrodden. The Lord wants you to "bee" joyful. There is great strength in joy, "*...the joy of the LORD is your strength*" (Nehemiah 8:10). Those were the words of Nehemiah to the people after they mourned and wept over their sin. Nehemiah encouraged them to become joyful. Today, joy is needed in abundance to live with the pressure and rush of society. It seems that most people are in a hurry to do something, but they don't take time to think joyful thoughts or to sing joyful songs that bring courage and inspiration.

Every day should be filled with joy. This is not fantasy, but an important habit to possess. You may say, "But suppose something bad happens?" We all face situations in life that can be discouraging and perplexing. Keep in mind, joyfulness is a decision. Joyfulness brings you to a place of expectation. You expect good things to come your way.

For years, Norman was a joyful, cheerful optimist. Every time I met him, he was the same joyful person. One day, unexpectedly, Norman's wife died. As I entered the funeral home, I wondered how this joyful person would respond to this loss. As soon as he saw me, he joyfully said, "Oh, Brother Rodes, my dear wife made it to Heaven before me. Praise God! She's in a wonderful place." What a blessing to see real joy being expressed in a person who faced a sudden death in his family. This is the kind of joy spoken of in Isaiah 51:11: "*Therefore the redeemed of the LORD shall return, and come with singing unto Zion; and everlasting joy shall be upon their head: they shall obtain gladness and joy; and sorrow and mourning shall flee away.*" "Bee" joyful. Make it a way of life. Join the Psalmist as he says, "*...Shout for joy*" (Psalm 132:9). Joy is the "bee" that never leaves a painful sting.

SMILE

Some people like to tell you,
When you're feeling rather sad,
To start the day out smiling
And you'll soon be feeling glad.

I tried this thing of smiling;
While my smile was on display,
I felt so out of order
Since I didn't feel that way.

So I thought the matter over
And I feel I must conclude,
You got to have a heart change
Before you change a mood

It's nothing less than folly
Putting troubles in a file
To use for future reference.
No wonder I can't smile.

Well, I finally got the answer;
Should have known all the while;
You got to count your blessings
If you really want to smile.

Bee Just

In the book of Leviticus, God commanded His people to "bee" just and have "*Just balances, just weights, a just ephah, and a just hin*" (Leviticus 19:36). What does "just" mean? According to the Bible dictionary it simply means to be legal and right; not dishonest in weights, measures or anything else. The Lord expects your way of life to "bee" just. He commands you to "bee" just. The Bible says the day will come when the Lord will send angels to "*sever the wicked from among the just.*" (Matthew 13:49). Then, in Revelation 22:11, we read where the Lord told John to write, "*He that is unjust, let him be unjust still: and he which is filthy, let him be filthy still: and he that is righteous, let him be righteous still: and he that is holy, let him be holy still.*"

In Romans 1:17 Paul mentioned, "*The just shall live by faith.*" Then, to enforce this truth, the Hebrew writer penned the same statement, "*Now the just shall live by faith*" (Hebrews 10:38). That should be enough to convince you that the Lord expects you to "bee" just, shouldn't it? According to these verses, to "bee" just is an important way to increase your faith. "Bee" just will never leave a painful sting!

Bee Justified

To "bee" justified means to render just or innocent; to be righteous. Jesus made a profound statement in Matthew 12:37: *"For by thy words thou shalt be justified, and by thy words thou shalt be condemned."* The use of proper words is important to our Heavenly Father. When the tongue is aflame with critical, judgmental, degrading words, it will not "bee" justified. You need to carefully guard your words.

When you are justified, your past sins are no longer held against you. *"Being justified freely by his grace through the redemption that is in Christ Jesus"* (Romans 3:24). Grace causes you to "bee" justified. *"That being justified by his grace, we should be made heirs according to the hope of eternal life"* (Titus 3:7). You can also be justified by faith: *"Therefore being justified by faith, we have peace with God through our Lord Jesus Christ"* (Romans 5:1). The Bible places great value on both grace and faith. Abraham was justified because he put his faith to work, *"Was not Abraham our father justified by works, when he had offered Isaac his son upon the altar?"* (James 2:21). "Bee" justified will never leave a painful sting.

Bee Kind

K indness can become a realization to everyone. A kind heart is a precious virtue in life. When King Rehoboam asked for advice from his father's counselors, they advised him wisely: "*...If thou be kind to this people, and please them, and speak good words to them, they will be thy servants for ever*" (II Chronicles 10:7). If Rehoboam would have obeyed their wise counsel and chosen to "bee" kind, the people would have gladly served him. Instead, he chose to heed the unwise advice of his friends; therefore, the people turned against their king.

Harsh, controlling people are miserable. They can't enjoy the calm rest that comes from being kind. You should show compassion, understanding and kindness toward others. Kind words have a healing effect on marriages and relationships. A home can become a peaceful and pleasant place to live if you learn to "bee" kind to your spouse. Life has enough problems. Why not add kindness to your marriage? "Bee" kind to your children. "Bee" kind to the elderly. "Bee" kind to your neighbors. "Bee" kind to your friends. "Bee" kind to your enemies: "*And be ye kind one to another, tenderhearted, forgiving one another, even as God for Christ's sake hath forgiven you.*" (Ephesians 4:32). God's blessing rests upon those who are kind to each other. "Bee" kind. This is a quality of great value.

Bee Known

E verywhere Paul traveled in his ministry, he was soon known. He wasn't well known because he was popular. In fact, in most cases he was hated. His main publicity came from those who opposed him. He was known by the court and the prison. He was known in numerous nations. Even the demon forces acknowledged they knew Paul when they demanded an answer from the seven sons of Sceva, *"Jesus I know, and Paul I know; but who are ye"* (Acts 19:15). Paul stood for something. He knew what he believed and why he believed it. He was not afraid to make known his faith in the work of the Lord Jesus. When questioned about his beliefs, he acknowledged, *"But this I confess unto thee, that after the way which they call heresy, so worship I the God of my fathers, believing all things which are written in the law and in the prophets"* (Acts 24:14). This man was known for his bold stand for what he knew was right.

You need to "bee" known. There are certain things you stand for that may seem a bit fanatical to those around you, but others should know where you stand and why you are taking that stand. It should "bee" known in your neighborhood that you are a child of God. You should "bee" known as a stable, unmovable, unshaken man or woman of faith. You should not be afraid to "bee" known.

Bee Labeled

In life, everyone is labeled in some way, whether good or bad. It is good to "bee" labeled as having a positive effect upon others. Abraham was labeled by Almighty God as a man who could be trusted: *"For I know him, that he will command his children and his household after him, and they shall keep the way of the LORD, to do justice and judgment; that the LORD may bring upon Abraham that which he hath spoken of him"* (Genesis 18:19). His faithfulness left a great impression upon his descendants. Moses was another man who was labeled by God as faithful: *"And Moses verily was faithful in all his house, as a servant, for a testimony of those things which were to be spoken after"* (Hebrews 3:5). He was faithful to bring the children of Israel through the wilderness to the borders of the promised land.

The prophet Daniel was labeled as a man without fault. Even his enemies had difficulty finding accusations to bring against him. That's quite a label! Such men and women, boys and girls are hard to find. Be the one who is labeled in your lifetime as one who stood for the right. Someone who left a good impression as a servant of the Lord on those around them. "Bee" labeled as righteous in this generation. Then, this "bee" will never leave a painful sting.

Bee Lasting

I once heard someone say, "That person won't last long." I wondered what he meant. He answered, "People who use illegal drugs, alcohol and tobacco are in danger of not lasting. There are certain principles in life we need to follow if we plan to 'bee' lasting. One of the most important is to have a positive outlook in life, using the Word of God as a pattern for our lifestyle." The Bible promises, *"With long life will I satisfy him, and shew him my salvation"* (Psalm 91:16). Salvation brings deliverance from harmful addictions and helps us to "bee" lasting.

We have all met people who were worn out and ready to retire at an early age. Worry, fret, negative speech and wrong thoughts can cause a person to age more quickly than their years. It is true, your body is subject to fatigue and tiredness, but you don't need to burn out or become worn out. Jesus once told His disciples, *"Come ye yourselves apart into a desert place, and rest a while"* (Mark 6:31). He knew they needed rest. Even Jesus himself would draw away from the crowds, at times, to be alone in some secluded place.

If you want to "bee" lasting, take care of your spirit, soul and body. II Corinthians 4:16 says, *"For which cause we faint not; but though our outward man perish, yet the inward man is renewed day by day."* One way to renew the inward (spirit) man is by studying and meditating on the promises in God's Word daily. When you confess the Word aloud, you are building up your inward spirit. Then you can "bee" lasting. This "bee" will never leave a painful sting.

Bee Learned

I saiah made a lovely statement concerning "bee" learned when he wrote, *"The Lord GOD hath given me the tongue of the learned, that I should know how to speak a word in season to him that is weary: he wakeneth morning by morning, he wakeneth mine ear to hear as the learned."* (Isaiah 50:4). How precious it is to learn the ways of the Lord. We all need to learn the right things in life. Laban told Jacob, *"I have learned by experience that the LORD hath blessed me for thy sake."* (Genesis 30:27).

Another man who was influenced by "bee" learned was the apostle Paul. In his epistle to the Philippians he wrote, *"Not that I speak in respect of want: for I have learned, in whatsoever state I am, therewith to be content."* (Philippians 4:11). Contentment is a lovely quality to learn. When you understand how to be content, you will learn to face life more successfully. Paul didn't learn contentment the easy way, but it was very valuable to him in the end. "Bee" learned is a very important "bee."

*To hear God is to fear God;
to fear God is to hear God.*

Bee Led

Whether you are aware of it or not, you are being led by someone every day. If you are led by the hand of God, you can expect to "bee" led in paths of truth and righteousness. In Psalm 31:3, the Psalmist says, *"For thou art my rock and my fortress; therefore for thy name's sake lead me, and guide me."* When you are secure in the fortress of the Lord, you have no need to fear the things around you. The hand that leads you will safely guide you on the path you need to go.

To "bee" led by the Lord is to "bee" led by wisdom. *"I have taught thee in the way of wisdom; I have led thee in right paths"* (Proverbs 4:11). Here wisdom is speaking: *"I have led thee."* Sometimes you may not know which way to turn or what decisions to make but when you are led by the Heavenly Father, His wisdom will teach you which way to go and what to do or leave undone.

We should all desire to "bee" led day by day, moment by moment, hour by hour by the gracious hand of our Heavenly Father and the precious Holy Spirit. *"But if ye be led of the Spirit, ye are not under the law"* (Galatians 5:18). The Holy Spirit will lead you day by day. Romans 8:14 says, *"For as many as are led by the Spirit of God, they are the sons of God."* Think about that statement! They are the sons of God because they are led by the Spirit of God. How beautiful it is to "bee" led by the Spirit of the Lord. Surely, this "bee" will never leave a painful sting.

Bee Lenient

To "bee" lenient does not mean that there is never a time for judgment, correction or discipline, but it does mean that you do not deal harshly or severely with those who may have disobeyed your instructions. To "bee" lenient is to be merciful, mild and gentle. Matthew 5:7 says, *"Blessed are the merciful: for they shall obtain mercy."* When you choose to "bee" lenient with others, you will obtain mercy.

A kind and loving father would "bee" lenient instead of harsh when punishing his child. I am not recommending that parents "bee" lenient toward their children without proper discipline, but there is a place to "bee" lenient instead of being a harsh disciplinarian.

A law official could choose to "bee" lenient in the way he deals with a criminal. A merciful judge may be motivated to "bee" lenient when metering out judgment. Of course, "bee" lenient could be used to the extreme and become a hindrance instead of an asset, but there is a proper way to "bee" lenient. Most of us could testify that someone has been lenient toward us, so why not "bee" lenient toward others?

"If you have a rebellious child, stick to the stick."

Bee Likeminded

To "bee" likeminded is similar to being in one accord. When two people are likeminded they do not think two different ways. When I established our churches, people came from many different denominational backgrounds. Because of this, it took time for us to become likeminded. When we searched the Word of God and discovered that we can "bee" likeminded, what a difference it made. Romans 15:5 says, *"Now the God of patience and consolation grant you to be likeminded one toward another according to Christ Jesus."* When a body of Believers becomes likeminded, the Holy Spirit will help them strengthen each other.

We should "bee" likeminded in the things pertaining to the kingdom of God. Paul encouraged the Philippians to "bee" likeminded: *"Fulfil ye my joy, that ye be likeminded, having the same love, being of one accord, of one mind"* (Philippians 2:2). If we are likeminded regarding the traditions of man, we will not have the unity of the Spirit. When we choose to be in agreement with God's Word, we can be unified and become likeminded.

When I was growing up alongside my siblings, mother had to train us to "bee" likeminded. After we became likeminded, we could play together without quarreling or being short-tempered with each other. We need to "bee" likeminded, whether at home, church or among other Believers. When we are truly likeminded in the things of the Spirit, there will be lasting joy, satisfaction and fulfillment in our lives. So, let's "bee" likeminded. This "bee" will never leave a painful sting.

Bee Longsuffering

The Bible instructs how to become longsuffering: "*Put on therefore, as the elect of God, holy and beloved, bowels of mercies, kindness, humbleness of mind, meekness, longsuffering*" (Colossians 3:12). Why would Paul specify the need to put on longsuffering if it wasn't valuable? Obviously, to "bee" longsuffering is something we all need in our lives to continue our walk as Believers. Those who choose to "bee" longsuffering are calm and stable. These people may go through difficult situations, but they cannot be stopped in their pursuits. They will not quit when things get tough. They will persevere until they come through in victory.

Paul instructed Timothy: "*Preach the word; be instant in season, out of season; reprove, rebuke, exhort with all longsuffering and doctrine*" (II Timothy 4:2). It was important for Timothy to remember to "bee" longsuffering toward others even if he needed to give a word of rebuke.

II Peter 3:9 describes that the Lord is longsuffering toward us: "*The Lord is not slack concerning his promise, as some men count slackness; but is longsuffering to us-ward, not willing that any should perish, but that all should come to repentance.*" When you heed the buzz of "bee" longsuffering, this "bee" will never leave a painful.

"To wait patiently doesn't take any longer than being uptight and it is much more pleasant and enjoyable."

Bee Lovable

Did you ever meet someone who was hard to love? They may have been harsh, judgmental or critical toward you. They may have hurt your feelings or made you feel degraded and unappreciated. They may not have seemed very lovable. You should "bee" loveable so others do not find it difficult to love you. Not only can you position yourself to be loved, but you can extend love toward those who show no love or kindness toward you. To "bee" lovable is a choice. When you choose to "bee" lovable, you will not be sarcastic and nasty toward other people. Some people who complain that no one loves them should consider the possibility that they themselves are not lovable. We must learn to "bee" lovable under all circumstances because this "bee" will never leave a painful sting.

"Love is a flower that blooms even in the coldest weather."

Bee Loved

S ome people have never learned to "bee" loved because they suffered injury from someone who claimed to love them or they were suspicious of those who attempted to show them love. To "bee" loved requires an openness to accept love from others, however, it does not open the door to everyone who claims to be loving.

To "bee" loved of God requires obedience: "*He that hath my commandments, and keepeth them, he it is that loveth me: and he that loveth me shall be loved of my Father, and I will love him, and will manifest myself to him*" (John 14:21). Notice the statement, "*shall be loved.*" You learn to "bee" loved by your Heavenly Father when you yield to His love.

The Apostle John knew what it was to "bee" loved. He referred to himself a number of times in the book that bears his name as the disciple "*whom Jesus loved.*" Why did Jesus love him? Because of John's loving attitude. How beautiful it is to love and "bee" loved. Surely, "bee" loved will never leave a painful sting!

Bee Loving

As I was growing up in the foothills of the Shenandoah Valley of Virginia, I was impressed by a man who had a loving personality. He had such a loving way that he reminded me of the verse in Romans 13:10: *"Love worketh no ill to his neighbour...."* He treated everyone with respect and was loving to his wife and children. This man left a deep impression on my young mind. I wondered how he became that way. Why did he have such a loving nature? I believe he chose to be loving.

Some believe certain people were born to be loving and others to have a more demanding nature. Nothing in life falls on you accidentally. You have choices to make. You can love your neighbor or you can hate him, but you will never have a good excuse for not loving your neighbor. When Jesus said, *"...love thy neighbour as thyself"* (Matthew 22:39), He didn't add, "If they are worthy of love," or "If they love you." Love is one sided. You love because you belong to God and God is love. God's love is infinite. When you love God, you love your fellowman. The nature of God is love. The nature of a Christian is love, *"By this shall all men know that ye are my disciples, if ye have love one to another"* (John 13:35). "Bee" loving will never leave a painful sting!

Bee Loyal

A loyal person is a valuable and much needed person. To "bee" loyal is to be faithful. The book of Proverbs asks, *"Most men will proclaim every one his own goodness: but a faithful man who can find?"* (Proverbs 20:6). To find such individuals is not impossible, but it may be difficult. Those who commit themselves to "bee" loyal are on their way to growth and maturity. They can reach out beyond the norm. They understand it is not easy to do a hard job, but they do not quit. Those who choose to "bee" loyal are those who can be trusted. To "bee" loyal should be a part of everyone's life, but few there be that find it.

When you are first loyal to the Lord, it will not be as difficult to "bee" loyal to others. A husband needs to "bee" loyal to his wife, a wife needs to "bee" loyal to her husband, and children need to "bee" loyal to their parents. The world is looking for people they know will be there when they are needed. Employers are looking for loyal workers. Pastors appreciate people in the pews who are loyal. The ministerial body needs leaders who are loyal. All Believers should set out to "bee" loyal in every area of their Christian lives, therefore, "bee" loyal!

Bee Manly

This generation needs to see men raise up to become men—brave, strong, able, honorable men. We need a man for the hour to display strong Christian manhood. To "bee" manly is an outstanding quality that we, as men, need to possess. To "bee" manly is to be brave enough to stand for the right while others are falling. To "bee" manly is to be well disciplined and have strong self-control. To "bee" manly is to show yourself a man. To "bee" manly is to take a bold stand to be a masculine figure among young men who are watching you. To "bee" manly is to be an honorable father of great courage to lead your children in the ways of the Lord. To "bee" manly is to treat your wife with honor and respect. To "bee" manly is to show respect to those of the opposite sex. To "bee" manly is to be pure and of a peaceable nature.

A true man takes full responsibility for wrong doing and has a heart to correct himself. The world needs to see men. Real men. Godly men. Men of integrity. Honest, reliable, dependable men with noble leadership qualities. Men, you need to choose to "bee" manly. It won't happen automatically, but you have within you what it takes—strong, godly willpower. If you have not chosen to "bee" manly in the past, you can change. Let those around you know that you have chosen to "bee" manly. Do you think "bee" manly would ever leave a painful sting? No! No! No! "Bee" manly!

Note: Although this is written specifically to men, women can apply the same principals to their lives.

Bee Master

C hoose to "bee" master over your life. No one can make your choices for you. Too long, it has been taught that we are not supposed to "bee" master over our lives because we are weak and unworthy. This has greatly hindered many Christians. Beloved, if you can't master your own life, how can you expect the Lord to help you? You are accountable and responsible to take control of your life. (Of course, that is impossible without the help of the Lord. That should be understood.)

You need to "bee" master over your life concerning your relationship with the Lord. No one can choose for you what kind of a relationship you will have with the Lord or your fellowman. You are accountable for that decision.

You need to "bee" master over your thoughts. If you do not choose to "bee" master over your thinking and deal with your mind Scripturally, you can end in disaster. You need to "bee" master over your behavior, what you do and how you do it. You need to "bee" master of the words you use and the way you say them. When you choose to "bee" master over your own life, you will not be blaming others for your failures, mistakes and weaknesses. Beloved, it is not wrong to take mastery over your life, but you must do it Scripturally. Paul tells the church, *"And every man that striveth for the mastery is temperate in all things"* (I Corinthians 9:25). What a worthy goal to strive to attain! Why not choose today to "bee" master over your own life if you haven't already made that decision? This "bee" will never leave a painful sting.

Bee Mature

Many Believers in today's society have lost the true value of what it means to "bee" mature. Ephesians 4:14-15 informs us: *"That we henceforth be no more children, tossed to and fro, and carried about with every wind of doctrine, by the sleight of men, and cunning craftiness, whereby they lie in wait to deceive; But speaking the truth in love, may grow up into him in all things, which is the head, even Christ."* Christians have become side-tracked with the toys and pleasures of this world. It is time to put away childish things and "bee" mature in God's Word. Paul said, *"When I was a child, I spake as a child, I understood as a child, I thought as a child: but when I became a man, I put away childish things"* (I Corinthians 13:11). You need to hunger and thirst for the things of God: *"As newborn babes, desire the sincere milk of the word, that ye may grow thereby"* (I Peter 2:2). Grow in the knowledge of your Heavenly Father so that you can become more like Him: *"But grow in grace, and in the knowledge of our Lord and Saviour Jesus Christ. To him be glory both now and for ever. Amen."* (II Peter 3:18). Become a man or woman of quality character. "Bee" mature in every area of your life. This "bee" will never leave a painful sting.

Bee Meek

J esus pronounced a special blessing upon the meek when He said, *"Blessed are the meek: for they shall inherit the earth"* (Matthew 5:5). Meekness is not what some conclude is weakness. True meekness is the strength, power and authority of God operating through one of His children. The word meek has to do with being gentle and humble. In other words, it displays a person with a calm character, not someone who is arrogant or quick to express themselves. To "bee" meek is to recognize that you have nothing and must depend totally upon the Lord.

The Bible refers to Jesus as being meek and lowly in heart. The Bible also tells us that Moses was very meek. In fact, according to Numbers 12:3, Moses was the meekest man on earth. How did he become that way? He chose to "bee" meek. Meekness, like any other characteristic, comes by choice. Whatever you desire in this life, choose that way. If everyone chose to "bee" meek, what a difference it would make in this world. When a person is meek and humble, God can help them and they can help others. "Bee" meek—it's the Bible way. This "bee" cannot leave a painful sting.

Bee Merciful

M ercy is a quality in which you should seek to excel. To "bee" merciful is a godly characteristic. The nature of God is to show mercy. The nature of a Christian is to "bee" merciful toward others. Jesus said, *"Be ye therefore merciful, as your Father also is merciful"* (Luke 6:36). The Lord has given you the choice to give and receive mercy. It is when you show mercy to others that the Lord will have mercy on you. In Matthew 5:7 Jesus said, *"Blessed are the merciful: for they shall obtain mercy"* (Matthew 5:7). What a glorious promise! Some people have cried out for justice in certain circumstances. Justice surely has its place, but, thank God, He deals with us in mercy instead of justice. If you think about all the times that God has been merciful to you, it will help you understand why you should be merciful to others. When you show tender love and mercy toward your own family members, you work for their good. Your children should be taught the value of showing mercy and compassion, even toward those who may have injured them. So many homes and churches would have less trouble if everyone would learn to "bee" merciful toward each other.

" Don't sense, use sense."

Bee Merry

The Bible says, *"A merry heart doeth good like a medicine"* (Proverbs 17:22). It would be good to take this medicine daily. It has been proven that laughter has cured people from their ailments. I remember reading an article about a group of scientists who chose to experiment on this theory. They gathered a group of cancer patients and instructed them to laugh several times a day. The patients needed to "bee" merry in order to make the project successful. It was not long before they saw a remarkable change in the health of their subjects. Since that time, it has been confirmed that others have also been cured from illnesses and ailments by having a merry heart and laughing throughout the day.

Years ago, a desperate elderly woman came to my wife and I for deliverance from depression. After numerous attempts to help her with little results, I asked, "Do you have an empty bottle somewhere in your house?" She did. I advised her to fill it with grape juice and place it in her refrigerator. I told her, "When you get up in the morning, take one teaspoon of this 'medicine' and laugh as hard as you can three times. Repeat this remedy at lunch and again before you go to bed." She thought this sounded strange but gave it a try. The next time we saw her, we asked how the "medicine" was working.

She laughed and said, "I knew the grape juice wouldn't work but laughter would. Now I laugh when I open the refrigerator to take my 'prescription.' I am no longer depressed."

You must serve the Lord with a merry heart. It's one thing to "bee" merry when life is pleasant, but the real test comes when you face uncertain circumstances. If you choose to "bee" merry every day, the problems you face will not disturb you. Singing and praising the Lord from a merry heart will keep you from becoming discouraged. *"Is any among you afflicted? let him pray. Is any merry? let him sing psalms*" (James 5:13). We all know that people who are discouraged or depressed cause the whole atmosphere to become gloomy; not only for themselves but those around them. If you would choose to "bee" merry, your atmosphere and countenance would change. *"A merry heart maketh a cheerful countenance: but by sorrow of the heart the spirit is broken"* (Proverbs 15:13). Of course, there will be times when sorrow, disappointment or grief may visit you, yet deep down inside the buzzing of "bee" merry reminds you better days are ahead for God's children.

A teeny weeny giggle
From a teeny tiny tot
Can top off any evening
In a family can it not?

Bee Mighty

The Bible refers to certain individuals as mighty men: "*Now Jephthah the Gileadite was a mighty man of valour*" (Judges 11:1). In Judges 6:12, the angel of the Lord declared to Gideon, "*...The LORD is with thee, thou mighty man of valour.*" II Samuel 23 described the mighty men who served King David. You can also become a mighty man or woman of God if you choose to "bee" mighty. The Bible characters did not become mighty just because they believed in God. To "bee" mighty, an individual must plan and make an effort to strive for excellence and reach beyond the average. If you choose to "bee" mighty, the Lord will help you become victorious and triumphant in every area of life. "Bee" mighty. This "bee" will never leave a painful sting.

"Some people think they have nothing to do
because they are doing nothing."

Bee Mindful

To "bee" mindful is to remember. The Apostle Paul remembered the struggle of Timothy when he endeavored to lead the church: *"Greatly desiring to see thee, being mindful of thy tears, that I may be filled with joy"* (II Timothy 1:4). We do not understand the cause of Timothy's tears, but Paul assured him they were valuable. He encouraged this young Pastor to keep pressing on.

The Apostle Peter explains the importance of "bee" mindful in II Peter 3:2, *"That ye may be mindful of the words which were spoken before by the holy prophets, and of the commandment of us the apostles of the Lord and Saviour."* He is warning us to "bee" mindful of the commandments.

The human race has a tendency not to always "bee" mindful of important things. You need to "bee" mindful of past mistakes and learn from your wrong decisions to avoid making the same mistake twice. You should "bee" mindful of those who have sacrificed their lives for the Lord. There is an old song that quotes, "that they would be mindful of the blood shed by the martyrs." You need to "bee" mindful of those around you who are struggling. The Apostle Paul reminds us, *"Now we exhort you, brethren, warn them that are unruly, comfort the feebleminded, support the weak, be patient toward all men"* (I Thessalonians 5:14). There are many areas in life you should "bee" mindful. This "bee" will never leave a painful sting.

Bee More

Today, "bee" more is buzzing around many people encouraging them to "bee" more than they are in life; to no longer be satisfied with a mediocre lifestyle. Only those who heed the encouraging buzz of "bee" more will reach their full potential. "Bee" more enthusiastic about what you can accomplish in your lifetime. Consider the promise to the winners in Romans 8:37, "*Nay, in all these things we are more than conquerors through him that loved us.*" Here, the writer is not suggesting a haphazard, non-productive lifestyle, but a ring of great victory. It's not just for someone else, you can "bee" more than a conqueror. Get a vision of yourself as a winner! Become all you can! "Bee" more reliable, dependable and trustworthy. "Bee" more cheerful. "Bee" more loving to your spouse and those around you. "Bee" more helpful. "Bee" more motivational toward yourself and others. "Bee" more is still encouraging all who will hear to "bee" more than what you are now. This precious "bee" will never leave a painful sting!

"You get what you think,
so think about what you will get."

Bee Motivational

Most of us face situations in life that tend to drag us down. It is in those times that we need to "bee" motivational. That is, we need to learn to motivate ourselves. If we cannot learn to motivate ourselves, it is doubtful if we will "bee" motivational to others. To "bee" motivational is a very important characteristic that all of us should endeavor to possess.

Some people are so filled with motivational suggestions that they are a pleasure to be around. There is a difference between being motivational and being bossy or involving one's self in other people's matters without invitation. To "bee" motivational is never to force your ideas on anyone. You should "bee" motivational at home, in the work place, around your friends and in your church. Wouldn't it be wonderful if all of us would decide to "bee" motivational in the things concerning the kingdom of Heaven? We could encourage one another, help to strengthen each other, and learn to lend a helping hand to those who may be facing some difficulty in life. To "bee" motivational is to be inspiring and to help lift others. This "bee" leaves a good influence, therefore, "bee" motivational.

IT IS YOUR CHOICE

So much of life is up to you,
To make it bright or make it blue;
So much depends on attitude
That has the force to change your mood

© Copyright Daniel D. Rodes

Bee Moved

Did you ever wonder how the Lord must feel to see multitudes everywhere with no one to lead them; no one to point them to the saving grace of our Lord and Savior? We need to "bee" moved as Jesus was, "*But when he saw the multitudes, he was moved with compassion on them, because they fainted, and were scattered abroad as sheep having no shepherd*" (Matthew 9:36). I can't help but "bee" moved when I think of all the pain and suffering around us on every hand.

An elderly gentleman was lying on his death bed. He had no one to tell Him about the plan of salvation. Someone stopped by our office and asked if I would visit him. When I saw this poor soul wasting away, I was moved with compassion. After this precious man received the Savior, he was moved with a desire to see his friends saved. He asked if I would visit his friends and explain to them how to be saved. When his friends heard how this dying man wanted them to be saved, they were moved and gave their hearts to the Lord.

Another time, I was asked by a dying 85 year old lady to pray that she would live. She said, "I still haven't finished my work on earth." I was moved with compassion and asked the Lord to spare her life. She died at the age of 95. The Lord granted her request. Thank God, we can "bee" moved to do something for Him. Someone may be waiting for you today to "bee" moved on their behalf!

Bee Natural

M any people are unnatural in their conduct and character when they are with others. They portray phony behavior or try to be like someone else, hoping to make an impression on their friends. II Corinthians 8:21 warns: *"Providing for honest things, not only in the sight of the Lord, but also in the sight of men."* A phony personality will not impress others. The way to win the heart of anyone is to "bee" natural.

Many years ago, I met a young lady I hoped would one day become my wife. I knew I had to "bee" natural in her presence. She was raised in a family with brothers and sisters who were genuine. To be phony would have been disastrous. By choosing to "bee" natural, I won the heart of that young lady who was my wife for over 50 years.

In the book of Acts, they needed men who were natural to fulfill the work of the Lord: *"Wherefore, brethren, look ye out among you seven men of honest report, full of the Holy Ghost and wisdom, whom we may appoint over this business"* (Acts 6:3). I would like to encourage all my preacher friends and church leaders to "bee" natural. If you, as a leader, are not genuine, your people will recognize it. Make a decision, today, to "bee" natural. This "bee" will never leave a painful sting.

Bee Needed

I t is good to "bee" needed, isn't it? You want to "bee" needed in the home, in the work place, in the church or in the community. What value are you to the community and those around you? Are you an asset? Who needs trouble makers or lazy, unproductive people?

Paul knew the church needed him. In writing to the church at Philippi, he expressed his conflict, *"For I am in a strait betwixt two, having a desire to depart, and to be with Christ; which is far better."* Then he concluded, *"...nevertheless to abide in the flesh is more needful for you"* (Philippians 1:23-24). Paul also was in need of others who could help him. He appealed to Timothy, *"Take Mark, and bring him with thee: for he is profitable to me for the ministry"* (II Timothy 4:11). Mark was needed. He had apparently proven himself to be valuable to Paul. This man had let Paul down at one time, but now Paul needed him. Maybe you have not been of great value to others in the past, but you can make changes and "bee" needed. Prepare yourself to be useful so you will "bee" needed. What a wonderful "bee" is "bee" needed!

"Lighting one's own candle is good,
but lighting another's is better."

Bee Neighborly

Isn't it great to "bee" neighborly to others? To "bee" neighborly is important in any neighborhood. Proverbs 18:24 tells us, "_A man that hath friends must shew himself friendly._" If someone chooses to "bee" neighborly, in most cases, his neighbors will return that gesture.

Years ago, we lived in a neighborhood where one of the neighbors obviously didn't appreciate those who called themselves Christians. He became very hostile toward us and tried his best to cause trouble. We made up our minds to "bee" neighborly and treat him and his family with respect, regardless of how he treated us. One day, a great change took place in this man. He proved to be friendly and became a good neighbor. We don't know why he acted as he did before, but the love of God brought peace between us and others in the neighborhood. We don't always know why people are unkind toward those who live around them, but one thing is sure, we can return good for evil. It may heal the hurt they are experiencing. The Bible still says in Matthew 22:39, "_Thou shalt love thy neighbour as thyself._" The Lord expects His children to love one another. That may be His way of winning some hostile soul to the Lord. Be a blessing to others. "Bee" neighborly. Surely this "bee" will never leave a painful sting.

Bee Next

A young man stood at the base, ready to hit the softball. His peers began to mock him saying, "You don't need to watch out for this fellow. He can't even hit a ball." I saw the courage and expectation fall from this young man's countenance. I wanted him to "bee" next in hitting a home run, so I stepped up to him and asked, "Do you see that fence down there?" He nodded. I said, "Hit that ball so hard that it goes over that fence and run as fast as you can." The ball went beyond the fence. Needless to say, he made a home run. So many people need encouragement to step out and "bee" next to accomplish something, not only on the material side, but on the spiritual as well.

How would you like to "bee" next to be promoted? If you want to "bee" next, you must also be considerate of others. It is not proper to push others back so you can get ahead. Don't become down-hearted and discouraged when someone else is promoted ahead of you. When you are considerate of others who have raised to a higher position, it often opens the door for you to "bee" next in line. Joseph had one backset after the other, but he wouldn't give up, even when he was sitting in prison after being wrongfully accused. The Lord saw this man's behavior in the midst of great loss. Little did Joseph know that he would "bee" next to be promoted under the jurisdiction of the king.

You need to encourage yourself, as well as others, to reach your God-given potential. You have a responsibility and a duty to be all that you can be, do all you can do and be an asset in the community in which you live. "Bee" next to go beyond the norm and do something that will benefit others. "Bee" next to be a great soul winner for the Lord. "Bee" next to help some backslider restore his relationship with the Lord. "Bee" next to help encourage others to reach their goal. Listen to the soft humming of this "bee" which says, "You can 'bee' next."

Bee Not

This "bee" may sound rather unusual, but "bee" not is a very important part of this "bee" family. Many people today are discouraged and feel like giving up, but we are instructed in II Thessalonians 3:13, "*...be not weary in well doing.*" "Bee" not be discouraged when things go wrong, but rather rise up and start again.

In Paul's letter to the Romans, he instructed them: "*Be not overcome of evil, but overcome evil with good*" (Romans 12:21). Paul writes in Galatians 6:7, "*Be not deceived; God is not mocked: for whatsoever a man soweth, that shall he also reap.*" He is giving a strong warning concerning the harvest that is sure to come. "Bee" not deceived—what you sow, you will reap. When you are doing right and sowing good seeds, you will be a blessing and benefit to others.

Another warning to "bee" not is found in Romans 11:20: "*Be not highminded, but fear.*" When you think too highly of yourself, you can fall. The answer is found in Romans 12:2: "*And be not conformed to this world: but be ye transformed by the renewing of your mind, that ye may prove what is that good, and acceptable, and perfect, will of God.*" Do not think like the world nor act like the world. Be transformed. This comes about by renewing your mind. "Bee" not is certainly a wonderful "bee" that will never leave a painful sting.

Bee Obedient

The Bible tells us to "*Exhort servants to be obedient unto their own masters, and to please them well in all things; not answering again*" (Titus 2:9). When you choose to "bee" obedient, there is no argument. You do what the master commands. The Scriptures tell us, "*Obey them that have the rule over you, and submit yourselves: for they watch for your souls, as they that must give account, that they may do it with joy, and not with grief: for that is unprofitable for you*" (Hebrews 13:17). God requires obedience in everything. If you have difficulty obeying God, you will have difficulty obeying your leaders. If you learn to "bee" obedient, you will be content and your life will be filled with blessing.

Every child should be taught at a young age how important it is to "bee" obedient. Ephesians 6:1 says, "*Children, obey your parents in the Lord: for this is right*." To "bee" obedient is to be prompt and without hesitation. "Bee" obedient. This "bee" will never leave a painful sting.

"Is it possible to serve God and not obey Him?"

Bee Occupied

Jesus told the parable of a master instructing his servants, *"...occupy till I come"* (Luke 19:13). The same message applies to each of us. There is a job we must do. We need to "bee" occupied with winning souls and serving others. We need to "bee" occupied with prayer. We all should "bee" occupied with the work of the Lord until Jesus returns. This gives no place for a weary, tired servant to become discouraged and quit. There is too much work to be done.

I would like to remind all pastors and teachers to apply this message to your lives: *"...occupy till I come."* It will help you remain focused and encouraged when things go wrong. It will help you to be faithful during the times of trials and tests. "Bee" occupied until Heaven springs open and Jesus comes in the clouds to receive you home. What a joy it will be to hear those precious words, *"Well done, thou good and faithful servant"* (Matthew 25:21). Choose to "bee" occupied with the work of the Lord. This "bee" will not leave a painful sting.

"Some people stay awake worrying while others stay awake planning."

Bee One

W hen Jesus prayed for His followers, He made this request to the Father, "*...that they may be one, as we are*" (John 17:11). What a prayer! What a request! That is the kind of relationship the Lord desires to have with each of His children. It's more than wishful thinking, but a possible experience. Through the death and resurrection of Jesus, we receive a position of son-ship with the Father which makes us one with Him. John wrote, "*Beloved, now are we the sons of God, and it doth not yet appear what we shall be: but we know that, when he shall appear, we shall be like him; for we shall see him as he is*" (I John 3:2). If you always choose to "bee" one with your Heavenly Father, your life will be filled with the blessings of Heaven.

To "bee" one is to be in unity and agreement and to have a close relationship. In Paul's epistle to the church at Corinth, he writes, "*Now I beseech you, brethren, by the name of our Lord Jesus Christ, that ye all speak the same thing, and that there be no divisions among you; but that ye be perfectly joined together in the same mind and in the same judgment*" (I Corinthians 1:10). What a lovely fellowship it is when the churches are in unity with the Spirit of God.

What a difference "bee" one could make in many marriages. Both the old and new covenant make it clear that you become one when you are married, "*And they twain shall be one flesh: so then they are no more twain, but one flesh*" (Mark 10:8). What a precious union it is when a husband and wife are perfectly joined in the bonds of love and peace. "Bee" one is a lovely bee which will never leave a painful sting.

Bee Optimistic

O ptimism is a good philosophy. To "bee" optimistic, one must also be realistic. True optimists do not live in a fantasy world. Optimists expects good things to happen. They help to make good things happen. They have a winning attitude and help others to be winners. They keep their eyes on the goal. Troubles don't stop them because they know the Lord will help them in every situation. They confess Psalm 37:23: *"The steps of a good man are ordered by the LORD...."*

The optimist is an encouragement to his spouse. He gives a certain measure of security to his family and fellowman. He doesn't pray haphazardly; he prays and expects the Lord to respond to his prayers. He expects his employer to favor him. If he is an employer, he expects his employees to favor him and do their job well. When hardships come, the pessimist quits. The pessimist expects to fail. Not so with the optimist. When others give up and quit, he keeps going. While some see the storm, he sees the harvest the rain will produce. Instead of judging a vulture for being a scavenger, the optimist sees him as a bird that helps keep the earth clean.

When Moses sent out the twelve spies to search the land, two were optimists and ten were pessimists. The pessimists saw the giants, the sons of Anak, and saw themselves as grasshoppers. The two optimists, Caleb and Joshua, saw the same giants and obstacles but they focused their attention on God's promise and the fruit of the land flowing with milk and honey. If Jesus had not been optimistic, He could have become discouraged with His disciples. The Bible says, *"For neither did his brethren believe in him"* (John 7:5).

Many optimists have faced defeat after defeat. Some experienced failure again and again, but they refused to waste their life with "what could have been." They have been mocked by the losing world, but they still dream. Because of this, they accomplish things others never achieve. A Jew once told me he could lose everything he had but would soon be a wealthy man again. The reason is simple. He was an optimist. He had a winning attitude. While the pessimist is crying over his loss, the optimist is seeking ways to rebuild. He motivates himself. He encourages himself: "*...But David encouraged himself in the LORD his God*" (I Samuel 30:6). So, learn to "bee" optimistic.

FROM FAILING TO SUCCESS

F - *Face the fact that everyone fails*
A - *Acknowledge where you missed it*
I - *Insist on learning new ways to win*
L - *Listen to advice from other successful people*
I - *Inspire yourself daily*
N - *Never, never give up*
G - *Go for it; you can make it!*

Bee Orderly

H ave you ever had things all messed up and out of order? Some people have a life that is very disorderly. That doesn't make you feel good, does it? That is why you should desire to "bee" orderly. Unless you choose to "bee" orderly, your life can become confusing and out of control. You need to "bee" orderly in every area of life. Paul wrote in I Corinthians 14:40, "*Let all things be done decently and in order.*" He didn't say just some things, but all things should be done decently and in order.

You need to "bee" orderly in conduct and behavior. You need to "bee" orderly in cleanliness and neatness. Our churches need to "bee" orderly. Paul instructed Titus, "*For this cause left I thee in Crete, that thou shouldest set in order the things that are wanting, and ordain elders in every city, as I had appointed thee*" (Titus 1:5). We all need to "bee" orderly. This can only be done when we choose to "bee" orderly.

"Lord, kindle a fire within me to burn out the trash."

Bee Organized

Y ou should "bee" organized in every area of your life to avoid confusion, delay and failure. Few things can be more frustrating than being unorganized. An office uses files to keep things organized. A public library must have their books organized to be able to locate the desired book. A pastor must "bee" organized or he will become frustrated with his own faulty leadership techniques. A CEO must choose to "bee" organized or he will not have organized employees. God uses organization in the way He appoints leaders as we discover in I Corinthians 12:28: "*And God hath set some in the church, first apostles, secondarily prophets, thirdly teachers, after that miracles, then gifts of healings, helps, governments, diversities of tongues.*"

You should have an organized lifestyle. Whether you are praying, studying the Scriptures, or playing with your children, you need to "bee" organized. I believe if people would teach their children to pick up their toys and clothes and put them in the proper place, those children could learn to "bee" organized at a young age. This "bee" is very important to maintain a successful life, therefore, "bee" organized.

"If you were a clock, would you be on time?"

Bee Original

O ver the years, I have talked with a number of people who expressed interest in writing articles, poems or songs. I tried to encourage them to "bee" original. Too many people just write lines that rhyme or reuse someone's thoughts. I'm not saying you can't reuse someone's thoughts, but you may need to be creative and re-word them to make it sound more original.

Years ago, I had an original statement: "If we live prepared to die, we will die prepared to live." It was later copied onto a plaque to be used as a wall hanging. People appreciate things that are original.

In the realms of the Spirit, to "bee" original means to be more than an average Christian. To supersede the average. To no longer be satisfied to live and die without accomplishing much for the Lord.

Paul chose to be an original Christian. He fulfilled what few others dared to accomplish. In his closing remarks, he said, *"For I am now ready to be offered, and the time of my departure is at hand. I have fought a good fight, I have finished my course, I have kept the faith: Henceforth there is laid up for me a crown of righteousness, which the Lord, the righteous judge, shall give me at that day: and not to me only, but unto all them also that love his appearing"* (II Timothy 4:6-8). Those words far exceed the goals of an average Christian. Some read those words, but feel they will never reach that level. If you choose to "bee" original, as Paul, you can excel the average Christian. Don't be satisfied with stale Christianity. Dare to "bee" original. This "bee" will never leave a painful sting.

Bee Overcomers

We need to "bee" overcomers. The Bible tells us, "*For what-soever is born of God overcometh the world: and this is the victory that overcometh the world, even our faith*"(I John 5:4). To "bee" overcomers, we must be established in faith according to the Word of God. There is something about faith which increases our ability to resist the influence of the devil. I've known people who faced the greatest tests of their lives and still came through in victory. Some overcame the stronghold of addictions and bad habits. Others overcame discouragement during great financial loss. Later, everything was fully restored.

To "bee" overcomers, as instructed in the Bible, we need to have a close relationship with our Heavenly Father. We are promised in Romans 8:37, "*Nay, in all these things we are more than conquerors through him that loved us*." We can "bee" overcomers by adjusting our lives to the Word of God. This "bee" will never leave a painful sting.

"Coping with your problems does more than wishing you didn't have them."

Bee Particular

I t is a good thing to "bee" particular. You should "bee" particular who you associate with and who your children have as friends. Romans 16:17 warns to avoid certain people, *"Now I beseech you, brethren, mark them which cause divisions and offences contrary to the doctrine which ye have learned; and avoid them."* That is why you need to fellowship with people who will leave a good influence on you and others.

You should "bee" particular the way you treat others and the way you talk to or about others. You should "bee" particular about your personal appearance and desire to be neat and clean. You should "bee" particular about your character and the way you act or behave yourself in the public. The Bible records that David was a young man of excellent behavior, *"And David behaved himself wisely in all his ways; and the LORD was with him"* (I Samuel 18:14). What a testimony that young man had!

I have heard people say that you can be too particular. There is a difference between being particular and being a perfectionist. Sometimes people who are perfectionists are difficult to work with. You can "bee" particular without being unreasonable. How important it is to "bee" particular!

Bee Patient

An elderly gentleman once told Esther and I that he had to wait longer than most people because he did not have the patience to wait. Job was an excellent example of patience. God greatly blessed this man because he was patient in a time of trouble. James, in writing his epistle, referred to Job's patience, "*Behold, we count them happy which endure. Ye have heard of the patience of Job, and have seen the end of the Lord; that the Lord is very pitiful, and of tender mercy*" (James 5:11).

I Thessalonians 5:14 gives this message, "*...be patient toward all men.*" This world needs more people who exercise this important virtue. Through patience, the patriarchs obtained the promises. In a hurried world, it is hard to "bee" patient, but it certainly is possible. "*For ye have need of patience, that, after ye have done the will of God, ye might receive the promise*" (Hebrews 10:36).

I have seen fathers become very impatient with their wives and children to such an extent that fear was placed upon the family. When parents show patience and lovingkindness toward each other and their children, a foundation of truth is established in the home. Impatient people can do a lot of damage in a home or community. Think of what a difference you can make in your surroundings if you exercise patience. This virtue appears to be very difficult for some people. Learning to be patient is not easy, but it can be very rewarding and it is God's way. When you exercise patience toward others, you can expect the Lord to exercise patience toward you. "Bee" patient. Slow down and enjoy life. This "bee" will never leave a painful sting.

Bee Peaceful

In the midst of all the tumult and confusion in this world, multitudes of hurting people do not know the value of sweet, perfect peace. It is difficult to live in peace with some people. Sometimes it seems impossible, but it is worth trying. Paul, in writing to the Romans, instructed them, *"If it be possible, as much as lieth in you, live peaceably with all men"* (Romans 12:18). People may not always respond favorably to your peaceful attitude, but to "bee" peaceful is God's way. When you live in peace with yourself and your fellowman, the peace of God will rule in your heart.

Most people would welcome having a peaceful person around them. A peaceful husband may win a less peaceful wife. A peaceful wife may be an instrument in helping a husband who is not peaceful to live in harmony with her. Peace has such sweet tranquility that it is hard to describe in words. We all need to practice what Paul wrote in I Thessalonians 5:13: *"...be at peace among yourselves."*

Where could you improve in peacefulness? This whole world is plagued with fear and trouble, but you can live peacefully in this time. Many little children have never had the privilege of growing up in a peaceful atmosphere. All they have ever known is parents fighting and quarreling. You have an opportunity to show them a true example of peace and victorious Christianity. As you pray and minister to these families, you can help bring healing to those troubled hearts.

There is a lovely old hymn that we used to sing, "Sweet peace, the gift of God's love." Think about that, sweet peace is indeed a gift of God's love. The peace of God will help to bring peace to a hurting world. So, "bee" peaceful.

Bee Peculiar

When Peter was writing to the Believers, he said, *"But ye are a chosen generation, a royal priesthood, an holy nation, a peculiar people; that ye should show forth the praises of him who hath called you out of darkness into his marvelous light"* (I Peter 2:9). The way we use the word "peculiar" in our everyday language is often negative as meaning "strange" or "odd," but the Bible uses peculiar in the positive form. To "bee" peculiar in the Biblical way is an honorary position. To "bee" peculiar means you are a special person—above average—in the eyes of the Lord. There are certain groups of people who are distinctively unique to others because of their relationship to the Almighty God. God said to the nation of Israel, *"Now therefore, if ye will obey my voice indeed, and keep my covenant, then ye shall be a peculiar treasure unto me above all people: for all the earth is mine"* (Exodus 19:5). Not only would Israel be a peculiar people, but all of God's children in every race and kindred are a peculiar people.

Apostle Paul gave us a description of this unique class of people when he said, *"Who gave himself for us, that he might redeem us from all iniquity, and purify unto himself a peculiar people, zealous of good works"* (Titus 2:14). You may appear peculiar to this generation who is quick to remind you we are not saved by works. That is correct, you are not saved by works, but works are the evidence of being saved. The Believers Paul referred to as peculiar were zealous of good works. You are redeemed to "bee" peculiar. That is a lofty position, so "bee" peculiar.

Bee Perfect

When someone suggests that you can "bee" perfect, I can almost hear the protest: "Nobody is perfect." Before you accept that conclusion, let's see what the Bible has to say. In writing to Timothy, Paul said, *"All scripture is given by inspiration of God, and is profitable for doctrine, for reproof, for correction, for instruction in righteousness: That the man of God may be perfect, thoroughly furnished unto all good works"* (II Timothy 3:16-17). The word "perfect" in this verse means "to be complete." It does not mean you become infallible. It means you can raise to a higher standard of perfection than most people are willing to achieve. If you are not living up to God's standard, change. God expects you to be complete in Him. In the book of Hebrews, we read *"Now the God of peace, that brought again from the dead our Lord Jesus, that great shepherd of the sheep, through the blood of the everlasting covenant, Make you perfect in every good work to do his will, working in you that which is wellpleasing in his sight, through Jesus Christ; to whom be glory for ever and ever. Amen"* (Hebrews 13:20-21). You no longer need to make excuses for your mistakes, failures and sin because, according to the Bible, you can "bee" perfect. This "bee" will never leave a painful sting.

Bee Persistent

Those who achieve the greatest accomplishments in life are those who learn to "bee" persistent. Persistence divides the loser from the winner. The winner has learned to "bee" persistent and the loser has not. The persistent are determined to accomplish something. They accept an assignment that may appear impossible and put forth every effort to fulfill the task.

Jesus told the story of a man who had some unexpected visitors. He didn't have sufficient bread to feed them, so he went to his friend's house. He was told they were in bed and were unable to help him. Most people would have returned without the bread. Not this man. How did he persuade his friend to give him his request? Jesus explained, "*I say unto you, Though he will not rise and give him, because he is his friend, yet because of his importunity he will rise and give him as many as he needeth*" (Luke 11:8). He learned to "bee" persistent. His importunity brought results, didn't it? Jesus is not teaching us to force others to respond to our demands, but rather to understand the value of true persistence.

Men and women who became a great success in the business world and in the Spiritual realm were those who knew they had to "bee" persistent. They wouldn't take "no" for an answer. Often, you are faced with situations that look almost impossible, yet to "bee" persistent can bring amazing results.

Bee Persuaded

To "bee" persuaded means to be settled in a matter. You are persuaded that you can do what the Lord called you to do. Nothing shall be impossible to you. "Bee" persuaded that you can accomplish the most difficult tasks in life by simply following the leading of the Lord and obeying the Scriptures.

"Bee" persuaded that your marriage can be a good marriage. "Bee" persuaded that your children can be children of God. "Bee" persuaded that you can live in peace with your family, friends and neighbors. It may be hard at first, but remember that all things are possible to him that believeth.

"Bee" persuaded that you will be faithful unto death. Paul made an astounding statement when he said, *"For I am persuaded, that neither death, nor life, nor angels, nor principalities, nor powers, nor things present, nor things to come, Nor height, nor depth, nor any other creature, shall be able to separate us from the love of God, which is in Christ Jesus our Lord"* (Romans 8:38-39). Notice, he said nothing would turn him away from the Lord. In fact, he even emphasized that nothing could separate him from the love of God. He was persuaded that the Lord would do exactly what He promised and that he could live in victory every day of his life. You can be just as persuaded that the Lord can work great things in your life. "Bee" persuaded that what God has promised, he will do. This "bee" will never leave a painful sting.

Bee Pessimistic

Y ou need to "bee" pessimistic. This statement may be rather shocking since I have been emphasizing optimism, but there are certain times when pessimism is good. "Bee" pessimistic when you are facing temptation. Think about the results. Jesus said, *"He that committeth sin is of the devil..."* (I John 3:8).

"Bee" pessimistic before you join a rebellious conspiracy against someone. "Bee pessimistic" about gossip and slander. The Bible says, *"...the poison of asps is under their lips"* (Romans 3:13). It is not the rattlesnake bite that causes the problem, it is the poison that has been injected into the victim that does the damage. People seldom consider the consequences before they talk against others.

Before you consider moderate drinking of alcoholic beverages, you may want to "bee" pessimistic. If you research what happens to "moderate" drinkers, you will find that many become alcoholics. *"Look not thou upon the wine when it is red, when it giveth his colour in the cup, when it moveth itself aright"* (Proverbs 23:31).

Don't want to dwell too long on pessimistic thoughts or you will become a pessimist. Only use pessimistic thoughts to avoid future problems. Your goal should still be optimism. When you use "bee" pessimistic in the right way, it will not leave a painful sting.

Bee Pitiful

The Bible says, *"Finally, be ye all of one mind, having compassion one of another, love as brethren, be pitiful, be courteous"* (I Peter 3:8). To "bee" pitiful does not mean to have a pity-party mentality. To "bee" pitiful is to be compassionate and understanding toward those who are going through very difficult times.

Several years ago, a man went into the barn to milk his cows. He heard an unusual noise from outside and turned toward his house. To his horror, his home was engulfed in flames. He ran toward the house in the hopes of rescuing his wife and three children, but was too late. The flames had consumed the house and his precious family. This would be a time to "bee" pitiful. This man needed someone to show compassion and pity toward him after his hour of tragedy. The Bible speaks of having pity on those who are suffering: *"Shouldest not thou also have had compassion on thy fellowservant, even as I had pity on thee?"*(Matthew 18:33).

There are others who may be facing misfortunes, tragedies or problems. There are some who are handicapped and unable to do much for themselves. Remember to "bee" pitiful, compassionate, sympathetic and understanding toward those who are facing these situations. This "bee" will never leave a painful sting when you use it to help others.

Bee Pleasant

P leasant people have a beautiful personality. They are a blessing to those around them. I once knew a young girl who had pleasant characteristics. I saw this girl weeping and almost smiling at the same time. She often visited our home and was always pleasant. At a young age, she lost her life in an auto accident. This girl left behind memories of a pleasant person.

How refreshing it is to be in the presence of a pleasant person. Even those with a bitter, irritable, melancholy disposition are affected when they come in contact with a pleasant individual. To "bee" pleasant is not a matter of circumstances; it's a matter of choice. You must choose to "bee" pleasant. It is good to practice developing a pleasant attitude and speaking pleasant words, "*...the words of the pure are pleasant words*" (Proverbs 15:26). A person who is pleasant, respectable and agreeable is already well on his way to success. "Bee" pleasant. This "bee" will never leave a painful sting!

"Make the best out of the worst.
Make the best out of the best."

Bee Polite

When you choose to "bee" polite, it reveals respect and appreciation for others. Romans 12:10 instructs how to "bee" polite: *"Be kindly affectioned one to another with brotherly love; in honour preferring one another."* Even in a restaurant, remember to "bee" polite to those serving you. Throughout our travels, waitresses or store employees would notice our polite conduct and ask where we were from. We appeared to them as if we were from another planet. There was a time when people knew how to "bee" polite. They knew how to address each other with respect. Children were taught to "bee" polite, especially to the elderly. It appears today's generation has lost the beauty of "bee" polite. Although, politeness has been lost in much of the younger generation, it is still a very important "bee" that needs to be restored.

" Truth will never argue."

Bee Positive

To "bee" positive is a matter of choice. We are living in such a negative world that those with a positive approach to life are classified as New Age philosophers. Somehow, many have the unscriptural belief that we must expect to be sad, bored, weary and down-trodden. No wonder so many Christians are depending on tranquilizers to help them cope with life. Many people who are emotionally disturbed, suspicious and fearful of others could trace part of their problem back to a negative attitude. A negative lifestyle causes you to lose confidence and trust in others.

Beloved, it is time for Christians to "bee" positive—positive in faith, positive in prayer, positive at home and positive at work. Negative people cannot praise the Lord the same as positive Christians. It is time to get, "*...the oil of joy for mourning,*" and put on, "*...the garment of praise for the spirit of heaviness...*" (Isaiah 61:3).

A positive person doesn't sit around waiting for bad things to happen, he expects something good to come out of the bad experiences. He sees every trial as an opportunity: "*And we know that all things work together for good to them that love God, to them who are the called according to his purpose*" (Romans 8:28). Positive people are not afraid to face an unknown future. They refuse to dwell on the negative. Let the world think their negative thoughts, talk their negative talk and walk their negative walk. While others lose, we will win. After all, God said the person who meditates upon His Word day and night, "*...whatsoever he doeth shall prosper*" (Psalm 1:3).

A positive person has a vision, a goal and a plan. He doesn't just talk about doing something, he does it. He is a man of perseverance. He refuses to procrastinate. There is a job that must be done and he will do it. If he hears, "It can't be done," he is motivated to accomplish it. Positive people are explorers. They explore new ways to accomplish great tasks. From their visions have come great inventions such as earth moving equipment or airplanes capable of transporting numerous travelers across the sky zipping at hundreds of miles per hour.

Positive people are energizers. They achieve their maximum potential. They are not all people of a high IQ. Many of them are not even intellectually superior to their peers, but they are not satisfied with a "that's good enough" mentality. I am convinced that a positive approach can transform your whole life. It can change your way of thinking and your way of planning your goals. That is why the wise man said, *"For as he thinketh in his heart, so is he..."* (Proverbs 23:7). You are what we think. "Bee" positive. It's the way to live!

"One creative thought at a time built our modern conveniences. An airplane was built from one creative thought."

Bee Powerful

T he Bible portrays Samson as an extremely powerful man. One example is recorded in Judges 16:3: *"And Samson lay till midnight, and arose at midnight, and took the doors of the gate of the city, and the two posts, and went away with them, bar and all, and put them upon his shoulders, and carried them up to the top of an hill that is before Hebron."* It is also recorded that he killed one thousand Philistines with the jawbone of a donkey. He recognized his supernatural strength came from obedience to Almighty God. When he disobeyed by revealing the secret of his strength to a deceptive woman, his power was taken from him. Some people lose the power of God because they do not use it correctly. You should "bee" powerful in a way that is effective and helpful to others.

The book of Acts tells us the early Believers were powerful: *"And with great power gave the apostles witness of the resurrection of the Lord Jesus: and great grace was upon them all"* (Acts 4:33). The powerful hand of God was working with them and through them. Miracles followed wherever they went and people marveled. Peter explained, *"...Ye men of Israel, why marvel ye at this? or why look ye so earnestly on us, as though by our own power or holiness we had made this man to walk?"* (Acts 3:12). The apostles confessed they could not "bee" powerful on their own, but depended completely on the Holy Ghost for miracle working power.

Paul was a preacher—a great preacher—but he also realized that his power to preach came from heaven and not man. He declared, *"For I am not ashamed of the gospel of Christ: for it is the power of God unto salvation to every one that believeth; to the Jew first, and also to the Greek"* (Romans 1:16). Not everyone may be called to preach, but everyone is called to "bee" powerful in the Holy Ghost. In Ephesians 3:20-21, Paul explained that the Lord can use anyone according to the power that works in them: *"Now unto him that is able to do exceeding abundantly above all that we ask or think, ac-*

cording to the power that worketh in us, Unto him be glory in the church by Christ Jesus throughout all ages, world without end. Amen."

Before the Lord can trust you with His great power, you need to humble yourself before Him and acknowledge that you can do nothing on your own. You must totally and completely trust the Lord to empower you for the work. Remember, it is more important to "bee" powerful in spiritual things than in the physical. Then, "bee" powerful will not leave a painful sting.

DESTINED TO WIN

We're armed for the battle
And ready for war.
We once were defeated
But not anymore.
All Heaven is with us
And courage within;
With Christ as our Caption
We're destined to win!

Bee Prayerful

It is good to start the day by choosing to "bee" prayerful. Someone who prays and gives thanks for their spouse and family members can change the whole atmosphere of a home. The prayer of faith can do wonders. The Bible tells us to pray for each other. Your words, your actions, your caring, in addition to your prayers, can change lives. Ask the Lord to make you a blessing and help you give encouragement to someone facing a problem. It is good to pray for those who seldom have anyone to pray for them. There are some senior citizens who may be neglected or little children who are abused who need the prayers of the saints. There may be a lonely person who needs your prayers. It is good to tell people you are praying for them, but be honest and pray. Words like this can add much to a lonely person's life.

In recent years, there has been a teaching that if you pray about something more than once, you pray in unbelief. This is unscriptural. Jesus gave an illustration of a woman who insisted on being delivered from her circumstances. He said those who pray in like manner shall receive an answer: "*And there was a widow in that city; and she came unto him, saying, Avenge me of mine adversary. And he would not for a while: but afterward he said within himself, Though I fear not God, nor regard man; Yet because this widow troubleth me, I will avenge her, lest by her continual coming she weary me. And the Lord said, Hear what the unjust judge saith. And shall not God avenge his own elect, which cry day and night unto him, though he bear long with them? I tell you that he will avenge them speedily...*" (Luke 18:3-8). This message is especially important to a spouse or child who may be a victim of abuse. When someone humbly seeks the Lord's help, He will hear their cry. It may seem when you are praying for a certain situation in your own life or in the life of someone near you that there is no answer. But the Bible tells us, "*Pray without ceasing*" (I Thessalonians 5:17). It may take days, weeks or sometimes years to change circumstances, but God still answers prayer. Therefore, "bee" prayerful.

Bee Preferred

To "bee" preferred may sound arrogant to the carnal mind, but you can "bee" preferred without becoming proud. There are many saints in the Bible who were preferred above others because of their decision to serve the Lord with their whole heart. These men and women of the Lord were highly favored. Daniel was preferred because an excellent spirit was in him: "*Then this Daniel was preferred above the presidents and princes, because an excellent spirit was in him; and the king thought to set him over the whole realm*" (Daniel 6:3).

Esther was preferred above all other virgins. She was not only chosen for her beauty, but for the spirit that dwelt within her: "*And the maiden pleased him, and she obtained kindness of him; and he speedily gave her her things for purification, with such things as belonged to her, and seven maidens, which were meet to be given her, out of the king's house: and he preferred her and her maids unto the best place of the house of the women*" (Esther 2:9). If you make a decision, like the saints of old, to serve the Lord with all your heart, you can "bee" preferred. You will find favor both with God and man.

It is important you remember to prefer others also. In Romans 12:10, Paul instructs us: "*Be kindly affectioned one to another with brotherly love; in honour preferring one another.*" "Bee" preferred will never leave a painful sting if you seek the favor of the Lord.

Bee Prepared

M any are the heart cries of people who were not prepared for the situations that happened in their lives, "I wasn't prepared for this. If I had known, I would have prepared." You need to "bee" prepared for whatever may take place. People who are prepared can face some of the most difficult times in life and come through with victory.

Many years ago, I was to scheduled to speak at a conference. While the emcee was introducing me as the next speaker, I was handed a bulletin which stated that I was assigned to speak on a specific subject. I had planned to speak on something completely different and was not prepared to speak on this topic. Before I could collect my thoughts, the emcee said, "Help me welcome Pastor Rodes." Although I was unprepared for what took place, I was prepared to expect the unexpected. Because of human error, someone had failed to inform me I was assigned a subject for that meeting. No one knew I hadn't studied the subject as I presented the Word that day.

Another time, I didn't even know I was scheduled to speak in a session. Someone came to me and said, "Brother Rodes, as soon as they finish singing this song, you may deliver the message." "Bee" prepared. You don't always know when you will be called upon. If you choose to "bee" prepared for the unexpected, you won't be caught off guard.

Bee Prevailing

To "bee" prevailing is to gain victory or superiority, to succeed. What an opportunity awaits those who refuse to be defeated. Jacob was a prevailing man. The prophet, Hosea, records his prevailing attitude even at the time of his birth, "*He* [Jacob] *took his brother by the heel in the womb, and by his strength he had power with God*" (Hosea 12:3). Many years later, this same man had to face his angry brother, Esau. The night before their meeting, he wrestled with an angel, "*Yea, he had power over the angel, and prevailed: he wept, and made supplication unto him: he found him in Bethel, and there he spake with us; Even the LORD God of hosts; the LORD is his memorial*" (Verses 4-5). Despite Jacob's weakness, he gained superiority over circumstances that troubled him. When his Uncle Laban took advantage of him, he still prevailed. Jacob was a fighter throughout his life. His mind was made up to be a winner and God blessed him exceedingly.

If you hope to prevail, you must listen to the warning buzz of "bee" prevailing. "Don't quit; don't give up" is what he is saying to each of us.

Bee Productive

The difference between a productive person and a nonproductive person is choice. One person chose to "bee" productive while the other did not. Someone may have a good paying job while another person has a lower paying job. This is a result of choice. Those who choose to "bee" productive usually excel.

People who decided to "bee" productive gave us many of the conveniences we enjoy today. Refrigeration, electricity, air travel, computers and a host of other inventions came about because someone chose to "bee" productive. They put to practice what Solomon said in Ecclesiastes 9:10, *"Whatsoever thy hand findeth to do, do it with thy might."* They did it and so can you. No, you may not be an inventor, but you can always do your best. You will only do a good job on your assignments when you choose to "bee" productive. This is the way to get a job done. Who knows what you can become if you choose to "bee" productive!

"The loss of a job does not necessarily mean a loss of opportunity."

Bee Prompt

When the congregation of the children of Israel rose up in rebellion against Moses and Aaron, Moses knew something had to be done quickly: *"And Moses said unto Aaron, Take a censer, and put fire therein from off the altar, and put on incense, and go quickly unto the congregation, and make an atonement for them: for there is wrath gone out from the LORD; the plague is begun"* (Numbers 16:46). If these two leaders had not learned to "bee" prompt, many more people would have lost their lives.

When Peter was in prison for preaching the Gospel, the Bible says, *"And, behold, the angel of the Lord came upon him, and a light shined in the prison: and he smote Peter on the side, and raised him up, saying, Arise up **quickly**. And his chains fell off from his hands"* (Acts 12:7). His response to the angel required haste. Suppose he would have said, "I'm sleepy, wait until morning to get me out of here." The angel would have gone his way and left Peter in prison. Peter was set free because he understood the importance of prompt obedience.

I watched a parent instruct one of their children to do a job or run an errand. The child had to be told several times before the instruction was obeyed. I am blessed when I see a child respond immediately. My wife and I were in a home when one of the daughters (possibly twelve years old) was given a job. This young girl was playing a game. She stopped and said, "I need to do something for Mom; I'll be right back." At least three times, this game was interrupted by the mom asking her to do something. Every time, she promptly obeyed. How refreshing it was to see a young person who was trained right. When children are trained to "bee" prompt to obey their parents, they will "bee" prompt to obey the Lord and others in leadership as well.

If "bee" prompt is not accompanying you from day to day, why not make this "bee" your friend today? I'm sure you will, one day, be glad you did. This "bee" helped Aaron and Peter and it will help you. "Bee" prompt will never leave a painful sting.

GOOD INTENTIONS

You had good intentions
For things you planned to do;
Yet one thing led to another
And you couldn't see it through.

You may have made a promise;
Of course, you didn't know
You couldn't keep your promise,
Or you'd have told them so.

It may be a sick neighbor;
You'd visit them some day;
You had so many things to do,
Your time just slipped away.

You had good intentions;
But, will they see you through?
When at the day of Judgment
Will "good intentions" do?

Bee Prosperous

A sk the average person what it means to "bee" prosperous. The answer would likely be centered around having plenty of money or possessions. That can be considered prosperity, but it is only a small part of what it means to "bee" prosperous. The Psalmist shows us what the Lord sees in a prosperous person. *"Blessed is the man,"* he writes, *"that walketh not in the counsel of the ungodly, nor standeth in the way of sinners, nor sitteth in the seat of the scornful. But his delight is in the law of the LORD; and in his law doth he meditate day and night. And he shall be like a tree planted by the rivers of water, that bringeth forth his fruit in his season; his leaf also shall not wither; and whatsoever he doeth shall prosper"* (Psalm 1:1-3). According to these verses, if you want to "bee" prosperous, you must not walk in the counsel of the ungodly. You must not stand in the way of sinners. You must not sit in the seat of the scornful. You must love the Word of God. This kind of prosperity is superior to money and possessions.

Abraham was a man whom God prospered greatly. He recognized that his prosperity was not from man but from the Lord. He told the king of Sodom, *"That I will not take from a thread even to a shoe-latchet, and that I will not take any thing that is thine, lest thou shouldest say, I have made Abram rich"* (Genesis 14:23).

Joseph was a prosperous man. Potiphar entrusted him with everything in his house: *"And his master saw that the LORD was with him, and that the LORD made all that he did to prosper in his hand"* (Genesis 39:3). Not only was Joseph prosperous, but *"The LORD blessed the Egyptian's house for Joseph's sake; and the blessing of the LORD was upon all that he had in the house, and in the field"* (Genesis 39:5). If the Lord could entrust you with prosperity, it would not only be a blessing to your own life, but also to those around you.

The Lord wants you to "bee" prosperous. He takes pleasure in the prosperity of His servants in every area of life, whether financially, spiritually or mentally. We read in Psalm 35:27: *"Let the LORD be magnified, which hath pleasure in the prosperity of his servant."* God is never pleased nor rejoices in the prosperity of a greedy or wicked person. Therefore, "bee" prosperous, but let that prosperity come from the blessings of the Lord.

I WILL WIN

You tried and tried and tried and failed
And yet you wouldn't quit.
You may have thought a dozen times,
"I'm quitting, this is it."
But then you heard that little voice
Deep down within you say,
"I may have failed a thousand times,
But I will win today!"

Bee Protected

We all need to "bee" protected in the evil times in which we live. To "bee" protected on a day to day basis requires a quality decision. You will not allow anything to come between you and the Lord. The Word has a tremendous protecting power for those who walk in the ways of the Lord. The Psalmist knew the importance of this precious "bee" when he wrote, *"For thou hast been a shelter for me, and a strong tower from the enemy"* (Psalm 61:3). The Lord is your strong tower in times of temptation. He will keep your marriage strong, stable and loving.

According to Psalm 34:7, *"The angel of the LORD encampeth round about them that fear him, and delivereth them."* You need this "bee" to remind you continuously that you are protected and delivered by the Angel of the Lord. When you neglect to heed the warning buzz of "bee" protected, you lose the protection that belongs to God's children.

"Treat fear as the worst of enemies."

Bee Protective

To "bee" protective is a very important "bee." You need to "bee" protective of your marriage, your household and your choice of friends. You need to "bee" protective of your morals and goals. You need to "bee" protective when you are driving on the highways. You need to "bee" protective of your children. You should know where they are, what they are doing and what kind of friends they have.

One time, when I was out seeking to win souls, a mother asked me to pray for her daughters who were turning out wrong. I asked her if she knew the current whereabouts of her 12 year old daughter. She replied, "She went out with some boys tonight." This mother had never learned how important it is to "bee" protective of her children.

Many are the sorrows in life because someone failed to listen to "bee" protective. The buzzing of this "bee" is saying, "be careful." Remember, "bee" protective will never leave a painful sting!

Bee Pure

W e are living in an evil generation. There seems to be so much filth on every hand. Television, internet and magazines have become impure. Even the manner of most people's dress is impure. It is time for the people of God to separate themselves from this unclean world and choose to "bee" pure.

In I Corinthians 6:18, Paul admonished the church to *"flee fornication."* Courtship, as we know it here in America, has lost purity and virginity and has become filthy. People seem to think it is "cool" to commit wickedness and do that which is evil in the sight of the Lord. There is nothing "cool" about it. It is filthy, dirty and unclean. Marriage, as holy matrimony, has almost become obsolete in some circles. Hebrews 13:4 warns, *"Marriage is honourable in all, and the bed undefiled: but whoremongers and adulterers God will judge."* So many people seem to take this warning lightly, but beloved, you must "bee" pure. God warns that nothing will enter into Heaven that is unclean.

God is calling His people to true repentance and separation from the world. He will forgive those who have trespassed His law of purity, but He requires them to turn away from sin and go in the right direction. You can "bee" pure, so *"keep thyself pure"* (I Timothy 5:22). "Bee pure" will never leave a painful sting.

"The only vision some people have is television."

Bee Purified

How precious it is to "bee" purified, especially when the Lord purifies you, "*Many shall be purified, and made white, and tried*" (Daniel 12:10). We, as humans, are often contaminated by the evil world and need the purifying fire of the Lord to keep us clean, pure and useable. In the book of Malachi, we read, "*And he shall sit as a refiner and purifier of silver: and he shall purify the sons of Levi, and purge them as gold and silver, that they may offer unto the LORD an offering in righteousness*" (Malachi 3:3). The Lord purified the sons of Levi to qualify them for His work.

Those who are in the glorious Kingdom of God are very special to the Lord. He wants His children free from the corruption of the world: "*He gave himself for us, that he might redeem us from all iniquity, and purify unto himself a peculiar people, zealous of good works*" (Titus 2:14). We have been redeemed, but it is important to "bee" purified from time to time because we are all subject to mistakes. Those mistakes may not seem to be major, but we still need to "bee" purified.

Not only does the Lord purify you, but James 4:8 explains your responsibility to purify yourself: "*Draw nigh to God, and he will draw nigh to you. Cleanse your hands, ye sinners; and purify your hearts, ye double minded.*" This can only be done by acknowledging the shed blood of the Lord Jesus Christ in your life. What an important "bee" is "bee" purified! This "bee" will never leave a painful sting.

Bee Qualified

S ome employers are looking for people to work for them, but are unable to find someone who qualifies for the position. Many people may apply, but are not chosen because they lack experience, education or do not meet the approval for some other reason.

The Bible tells us in Matthew 22:14, *"For many are called, but few are chosen."* There are people who could be mightily used of the Lord, but they are not qualified to obtain the fullness of their calling. Why? It may be they desire to do things their own way instead of the way of the Lord. It may be they carry a wrong attitude and do not know how to approach situations correctly. It may be they express their own opinion on situations. Or, it may simply be they have no understanding of the Word. The Bible seems strange to them because they have a carnal mind. Only spiritually minded people are able to discern the things of the Spirit: *"But the natural man receiveth not the things of the Spirit of God: for they are foolishness unto him: neither can he know them, because they are spiritually discerned"* (I Corinthians 2:14).

In order to "bee" qualified to be used by the Lord, you must learn to walk according to His ways and plans. God does not need someone who is eloquent or highly educated. He is looking for people who are willing to do what He requires without hesitation or excuse. Then, He will be able to mightily use them. Seek to "bee" qualified in the kingdom of God. This "bee" will never leave a painful sting.

Bee Quick

S ome things require haste. Paul was instructed to "bee" quick in Acts 22:18: "...*Make haste, and get thee quickly out of Jerusalem: for they will not receive thy testimony concerning me.*" The Lord requires quick obedience. If Paul would not have been quick to obey, he could have lost his life.

In Luke 14, we read the account of guests invited to a wedding supper. After those guests had made excuses for their inability to attend, an urgent instruction was given. "...*Then the master of the house being angry said to his servant, Go out quickly into the streets and lanes of the city, and bring in hither the poor, and the maimed, and the halt, and the blind*" (Luke 14:21). The word "quickly" in this verse means "speedily, rapidly, hastily, shortly, soon or suddenly." You need to "bee" quick to respond when an instruction is given. If you hesitate, you may miss the invitation.

One of the best ways to heal a wound resulting from what someone said about you is to "bee" quick to forgive. Jesus told us, "*Agree with thine adversary quickly, whiles thou art in the way with him; lest at any time the adversary deliver thee to the judge, and the judge deliver thee to the officer, and thou be cast into prison*" (Matthew 5:25).

"Bee" quick to love. "Bee" quick to make corrections when you are wrong. "Bee" quick to change the way you do things. If you would learn to "bee" quick, you wouldn't be tormented with procrastination. There may be a job you know you should do, but you keep putting it off. "Bee" quick to finish that job. Listen to the buzzing of "bee" quick. This "bee" will help you stay far away from procrastination.

Bee Quiet

It is refreshing to have quiet moments alone with God. When you walk alone in some serene place, sit under the shade of a tree or lay in bed at night just absorbing the presence of the Lord, you find peace and tranquility. These are precious moments away from the stress, pressure and confusion of this world. It is in these quiet moments that you are able to relax your weary mind. Jesus instructed His disciples, "...*Come ye yourselves apart into a desert place, and rest a while: for there were many coming and going, and they had no leisure so much as to eat*" (Mark 6:31). If you do not spend some quiet time alone, you can become overcharged with the cares of this life (Luke 21:34).

A busy mother may find it difficult to spend time alone because of her family duties, yet in the stillness of the night, she can rest in the presence of the Lord. This helps to renew her strength to be a strong and capable mother.

Parents may want to consider taking their family to some quiet stream where the breeze is sifting through the leaves and the birds are filling the air with their melodious music. This is a beautiful place to train your children to "bee" quiet and listen to the peaceful surroundings of nature and sense the presence of the Lord: "*The heavens declare the glory of God; and the firmament showeth his handywork*" (Psalm 19:1). In these quiet moments, you can regain your composure and renew your spiritual strength. Why not start today? Have some quiet time alone with God. Learn to "bee" quiet. This "bee" will never leave a painful sting.

> Come ye apart
> From your daily toil,
> And pray awhile
> Lest care should spoil
> Your peace with God
> And rob your heart.

Bee Rational

To "bee" rational is to be able to reason logically by drawing a conclusion without inference from fear or emotions. To "bee" rational is more than basing one's reasoning or opinion on a philosophy or theological theory. A rational mind must have knowledge superior to that of theory. The carnal mind may reject the supernatural or miraculous power of God. A person with a truly rational mind has faith to believe God and His Word because his beliefs are based on fact, not theory.

I once heard of a man who believed the Bible was no more than a book of theory. He believed that an intellectual or intelligent person would not believe the Bible. Beloved, not only do we, as Believers, believe all the accounts in the Bible, but we believe, "*Whatsoever things were written aforetime were written for our learning, that we through patience and comfort of the scriptures might have hope*" (Romans 15:4). Thank God, a rational mind can understand and believe the Scriptures. Therefore, it is important to "bee" rational.

"Most of our problems start in the brain."

Bee Ready

Y ou need to "bee" ready to expect great things to come your
way. If you are not ready for wonderful experiences in life,
you may miss great opportunities. People who are ready to face difficulties, challenges or blessings are more capable of receiving the
best in life. Someday, you may face the unexpected, but if you are
ready, it won't be as difficult.

One day, David, a young shepherd, was asked by his dad to take
some supplies to his brothers who were in the army of Israel. He
was also given the orders to investigate their well-being. David did-
n't know that he would be faced with a challenge that would change
his nation. When he heard the threat of Goliath, he was ready to
fight the battle. King Saul wasn't sure this young man was eligible
for such an assignment. He looked at David and said, *"Thou art not
able to go against this Philistine to fight with him: for thou art but a
youth, and he a man of war from his youth"* (I Samuel 17:33). David wasn't moved by Saul's negative challenge but narrated to Saul
how he killed a bear and a lion: *"Thy servant slew both the lion and
the bear: and this uncircumcised Philistine shall be as one of them,
seeing he hath defied the armies of the living God."* Then in faith,
*"David said moreover, The LORD that delivered me out of the paw
of the lion, and out of the paw of the bear, he will deliver me out of
the hand of this Philistine. And Saul said unto David, Go, and the
LORD be with thee."* (I Samuel 17:36-37). I would call this man
ready, wouldn't you? Because David was ready, Goliath and the
enemy nation were defeated and the nation of Israel could shout the
victory. Would you "bee" ready if the Lord asked you to do something others were afraid to do?

To "bee" ready is to keep looking for opportunities to do something
for God and man. People who make up their minds to "bee" ready
are not afraid to live or die. You must "bee" ready to leave this
world at any time. You need to "bee" ready for the coming of the

Lord is drawing nigh. Jesus said He is returning for His children. He gave us these very important instructions: "*Be ye therefore ready also: for the Son of man cometh at an hour when ye think not*" (Luke 12:40). Whatever today or tomorrow may hold, "bee" ready.

BEARING ONE ANOTHER'S BURDEN

If I meet one along the way
And do not understand,
Just why he suffers such heartache
Still, let me give a hand,
And help how little it may be,
The part that's mine to share:
For what becomes another's load
Is partly mine to bear.

Bee Realistic

Y ou should have big visions and lofty dreams, yet remember to "bee" realistic. Some highly motivated people have a tendency to become unrealistic. Let me drop a word of caution here not to discourage those who aim for the top. I like to encourage people to become more than the average. Yet, in the midst of your enthusiasm, "bee" realistic. You may have ever so much zeal, but unless you have knowledge with your zeal it could be harmful. In Romans chapter ten and verse two, Paul referred to some of his fellow Israelites, *"For I bear them record that they have a zeal of God, but not according to knowledge."* After you are motivated, it is sometimes hard to stay balanced. One time, you may have zeal but have limited knowledge. Another time, you may have knowledge but lose the zeal.

To "bee" realistic does not mean you can't accomplish great things, just don't set your goals too high that you become discouraged if you don't reach them. You may have to become a great employee before you can become a great employer. You may need to set a goal to pastor a church of 100 people before you work toward 1,000. Set big goals and have great dreams, but "bee" realistic.

Remember to "bee" realistic in prayer. There are people who think they have great faith because they ask the Lord for a large request. They are not making requests with faith, but are asking for something that is not realistic. I was at a prayer meeting where one of the men asked the Lord to give him a beer manufacturing company to transform into a Christian campground. That was many years ago and his request is still unanswered. It never will be fulfilled because his prayer was not realistic. James 4:3 says, *"Ye ask, and receive not, because ye ask amiss, that ye may consume it upon your lusts."* If you ask the Lord for something beyond your faith level, it can hinder you. As your faith grows, you will understand how to "bee" realistic and ask for bigger things. Learn to "bee" realistic. This "bee" will never leave a painful sting.

Bee Reborn

In the third chapter of John, Jesus explained what it means to "bee" reborn. When Jesus told Nicodemus (a ruler of the Jews) *"Ye must be born again,"* Nicodemus responded, *"How can these things be?"* (John 3:7, 9). The new birth doesn't make sense to the carnal mind because the carnal mind cannot understand spiritual things. Peter wrote in I Peter 1:23, *"Being born again, not of corruptible seed, but of incorruptible."* To "bee" reborn is not natural. A spiritual birth takes place within you when you receive Jesus as Lord and Savior. Paul explained what happens when a person is born again. A major change takes place: *"Therefore if any man be in Christ, he is a new creature: old things are passed away; behold, all things are become new"* (II Corinthians 5:17). When the Lord Jesus comes into your hearts, He not only forgives your sins, but He removes them out of His sight and gives you victory over sin. What a glorious experience—to be redeemed from all sin because of Jesus: *"In whom we have redemption through his blood, even the forgiveness of sins"* (Colossians 1:14).

One immoral person said he was born that way. I responded, "If you weren't born right the first time, you can be born again." No matter how wicked a person may be, he or she can "bee" reborn and be set free from all sin. Forgiven! What a wonderful Savior! If you have never asked Jesus to come into your heart or if you are backslidden, you can "bee" reborn, today. "Bee" reborn will never leave a painful sting.

Bee Recognized

When I refer to "bee" recognized, I am not suggesting promoting ego or pride. To a measure, all of us are recognized for who we are. It is good to "bee" recognized for what you stand for. "Bee" recognized as a stable, godly, courageous Christian. "Bee" recognized as a servant with a peaceable and pleasant attitude. Paul told the Romans that their faith was recognized throughout the whole world (Romans 1:8). Imagine a body of Believers who had such great faith that they were recognized worldwide!

Many so-called "Christians" have been cheated from becoming all they desired to become because they were sharply and sternly taught false humility. Humility is a requirement in the Kingdom of God, but true humility does not take second place to achievement. It is proper and right to "bee" recognized as a diligent person who accomplishes something. You should "bee" recognized as a hard, honest worker. A faithful, dependable, reliable person is an asset in any work place. If "bee" recognized leaves a painful sting, it is not truly "bee" recognized. Go ahead, "bee" recognized.

*"Put your trust in God each day
And He will help you find the way."*

Bee Reconciled

W hat a beautiful experience it is when you are an instrument that brings harmony and reconciliation to people. God has given you the precious ministry of reconciliation: *"To wit, that God was in Christ, reconciling the world unto himself, not imputing their trespasses unto them; and hath committed unto us the word of reconciliation"* (II Corinthians 5:19). Before you can be reconciled to others, *"Be ye reconciled to God"* (Verse 20). You need to learn to be reconciled so you can help others. In a time of distress when marriages are pulling apart, family members are raising against each other and churches are building great walls between themselves, you need the ministry of reconciliation. Anticipate people being reconciled as you minister to them. When you help people settle their differences and encourage those who were hurt to forgive, you see the beauty of reconciliation.

To "bee" reconciled you may need to submit to the wishes of others. My wife and I found a precious verse in the Bible that was a blessing to us for years, *"Submitting yourselves one to another in the fear of God"* (Ephesians 5:21). We may not have seen everything exactly alike or always enjoyed the same things but we could still walk in perfect harmony. When husbands and wives have different opinions, the situation can "bee" reconciled in a peaceable manner. If a problem arises between you and others, you have an opportunity to "bee" reconciled! "Bee" reconciled. This "bee" will never leave a painful sting!

Bee Refreshed

We all need a time to "bee" refreshed, a time to get away from the busy hustle and bustle of life. Peter speaks of a time of refreshing that comes from the presence of the Lord: *"Repent ye therefore, and be converted, that your sins may be blotted out, when the times of refreshing shall come from the presence of the Lord"* (Acts 3:19). In times of life when you make mistakes, you cannot be refreshed until you repent. It is then that you are refreshed by the sweet presence of the Lord. When you are under stress or tension, it is good to set aside a time to meditate upon the Lord and His goodness. This helps you to "bee" refreshed as you bathe in the presence of the Lord.

David recognized a need to "bee" refreshed when he prayed, *"I shall be anointed with fresh oil"* (Psalm 92:10). That oil refers to the anointing that destroys the burdens that weigh upon you when you have been too busy to find the true refreshment that comes from the Lord. You need to "bee" refreshed daily in order to stay alert and sensitive to the voice of the Lord so He may lead you step by step in life. Everyone needs a time of refreshment, so set aside a time each day to "bee" refreshed. A good time for this is just before retiring for the night. Before you go to sleep, allow that refreshment to come from the presence of the Lord. How precious it is to "bee" refreshed.

Bee Rejected

With the pen of inspiration, the scribe narrated an amazing statement about our Lord: *"He is despised and rejected of men; a man of sorrows, and acquainted with grief"* (Isaiah 53:3). Why was He rejected? Why was He a man of grief? Why was He a sorrowful Savior? Because His doctrine, teaching and way of life did not match up with the doctrines, teachings and way of life of the religious crowd of His day. The holy life of Jesus brought conviction on His adversaries. The truth caused friction.

If you live according to the Scriptures, you also will "bee" rejected for disturbing the carnal mind. Carnality and spirituality are not compatible. That is why Jesus was rejected and it shouldn't seem strange if you are also rejected.

To "bee" rejected is not a pleasant thing, but to live right among those who live wrong is sure to cause rejection. Jesus told us how to respond, *"Rejoice ye in that day, and leap for joy: for, behold, your reward is great in heaven"* (Luke 6:23). In other words, don't be disturbed when you are rejected. If you are rejected here, your reward will be great in Heaven. My friends, it is far better to "bee" rejected by the world and the apostate church than to "bee" rejected by the Lord. If you choose not to take rejection personally, "bee" rejected will not leave a painful sting.

Bee Rejuvenated

To "bee" rejuvenated is to be refreshed and restored to strength. We all need to "bee" rejuvenated at times, especially when we are under heavy pressure or stress. When you face a difficult task, you need to "bee" rejuvenated. If you learn to "bee" rejuvenated, you can learn to overcome a lot of those "down days" that people face. I am not saying it is sin to have "down days," but there certainly is a better way to live, so why not choose to "bee" rejuvenated? You can do this by finding helpful, encouraging Scriptures from the Word of God. Read verses aloud such as, *"I can do all things through Christ which strengtheneth me"* (Philippians 4:13) or *"...nothing shall be impossible unto you"* (Matthew 17:20). Believe what the Lord has promised and expect to "bee" rejuvenated. People who can "bee" rejuvenated often accomplish more in life than those who do not practice rejuvenating themselves.

Sometimes you may have to take off from a busy schedule and rest awhile to "bee" rejuvenated. This is especially true for those in leadership positions who are under heavy pressure most of the time. Whether you're a CEO over a large corporation, a pastor, a teacher, a manager or in any other leadership position, there will come a time when you need to "bee" rejuvenated. Your fellow laborer may be weary of the way and need to "bee" rejuvenated. You can only help him if you keep yourself rejuvenated on a daily basis.

Taking time to "bee" rejuvenated is not time lost. It helps in, *"Redeeming the time"* (Ephesians 5:16). You could keep yourself from a lot of trouble if you would take time out to "bee" rejuvenated. "Bee" rejuvenated lest you yield to a "bee" that leaves a painful sting.

Bee Relaxed

It seems that many people find it hard to "bee" relaxed. I have prayed for people who were "up-tight" and had to tell them to relax if they hoped to receive from the Lord. Isaiah 40:31 says, *"But they that wait upon the LORD shall renew their strength; they shall mount up with wings as eagles; they shall run, and not be weary; and they shall walk, and not faint."* When you learn to "bee" relaxed, you can head off a lot of unnecessary stress and tension. "Bee" relaxed when you read or study the Bible. Children who learn to "bee" relaxed can do better in school than those who are stressed. If we could all learn to "bee" relaxed, I believe we would enjoy life more fully and receive more of the blessings the Lord has for us. Let's all make that important decision to always "bee" relaxed!

A GLIMPSE OF HEAVEN

When I see the woodland flaming
In a brilliant red and gold,
I can only stand and marvel
At the splendor I behold.

Only could the Master Painter
Clothe a tree in such array;
Seems I get a glimpse of Heaven
Every sunny Autumn Day.

Bee Reliable

A reliable person is a person with trustworthiness, integrity and dependability. He does what is expected and required of him whether anyone is watching or not. This world needs more reliable people. A businessman once said, "It is difficult to find reliable employees in our day." To "bee" reliable is both your choice and responsibility. Paul reminded Timothy of the importance of being reliable: *"O Timothy, keep that which is committed to thy trust, avoiding profane and vain babblings, and oppositions of science falsely so called"* (I Timothy 6:20). The Lord is still looking for reliable people—those He can trust, those who will be there when He needs them, those He knows will do a satisfactory job. The next time you feel like doing something dishonest, heed the buzz of "bee" reliable because this "bee" will never leave a painful sting.

" Don't rest until you do your best."

Bee Reluctant

There are times in life you need to "bee" reluctant. I have been reluctant when confronted by salesmen trying to convince me to purchase their product. In some cases, I later found they were dishonest and unreliable.

You should "bee" reluctant when someone tries to force you to do something you know is ungodly or would hinder your relationship with the Lord. You should "bee" reluctant when someone tries to persuade you to believe a new doctrine. You should be cautious and move slowly lest you be led astray: "*Beware lest any man spoil you through philosophy and vain deceit, after the tradition of men, after the rudiments of the world, and not after Christ*" (Colossians 2:8). Allow the Holy Spirit to signal you when someone is dishonest or trying to deceive you. This is a good time to "bee" reluctant; it may save you from much trouble.

"The fear of God is healthy.
There is a difference in fearing God and
being afraid of Him."

Bee Remembered

How would you like to "bee" remembered when the time comes for you to leave this world? Some people desire to "bee" remembered for their fame or for what they accomplished in life. Others are remembered, not because they set a goal to be noticed, but because they did something noteworthy One example is the woman with the alabaster box of precious ointment, *"There came unto him a woman having an alabaster box of very precious ointment, and poured it on his head, as he sat at meat"* (Matthew 26:7). This act was not done to get attention or to "bee" remembered. However Jesus said, *"Verily I say unto you, Wheresoever this gospel shall be preached in the whole world, there shall also this, that this woman hath done, be told for a memorial of her"* (Matthew 26:13).

Some people will "bee" remembered in a negative way. Luke 17:32 reminds us, *"Remember Lot's wife."* Lot's wife was remembered for looking back and becoming a pillar of salt. Some people will "bee" remembered as a blessing to others. Others, as a servant to many. Yet others will "bee" remembered for what they taught or for their labor among men. Paul encouraged the Corinthians to remember his labor: *"Now I praise you, brethren, that ye remember me in all things, and keep the ordinances, as I delivered them to you"* (I Corinthians 11:2).

Shadrach, Meshach, and Abednego were remembered because their faith and obedience delivered them out of the fiery furnace. Daniel was remembered as a man of prayer who was cast into a den of lions but came out victoriously. Jeremiah was remembered as a weeping prophet. Joseph of Arimathaea was remembered for giving Jesus his personal burial plot. Wouldn't you like to "bee" remembered for something upon which Jesus could place His benediction? Surely, "bee" remembered will never leave a painful sting.

Bee Reminded

B rother or Sister, if your memory goes on a vacation, you have a problem. Memory is a gift of God. You need to often "bee" reminded of the valuable things that have come your way over the years. I am reminded of my precious father and mother who brought their children up to be men and women of character. I am reminded of the good times I had with my parents and my fourteen brothers and sisters. It has been years since the passing of my parents, yet fond memories still linger. Some of my siblings are deceased, but I am glad for the good times we had that leave precious memories. I have pleasant memories of our children growing up in our home. It is good to "bee" reminded of the sweet fellowship you have had with family, friends and loved ones.

"Bee" reminded of the blessings that come to you every day and forget the hurts and problems. "Bee" reminded that your blessings come from God. "Bee" reminded of the promises you made. "Bee" reminded of your marriage vows. "Bee" reminded of your New Years' resolutions. "Bee" reminded of the promises of God, lest you forget. God reminded the children of Israel that it was not their ability or good management that caused them to possess the land. He gave them a very important warning: *"But thou shalt remember the LORD thy God: for it is he that giveth thee power to get wealth, that he may establish his covenant which he sware unto thy fathers, as it is this day"* (Deuteronomy 8:18). You need to often "bee" reminded of the good things the Lord has done. How important is "bee" reminded!

Bee Reprogrammed

What you did with yesterday is likely a repeat of what you will do with today. What you do with today will determine what you do with tomorrow. If you are satisfied with mediocrity, lack of enthusiasm or lack of achievement, you will remain the same day after day, year after year. But that can be changed if you are willing to "bee" reprogrammed. If you feel like nothing good ever happens to you, stop thinking that way. Get ready to "bee" reprogrammed in your mind. Instead of thinking everyone else gets the best jobs and you get what is left, reprogram yourself to say, "If others can do it, I can, too." It's not too late to become something you always wanted to be. You can still rise up with zest and zeal and accomplish what you didn't think you could accomplish. If you are willing to "bee" reprogrammed, you can change your failures into triumph, your sorrows into inspiration, your discouragement into courage, your losses into gain and your turmoil into peace. All this can happen to you if you are willing to "bee" reprogrammed. Remember, you are what you think, *"For as he thinketh in his heart, so is he"* (Proverbs 23:7).

Start to "bee" reprogrammed by looking for ways to improve your self worth. Ask the Lord to give you an idea, a plan and a purpose. You can change your whole outlook in life. Every time you think a negative thought, say, "No, I've been reprogrammed. I will think positive thoughts about my future." "Bee" reprogrammed.

Bee Rescued

L ike so many, you may need to "bee" rescued from the things of
this world. Many need to "bee" rescued from the spirit of fear,
the spirit of anger, the spirit of lust, the spirit of infirmity or a host
of other evils that have bound and ensnared good meaning people.

There is an old hymn that says "Rescue the Perishing." Many are
perishing in this world. Their sin is driving them farther away from
God. You and I need to be ready to help those who may not be
aware they need to "bee" rescued. If you have been rescued, help
rescue others who may be perishing. You can help by praying and
fasting for them.

Even in the natural realm, you may be called upon to rescue someone. My wife and I have a dear friend who was able to rescue a
drowning man. Though he didn't know the man, duty called for
quick action. He was able to deliver him from death.

Years ago, I needed to "bee" rescued from the bondage of the devil.
I submitted to God's plan for my life and was set free at last. "Bee"
rescued is ready to help release you from the bondage of sin and
rebellion against God. If you need to "bee" rescued, you must first
have a desire to be delivered. Ask the Lord to help restore you. Listen to the encouraging buzz of "bee" rescued. This "bee" will never
leave a painful sting.

Bee Resolved

To "bee" resolved is to be determined, resolute, steadfast and firm. You want to become familiar with this "bee." It will help you become a good leader, a good follower and a victorious Believer. When I see a young man or woman with a zeal and a resolution to stand true in the midst of opposition, I admire them. Some have made this resolution but did not stick to it. If that is your case, all hope is not gone. Start over again. "Bee" resolved in your mind that you will accomplish something of value in this world. You will become that special person who is pleasing to the Lord.

If you are married or preparing for marriage, "bee" resolved to have a good marriage. Whether you are single or married, "bee" resolved to make the best out of life for you and others. I often hear people express their desire, especially in court, to do "what is the best interest of the person involved." Our whole vision should be not only to have a beautiful life for ourselves, but to seek the benefit of others as well. "Bee" resolved to be an encouragement to others.

I was meditating on the story of Jonathan's armor bearer. He was resolved to guard Jonathan and help him achieve his goal in whatever decision he made. *"And his armourbearer said unto him, Do all that is in thine heart: turn thee; behold, I am with thee according to thy heart"* (I Samuel 14:7). Because someone cared, a great victory was won for Israel. When someone stands beside you in difficult times, it can strengthen you to persevere. There are times you need to "bee" resolved to stand with someone facing a hard situation. Heaven will assist you when you make this very important decision.

"Bee" resolved to serve only the Lord and none other. "Bee" resolved to obey the Biblical instructions given for your life. "Bee" resolved to pray for the needs of mankind all around you. What a wonderful "bee"! It will never leave a painful sting.

Bee Respectful

To "bee" respectful is to hold another in high regard, to esteem and show respect toward all people and to treat with deference, honor and consideration. To "bee" respectful is to be courteous and considerate of the feelings of others. To "bee" respectful is to respond politely to strangers and friends. You should "bee" respectful to those in authority over you. This generation has lost a lot of its respect toward others. In my travels across the USA, I have seen much disrespect, even between leaders. We, as Christians, must learn to "bee" respectful. No one ever reaches a position in life where they are no longer accountable for their conduct or have an excuse not to show respect to others, even those under them. Parents need to "bee" respectful to their children and teach their children to "bee" respectful toward them. Employers need to "bee" respectful toward their employees if they desire to receive respect in return. However, we are responsible to "bee" respectful to others whether they respect us or not.

You, perhaps, remember the story of Elisha who passed a group of children who mocked him "*and said unto him, Go up, thou bald head; go up, thou bald head*" (II Kings 2:23). Where did these children learn to be disrespectful to a man of God? Whatever caused these children to behave as they did brought a tragedy that affected a number of families. Perhaps the parents had never learned to "bee" respectful toward leadership. "Bee" disrespectful stung them and their children with a very painful and lasting sting. Learn a lesson from this tragedy and teach your children to "bee" respectful to leadership as well as to others.

You should "bee" respectful to those around you. Your peers deserve your respect. We are all human and subject to mistakes. We need each other. Let us help one another instead of being critical. Learn to "bee" respectful. This "bee" will never leave a painful sting.

Bee Responsible

A ny successful individual has learned to take responsibility. It is your duty to "bee" responsible in the spiritual, as well as the natural world. A person who does not take responsibility does not understand his ability to "bee" responsible. People who take responsibility for their acts, behavior and mistakes are well on their way to becoming a success. Such individuals can be trusted. They are the ones who find good jobs and keep them. They understand a job that is not well done is not done. They are not satisfied with a "that's good enough" attitude. They refuse to blame others for their failures or lack of accomplishments. Jesus told a parable of the man with five talents. His lord told him, *"Well done, thou good and faithful servant"* (Matthew 25:21). This man took responsibility for his talents and was rewarded accordingly.

People who choose to "bee" responsible are an asset at home, at church and in the work place. Responsible people become the leaders in the community. They accomplish things others only hope to accomplish. They are a blessing wherever they go. "Bee" responsible. This "bee" will never leave a painful sting.

"If you fail, admit it;
Reset your goal and hit it."

Bee Restored

W hen King David was notified by the prophet Nathan that his sin had grieved God, he frantically cried out to the Lord, *"Cast me not away from thy presence; and take not thy holy spirit from me"* (Psalm 51:11). When you fail the Lord, you often feel shame, remorse, fear and a sense of complete helplessness. You lose hope. David recognized how much his sin could cost him, yet he pled to the Lord for forgiveness. He saw his need to "bee" restored and prayed, *"Restore unto me the joy of thy salvation; and uphold me with thy free spirit"* (Psalm 51:12).

We all face times when we need to "bee" restored. It may be a broken relationship, a marriage or a commitment that needs to "bee" restored. We may need a restoration of love, faith, peace or joy. We may need to "bee" restored to our former walk with God.

When Peter failed the Lord, he needed to "bee" restored. I am fascinated by the words of Jesus to Mary as recorded in Mark 16:7: *"But go your way, tell his disciples and Peter that he goeth before you into Galilee: there shall ye see him, as he said unto you."* I see the Lord's loving response after Peter's fall—tell the disciples *"and Peter."* He wanted Peter to know he was forgiven and still included in His circle.

There may be someone reading this who feels their hope of restoration is gone. Remember how Peter responded after he failed the Lord; he wept bitterly. The Lord saw those tears of repentance and restored Peter back to the office of an apostle. When you truly repent from the heart, the Lord is ready to bring restoration. He is still in the restoring business, so "bee" restored. This "bee" will never leave a painful sting!

Bee Revived

O ften in life, we become weary, discouraged and tired and need to "bee" revived. People who are facing difficulties in life often need to "bee" revived to grasp a new approach to life. The Psalmist made a very important appeal to the Lord in Psalm 85:6. *"Wilt thou not revive us again,"* he asked, *"that thy people may rejoice in thee?"* He not only made the request to "bee" revived, but he gave the reason why he wanted to "bee" revived.

Years ago, I was asked to speak at a church. According to their leaders, this church had lost the fire and desperately needed to "bee" revived. Through prayer and the preaching of the Word, that church had a great revival.

You can help to revive yourself. Many scriptures are written to bring refreshment to your spirit and revival to your soul. One such scripture is found in Isaiah 3:10, *"Say ye to the righteous, that it shall be well with him: for they shall eat the fruit of their doings."* Another lovely promise is written in Isaiah 26:3, *"Thou wilt keep him in perfect peace, whose mind is stayed on thee: because he trusteth in thee."* Verses like these help to lift your spirit and revive you.

I believe many of the patriarchs of old needed to learn how to pray and put forth an effort to revive themselves before they could be a benefit to others who needed to "bee" revived. An evangelist who preaches a revival service must "bee" revived himself before he can help revive others. Since we all face pressures and have decisions to make on a regular basis, we should ask the Lord to revive us daily. For example, you could say, "Lord, this decision is rather difficult to make. I need to 'bee' revived so I don't become discouraged or weary of the way." "Bee" revived is a very important "bee" to have in your life.

Bee Right

T hink right. Talk right. Act right. Treat your spouse right. Treat others right. Treat your family right. Treat your neighbor right. Draw the line. Right is right and wrong is wrong. Make a quality decision, "I will always do what is right." Get on the right track and stay there. Make sure you are right. Remember, *"The way of a fool is right in his own eyes..."* (Proverbs 12:15). You cannot "bee" right until you know what the Scripture calls right. Study the Bible and do what it tells you to do. The Bible is always right.

You can't go by feelings, *"There is a way which seemeth right unto a man, but the end thereof are the ways of death"* (Proverbs 14:12). If you are tempted to falsify a deal, ask yourself if it is the right thing to do. Is it right to cheat? Is it right to take advantage of others? "Bee" right. Let your conscience rest in peace that all is well!

" A trained mind can pick up great ideas."

Bee Rivers

John 7:38 explains how to "bee" rivers: *"He that believeth on me, as the scripture hath said, out of his belly shall flow rivers of living water"* (John 7:38). It is interesting to note that Jesus didn't say "a river" would flow out of a Spirit-filled person; He said "rivers." These rivers are probably referring to different areas in your life where you can be a blessing to others. You need to understand that you are not the source of that river. The Holy Spirit will be working through you, causing these rivers to bring inspiration, comfort, help and strength to those in need.

Rivers may be held back for a while by a dam or some other structure, but eventually some break forth again because their source didn't fail. There are some rivers, however, whose source can fail. There is a river not far from where we live that is called Dry River. It gets its name from the fact that it completely dries up during the heat of the summer. We, as the people of God, need to make sure that we keep the rivers flowing out of us in the midst of obstacles and hindrances.

God wants us to "bee" rivers of blessing. This generation needs spiritual, mental and physical healing. It needs deliverance. It needs to be loosed from the bands of wickedness. Therefore, let us "bee" rivers that continue to flow year after year and bring nourishment and refreshment to our fellowman.

Bee Rooted

In Paul's letter to the church at Ephesus, he wrote, "*That Christ may dwell in your hearts by faith; that ye, being rooted and grounded in love*" (Ephesians 3:17). He desired that they all "bee" rooted and grounded in love. The fact is, this church that was once known for its love in the brotherhood lost much of that love. The Lord told John to write to the church of Ephesus: "*Nevertheless I have somewhat against thee, because thou hast left thy first love*" (Revelation 2:4). They had lost their first love. That should be a warning to everyone. If the church of Ephesus had remained rooted and grounded in love, they wouldn't have lost that love.

Jesus reminded us to "bee" rooted in the Scriptures. In the parable of the sower, He revealed what happens when you are not deeply rooted in the Word of God. He explained, they "*...have no root in themselves, and so endure but for a time: afterward, when affliction or persecution ariseth for the word's sake, immediately they are offended*" (Mark 4:17). When you are rooted in the Word, you can endure the afflictions, persecutions and temptations you face each day. To "bee" rooted is a decision you must make. It is when you are fully "*Rooted and built up in him, and stablished in the faith, as ye have been taught, abounding therein with thanksgiving*" (Colossians 2:7) that you can face life with triumph! You become firmly settled and rooted in the things of the Lord. When you choose to "bee" rooted in the love of God, this "bee" will never leave a painful sting.

Bee Sacrificial

R omans 12:1 instructs, *"I beseech you therefore, brethren, by the mercies of God, that ye present your bodies a living sacrifice, holy, acceptable unto God, which is your reasonable service."* To "bee" sacrificial is to give yourself for a cause. Jesus stated what seems to be a paradox in Mark 8:35, *"For whosoever will save his life shall lose it; but whosoever shall lose his life for my sake and the gospel's, the same shall save it."* One cannot "bee" sacrificial without reaping benefits from voluntarily giving of one's self.

John mentions the beautiful sacrificial love of God in I John 3:16: *"Hereby perceive we the love of God, because he laid down his life for us: and we ought to lay down our lives for the brethren."* Throughout history, there have been heroes who chose to "bee" sacrificial and were ready to face difficult circumstances for the benefit of others. Although, some would lose their lives, they knew someone else would benefit from the choice they made. Many martyrs have voluntarily laid down their lives for the Lord Jesus Christ. I believe that God is well pleased with those who chose to "bee" sacrificial.

Years ago, there was a poor family whom the father had deserted. The children scarcely had anything to eat. The mother was so sacrificial that she would let herself go hungry to feed her children. To "bee" sacrificial is indeed a beautiful way of life that most people have never understood. Was it not Jesus who chose to "bee" sacrificial and give His life on Calvary to redeem us from our sins? That sacrificial gift was beautiful. Years later, we are still reaping benefits from the One who gave His life that we may live.

Bee Saintly

It seems most people misunderstand the word "saint." They think it is referring to some super Christian who soared far above the normal in a quest for God. Some may say, "We will be saints in Heaven, but not here on the earth." Beloved, if we are not saintly here, we will not be saints in Heaven. To "bee" saintly is simply to be Christ-like with an intimate relationship with the Almighty that supersedes the carnal way of pursuing God. Any born again child of God can "bee" saintly. In Paul's writings to the churches, he addressed the Ephesians as *"the saints which are at Ephesus"* (Ephesians 1:1). He referred to the Romans as *"called to be saints"* (Romans 1:7). He also refers to those at Corinth as *"called to be saints"* (I Corinthians 1:2). To "bee" saintly is to exercise a Scriptural lifestyle and to walk before the Lord in holiness. "Bee" saintly. It is God's way.

THE FANCY PRAYER

The prayer that's prayed
With the perfect word,
May be the prayer
That is never heard.

© Copyright 1978 *Sunbeams of Inspiration*

Bee Sanctified

S ome people believe that sanctification is a mere separation from the world. It goes much deeper than that. To "bee" sanctified is to be consecrated and to be suitable for the work God has called you to do. The Bible says that Jesus sanctified Himself. In other words, He was fully consecrated to His Heavenly Father. He prayed, "*And for their sakes I sanctify myself, that they also might be sanctified through the truth*" (John 17:19). If Jesus needed to "bee" sanctified, how much more should you, as His follower, "bee" sanctified! When you are sanctified, you are no longer in charge of your life. You are no longer a part of the world but sanctified unto the Lord.

To "bee" sanctified is so important that the Bible explains how family members can have a sanctifying effect upon each other: "*For the unbelieving husband is sanctified by the wife, and the unbelieving wife is sanctified by the husband: else were your children unclean; but now are they holy*" (I Corinthians 7:14). According to this verse, it is extremely important to "bee" sanctified to the Lord because it affect others. Surely this "bee" will never leave a painful sting.

Bee Satisfied

O ver the years, I have known people who were dissatisfied with the direction the Lord was leading them. I was one of those people. When the Lord called me to an international ministry (traveling to other countries, preaching on worldwide radio and sending out literature worldwide), I was dissatisfied. Why would God choose me for that work when there were others more able than myself? It's not that your Heavenly Father enjoys giving you a job you dislike, He wants to change your thinking so you can "bee" satisfied with the direction He leads. My wife and I allowed the Lord to change our thinking. We learned to "bee" satisfied and surrender to God's will for our lives. Even though I was sometimes away from home for weeks, I was satisfied to travel in obedience to God's call. Now, I look back with satisfaction because I was obedient to the will of God.

Many people, today, are dissatisfied. Something is missing. Something is stealing their joy. I believe "bee" satisfied is buzzing around them, trying to lead them to the answer. Proverbs 12:14 explains: *"A man shall be satisfied with good by the fruit of his mouth."* A few chapters later, this statement is reinforced: *"A man's belly shall be satisfied with the fruit of his mouth"* (Proverbs 18:20). The Psalmist echoes a similar message in Psalm 63:5: *"My soul shall be satisfied as with marrow and fatness; and my mouth shall praise thee with joyful lips."* To "bee" satisfied, you must guard the words of your mouth. Fill your mouth with joy and praise to the Lord.

Are you satisfied with your life? Where you live? Where you work? Where you go to church? It is important that you learn to "bee" satisfied. If you are not satisfied with your life, pray and ask the Lord to help you become satisfied.

Bee Saturated

W hen David said, *"My cup runneth over"* (Psalm 23:5), he was saying that he was saturated with the wonderful things of the Lord. Wouldn't it be great if you were saturated with the Holy Spirit? You can "bee" saturated with the Word of God and be familiar with every verse.

You can "bee" saturated with the love of God: *"If we love one another, God dwelleth in us, and his love is perfected in us"* (I John 4:12). What a wonderful possibility—to "bee" saturated with the love of God. When this becomes a realization, you can love your enemies and pray for those who despitefully use you.

Think of what it would be like if you were saturated with the joy of the Lord. In John 15:11, Jesus said, *"These things have I spoken unto you, that my joy might remain in you, and that your joy might be full."* Notice He said, *"My joy."* He knew human joy doesn't last, but His joy would remain. What a blessing to "bee" saturated with the joy of the Lord.

You can "bee" saturated with the peace of God. Here again, Jesus knew that human peace is subject to fail so He gave His peace. How would you like to "bee" saturated with the peace of God every day of your life? It is possible because Jesus said, *"Peace I leave with you, my peace I give unto you: not as the world giveth, give I unto you"* (John 14:27). Philippians 4:7 gives a glimpse of what happens when you choose to "bee" saturated with the peace of God: *"And the peace of God, which passeth all understanding, shall keep your hearts and minds through Christ Jesus."* When you choose to "bee" saturated with the Word of God and the fruit of the Spirit, this "bee" will never leave a painful sting.

Bee Saved

According to I Timothy 2:4, God desires for all people to "bee" saved: *"Who will have all men to be saved, and to come unto the knowledge of the truth."* That is why He sent His Son to redeem us, *"For God sent not his Son into the world to condemn the world; but that the world through him might be saved"* (John 3:17). If you are not saved, the Lord is offering you the free gift of salvation. You may say, "O, but I am too bad to 'bee' saved." The good news is that all can "bee" saved: *"Wherefore he is able also to save them to the uttermost that come unto God by him, seeing he ever liveth to make intercession for them"* (Hebrews 7:25). No matter how far you have gone, the Lord can still save to the uttermost.

Paul and Silas were thrown into prison for preaching the gospel. When the prison doors were miraculously opened, the keeper of the prison was afraid. After realizing no one had escaped, the jailor asked, *"Sirs, what must I do to be saved?"* (Acts 16:30). Paul and Silas were able to instruct the keeper of the prison how to "bee" saved: *"And they said, Believe on the Lord Jesus Christ, and thou shalt be saved, and thy house"* (Acts 16:31). Through believing in Jesus Christ, he was born again and they rejoiced together. There is much rejoicing when a sinner chooses to "bee" saved.

"Bee" saved from your sins, today. We all need to heed the buzzing of "bee" saved. This "bee" never tires warning of danger to those who will listen.

Bee Scriptural

I t is possible to believe you are Scriptural, but still be wrong. The Lord will hold you responsible for how you interpret the Word of God; whether you have slanted its instructions to suit your religious theology or whether you have rightfully divided the Word of Truth. You cannot choose to believe only part of the Bible. Your beliefs must "bee" Scriptural. Your conduct and behavior must "bee" Scriptural. You may remember the story of a pastor who wrote in the front of his Bible, "This Book will keep you from sin or sin will keep you from this Book." How true!

To "bee" Scriptural should be the desire of every Believer. The way you learn to "bee" Scriptural is by reading, studying and meditating upon the Word. The Bible teaches you how to treat your fellowmen, how to love your enemies, how to forgive those who trespass against you, how to serve the Lord, how to praise the Lord and how to respond to those who revile you. I Peter 2:21-23 explains, *"For even hereunto were ye called: because Christ also suffered for us, leaving us an example, that ye should follow his steps: Who did no sin, neither was guile found in his mouth: Who, when he was reviled, reviled not again; when he suffered, he threatened not; but committed himself to him that judgeth righteously."*

It is your responsibility, obligation and duty to "bee" Scriptural in what you believe and teach. You can have a sweet trust and confidence in the Lord when you are Scriptural. "Bee" Scriptural is an extremely important "bee."

Bee Searched

The human race has a tendency not to be completely honest when evaluating what lies within. There is an interesting prayer recorded in Psalm 139:23 which reads, *"Search me, O God, and know my heart: try me, and know my thoughts."* David was aware that he could not properly examine his own life. Because his heart was so much in tune with the heart of his Heavenly Father, he was not afraid to "bee" searched by the Lord. He wanted the Lord to examine him. He needed his Heavenly Father to help him have a heart that was well pleasing in His sight.

Job made a similar statement in Job 23:10, *"But he knoweth the way that I take: when he hath tried me, I shall come forth as gold."* Here, Job is crying out to "bee" searched. Notice the expression, *"I shall come forth as gold."* He knew that after things were burned out of his life, it would free him from his own self-centeredness.

Follow the examples of these two great men and cry out to the Lord to "bee" searched. Allow Him to go through your life to take out anything that may hinder your relationship with the Heavenly Father. You should be ready at all times for the Lord to use His searchlight to expose the things that matter to Him. There is nothing hidden from His all-seeing eyes. *"Shall not God search this out? for he knoweth the secrets of the heart"* (Psalm 44:21). The fact is, God knows your heart better than you do. What you may consider a small matter, may not be small in the sight of your Heavenly Father. Did you ever have a tiny, almost invisible splinter in your finger? That splinter can affect the whole body until it is removed. It may be an accumulation of little things that are displeasing to the Lord that keep you from becoming useable.

It may be good for you to pray as the Psalmist and ask the Lord to search you. You may not be aware there are things in your human nature which are hindering you. So, welcome "bee" searched into your life.

Bee Secondary

We used to sing a little song that says, "Jesus first, yourself last and others in between." That's a good philosophy. Paul writes, *"Let nothing be done through strife or vainglory; but in lowliness of mind let each esteem other better than themselves"* (Philippines 2:3). That doesn't mean you should consider yourself inferior to others, but it does keep you from exalting self and feeling you are more important than others. Jesus said, *"For whosoever exalteth himself shall be abased; and he that humbleth himself shall be exalted"* (Luke 14:11). According to this scripture, the Lord wants you to be exalted; the problem lies in exalting yourself. Behind self exaltation is pride and pride is destructive.

No matter how educated, brilliant or intelligent you may be, you are not superior to others. We are all human beings, subject to failure and mistake. When you choose to "bee" secondary and exalt others better than yourself, you become aware of your need for others. Go ahead, "bee" secondary; it's the right thing to do. This "bee" will never leave a painful sting!

Bee Secure

To "bee" secure does not guarantee that you will be free from trouble, but it does keep you from anticipating problems. No one can be truly secure without putting their faith, confidence and trust in the Lord. To "bee" secure means that you are not anxious, disturbed or fearful concerning the future, but completely trust Him who has promised, "*I will never leave thee, nor forsake thee*" (Hebrews 13:5). To "bee" secure means that you expect God to move on your behalf, even in the most difficult circumstances. Psalm 91 speaks of that security in the first verse: "*He that dwelleth in the secret place of the most High shall abide under the shadow of the Almighty*." Here, you have a picture of the safety and security that God offers His children. Picture an eagle who nests high in the cleft of a rock. The storms may be violent, but the eagle is secure in the cleft of the rock. You, too, can "bee" secure from life's storms when you rest upon the Rock, Jesus Christ. Only in Him are you safe and secure.

"Some people stay awake at night worrying about staying awake at night."

Bee Selective

There comes a time when you need to "bee" selective. Lot should have chosen to "bee" selective when he cast his eyes on the well watered plains of Sodom. According to Genesis 13:10, *"Lot lifted up his eyes, and beheld all the plain of Jordan, that it was well watered every where...."* He saw only the fruitful land instead of the spiritual future of his family. It is natural to "bee" selective concerning the kind of car you drive, the kind of home you live in, where you work and where you go to church, but it is more important to "bee" selective of those with whom you and your children associate. Do your associates and friends help or hinder you? You should "bee" selective of what kind of school your children go to and the places they go. Sad is the day when children are lost to the world because we didn't choose to "bee" selective. You could save yourself a lot of trouble if you learned to "bee" selective, couldn't you? This "bee" will never leave a painful sting.

"There are no atheists in the casket;
by then they believe there is a God."

Bee Sensible

A sensible person has discernment, good understanding and good judgment. To "bee" sensible is to be equipped with common sense (which is still of great value today). You need to "bee" sensible when making decisions. Many have made hasty decisions which they later regretted. They wished they had taken time to think sensibly before making the decision. To "bee" sensible keeps you from a lot of trouble.

You need to "bee" sensible with your words. Proverbs 6:2 warns, *"Thou art snared with the words of thy mouth, thou art taken with the words of thy mouth."* Foolish or hasty words can cause much heartache. Learn to "bee" sensible in every area of life. This "bee" will never leave a painful sting.

" Being tense doesn't make sense."

Bee Sensitive

We live in a generation where too many people are not sensitive to those around them. They may not mean to be rude or disrespectful, but they say things that can be both injurious and degrading. To "bee" sensitive is to be considerate of the feelings and opinions of others. That doesn't mean you have to agree with them, but you should at least be respectful.

You need to "bee" sensitive and considerate of your friendship with other people. Many friends have injured each other unintentionally by some deed or action. You should "bee" sensitive to those who may be struggling with a problem. "Bee" sensitive to those who have fallen. They need your encouragement instead of your criticism, your love instead of your opinion, your help instead of your judgment, restoration instead of rejection. You need to "bee" sensitive to those who have suffered a tragedy or lost a loved one. Their loss can be very painful and they need comfort. This gives us an opportunity to not only express your sympathy, but to speak kindly and gently to those who are grieving.

You should learn to "bee" sensitive to those around you. You don't always know why people are "touchy" or respond as they do. If you knew, you may treat them differently. I once met a person who was in great distress. When I found out his life story, I understood he needed my help and not my judgment. I was only able to offer help because I chose to "bee" sensitive. What a difference this "bee" can make!

Bee Sentimental

In married life, we need to "bee" sentimental. I'm not suggesting that you be sentimental to everyone because this could be dangerous. I'm only encouraging you to be sentimental to your spouse and your little children. To "bee" sentimental helps to keep a good relationship between husband and wife. This helps a husband and wife work together as a team. To "bee" sentimental brings you together in one. Jesus reminds, *"Wherefore they are no more twain, but one flesh"* (Matthew 19:6).

God expects marriages to be joyful and full of love and peace. Loving acts and deeds are an important part of keeping a marriage strong and blessed. If you choose to "bee" sentimental toward your spouse, marriage can be a very sweet and precious union.

Matter-of-fact people are often difficult to live with. Sometimes they have a difficult time showing any kind of sentimentalism. It may be difficult at first, but you can learn to "bee" sentimental toward your spouse. Once you understand how valuable this decision is, it can be most rewarding.

According to Proverbs, there is extreme great value in a woman: *"Who can find a virtuous woman? for her price is far above rubies"* (Proverbs 31:10). If a husband would value his wife that much, he wouldn't find it difficult to "bee" sentimental toward her. Husbands, learn to "bee" sentimental. Wives, learn to "bee" sentimental. Then, that painful "bee" of separation that has stung so many married couples will fly away.

Bee Separated

I f you want to be a follower of Christ, you must understand sepa-ration. It is not possible to live in two worlds. Jesus taught us to "bee" separated from the world. He said, "*...My kingdom is not of this world*" (John 18:36).

Paul wrote to the church at Corinth that those who live according to the world's standards and those who are children of the Kingdom of God cannot be united. Therefore, he says, "*Wherefore come out from among them, and be ye separate, saith the Lord, and touch not the unclean thing; and I will receive you*" (II Corinthians 6:17). According to this scripture, the Lord cannot receive those into His kingdom who still have a hankering after the world.

There is a vast difference between righteousness and unrighteous-ness, right and wrong, good and evil. We are living in a generation where good and evil are often mingled together. What once was considered wrong has now become an acceptable way of life. If you don't separate yourself from the world now, you will be separated from God at the judgment, "*And before him shall be gathered all nations: and he shall separate them one from another, as a shep-herd divideth his sheep from the goats*" (Matthew 25:32). It is very important to listen to the sound of this "bee" when he says, "'Bee' separated." Otherwise, you will receive a very painful sting!

Bee Serene

To "bee" serene is to be in a state of calmness, tranquility and peace; free from trouble, fear and frustration. How precious to be in the presence of people who have a serene personality. These people are of great value in the world in which we live.

Over the years, I have noticed that people who chose to "bee" serene stood out above others. They had a characteristic that was not only beautiful, but was a benefit and blessing to those around them. I remember one elderly gentleman who could easily relieve the tension when those around him began to be disturbed. He would respond in a serene manner, "Let's not make this problem any bigger than it really is." His calm tone of voice and manner of life changed the atmosphere around him.

To "bee" serene is a choice. Not only will it benefit you, but also those around you. Let's learn how to "bee" serene.

GIVE ME A SERENE SPOT

Give me a mountain stream
that twists and rolls, crawls and turns
in and out among oak trees.
A spot to rest from the noon blaze
with a soft breeze
sweeping over the wild ferns.
A quiet place, only the sound
of birds and easy waters.
Often, my soul yearns
for such a spot, serene
where the weary world and its crude ways
are not felt, heard or seen.

Published by Gusto 1980, A Literary/Poetry Journal
© Copyright Daniel D. Rodes

Bee Serious

" Are you serious?" Perhaps we have all heard that question asked when someone wasn't sure if a person was telling the truth or not. Even when being humorous, you must always be truthful. The Bible warns against lying and jesting: *"Lie not one to another, seeing that ye have put off the old man with his deeds"* (Colossians 3:9). Ephesians 5:4 confirms this by saying, *"Neither filthiness, nor foolish talking, nor jesting, which are not convenient: but rather giving of thanks."* Jesting has to do with vulgar speech or foolishness. I, personally, feel that we have too much lying and jesting behind the pulpit under the disguise of humor. Good, clean humor is lifting, but seriousness should also have its place. There is a time to "bee" serious and there is a time to be humorous.

You need to "bee" serious when you make decisions in life. You need to "bee" serious about your relationship with your spouse and family. You must "bee" serious in your relationship with the Lord.

To "bee" serious is a very important "bee," but you don't want to be so serious that there is never a time of rejoicing and cheering the hearts of others. Over the years, there was some teaching that we are never to express joy or gladness. That is unscriptural. The book of Acts records the daily operation of the Believers, *"And they, continuing daily with one accord in the temple, and breaking bread from house to house, did eat their meat this gladness and singleness of heart"* (Acts 2:46). One of the shortest verses in the Bible admonishes us to *"Rejoice evermore"* (I Thessalonians 5:16). A person can "bee" serious and still have fun and live a joyful life. "Bee" serious; this "bee" will never leave a painful sting.

Bee Settled

There are people who never seem to "bee" settled on anything. They live here a while, then move. They are at this job a while, then they change jobs. They go to one church for a while, then to another, or they may even stop going to church altogether. They believe a certain doctrine today, but tomorrow they believe something completely different. No wonder Paul admonished, *"That we henceforth be no more children, tossed to and fro, and carried about with every wind of doctrine, by the sleight of men, and cunning craftiness, whereby they lie in wait to deceive"* (Ephesians 4:14). If you are not settled in what you believe, you can be deceived.

You should "bee" settled concerning your relationship with the Lord so you don't become discouraged and backslide. It is good for a husband and wife to "bee" settled in their minds to make their marriage work even if other couples may be separating. I believe one reason there are so many marriage problems is that people have not settled it in their hearts: "I have a marriage vow and that settles it." You need to "bee" settled concerning what is right or wrong. Then, when you are tempted, you will know what to do. People who choose to "bee" settled are stable and steadfast. They are not easily shaken when something goes wrong. They don't go into a panic if they lose their job. You can face the future in victory because you are settled in what you believe and know what the will of God is for your life. "Bee" settled in God's Word. This "bee" will never leave a painful sting.

Bee Shaken

There is a time when you need to "bee" shaken. To "bee" shaken is to tremble or shudder at the evil around you. When one sees what is labeled as Christianity today, it is time to "bee" shaken. I was reading, recently, where some professor spoke out against the Lord Jesus Christ in a blasphemous manner. He said, "We need to be aware that Jesus was human and made mistakes like the rest of us." You should "bee" shaken by such an ungodly statement. Obviously, this professor never met the Jesus Christ of the Bible. The Bible plainly declares, *"For we have not an high priest which cannot be touched with the feeling of our infirmities; but was in all points tempted like as we are, yet without sin"* (Hebrews 4:15). Yes, Jesus lived on earth as a human, but He never sinned.

You should "bee" shaken when the Word of the Lord brings correction. The Lord pays attention to those who can "bee" shaken and are ready to change, *"...to this man will I look, even to him that is poor and of a contrite spirit, and trembleth at my word"* (Isaiah 66:2). Learn to use this "bee" appropriately and it will never leave a painful sting.

"It's a good thing to fear if you fear the right thing."

Bee Silent

S ilence is a beautiful virtue when used correctly. The writer of Ecclesiastes wisely said there is, *"a time to keep silence, and a time to speak"* (Ecclesiastes 3:7). It takes wisdom to learn when to "bee" silent and when to speak. Not all statements or questions require an answer. We read in John 19:10 where Jesus refused to answer His accusers. Pilate asked Him, *"Speakest thou not unto me?"* Jesus knew this was the time to "bee" silent. It is important that you learn to do likewise. When you are accused (whether your accusers are right or wrong), it is often good to "bee" silent. Generally speaking, they are not looking for information that will benefit you but rather them. How often we could have saved ourselves from a lot of trouble if we had learned to "bee" silent. I am not promoting the "silent treatment" that has been used over the years where someone refuses to talk to a person for a week or so. I have never seen good come out of this kind of behavior. I am talking about holding your peace as written in Proverbs 11:12 *"...a man of understanding holdeth his peace."*

Once, I sat with a man who was trying to convince me that his unscriptural behavior was right. After a long speech of justifying himself, he waited for my response. I chose to "bee" silent. When he saw I wasn't planning to answer him, he also chose to "bee" silent. That was better than getting into an argument.

Habakkuk tells us there is a time to "bee" silent before the Lord. *"The LORD is in his holy temple: let all the earth keep silence before him"* (Habakkuk 2:20). When you come into the presence of the Lord, there is a time to speak and a time to "bee" silent. I believe the Lord will give you direction when to "bee" silent if you ask Him. It is good sometimes just to rest in His presence and let Him speak to your heart.

The writer of Ecclesiastes gives good instructions: "*Be not rash with thy mouth,*" he says, "*and let not thine heart be hasty to utter any thing before God: for God is in heaven, and thou upon earth: therefore let thy words be few*" (Ecclesiastes 5:2). It is important to learn when to speak and when to "bee" silent.

PASSING A STORY

If you hear a nasty story,
Be it false or true;
Would you pass it on to others
If the story was on you?

Bee Simple

O nce, after speaking at a meeting, an educated person came to me and said, "I never could understand that scripture, but to-night, you made it so simple that anyone could understand it." Some scholars have made the Word of God appear to be beyond the average human's understanding. The Word of God is not so sophisticated or overwhelming that it cannot be understood. *"But it shall be for those: the wayfaring men, though fools, shall not err therein"* (Isaiah 35:8). Jesus gave a surprising and disturbing message when He said, *"I thank thee, O Father, Lord of heaven and earth, because thou hast hid these things from the wise and prudent, and hast revealed them unto babes"* (Matthew 11:25). He will open the scriptures to the simple.

If you learn to "bee" simple instead of making things complicated, it is easier for others to receive directions from you. Some teachers, over the years, have been able to instruct their students in such a simple manner that the children could learn speedily. To "bee" simple can be a great benefit to the average person, so let's "bee" simple!

Bee Sincere

A sincere person has an honest heart. When they say, "I love you," they mean it. When they say, "Thank you," they mean it. When they say they appreciate that you came to visit them or that you listened to their problem, you know they are sincere. Years ago, I learned from an older gentleman the value of being sincere. He said you can train yourself to "bee" sincere and to speak words that have meaning and value.

People can usually discern between someone who is sincere or who is a phony, so learn to "bee" sincere. You may be at a workplace where you continually meet customers. Although you are not directly receiving the benefits, learn to say "Thank you" sincerely. After all, if it were not for those customers, you may not have a job. A minister who preaches a message from a sincere heart is much more powerful and effective than one who gives a message because of obligation and responsibility. You can train yourself to "bee" sincere and truly mean what you are saying. To "bee" sincere is a very valuable "bee."

Bee Skillful

To "bee" skillful is not necessarily a hereditary trait. To "bee" skillful is often the result of experience or training. You increase in your skills mainly because you desire to excel in an area. An artist may do a beautiful job painting a picture, but with desire to improve, he can become more skillful. You may need to increase your learning to become more skillful in an area of your life.

You can learn to "bee" skillful when studying and meditating upon the Word of God. II Timothy 2:15 instructs, "*Study to shew thyself approved unto God, a workman that needeth not to be ashamed, rightly dividing the word of truth.*" Learn to "bee" skillful in soul winning. By learning how to approach a person correctly, it may increase your opportunity to lead him to the Lord. Learn to "bee" skillful in your workplace. It is important not only to accomplish the job but to do it with excellence. When you learn to apply this "bee" to everything you do in life, you will be more productive. "Bee" skillful will never leave a painful sting.

To be successful:
think hard, work hard, keep guard.

Bee Slow

There are certain areas in life you should "bee" slow. Proverbs 18:13 explains why you need to "bee" slow. Here, the writer instructs, *"He that answereth a matter before he heareth it, it is folly and shame unto him."* If you answer a matter before you hear the full story, you could misinterpret what was said. That would be foolish, wouldn't it? Your words can do damage if you are careless and thoughtless in expressing your opinion. Even if something appears to be right, it could be wrong when you jump into conclusions. Many people have been hurt with words that leave unnecessary pain. You should learn to "bee" slow before you answer a matter. The Bible informs us to "bee" *"slow to speak"* (James 1:19). The latter part of this verse gives farther admonition to "bee" *"slow to wrath."* When you learn to "bee" slow to speak, you will "bee" slow to wrath. Proverbs 14:29 tells us: *"He that is slow to wrath is of great understanding."* Listen to the wise man's observation in Proverbs chapter 15 verse 18, *"A wrathful man stirreth up strife: but he that is slow to anger appeaseth strife."* There is a major difference between the temperament of these two men. When there is tension or strife, one stirs more contention while the other chooses to "bee" slow to anger.

Often it is good to "bee" slow in making decisions. A quick decision may be a lack of understanding and cost more than you are willing to pay. There have been people over the years who made hasty decisions and later regretted it. That is why you must "bee" slow in some of your planning and endeavors, but let us not forget that being too slow can also be detrimental. There is a time to "bee" slow; therefore, "bee" slow.

Bee Sociable

Everyone should learn how to "bee" sociable. To "bee" sociable is a clean, valuable and important part of Christian life. To "bee" sociable is to be characterized by a pleasant personality. A sociable person has an agreeable attitude, but does not agree with that which is wrong. It is important for you to "bee" sociable. To "bee" sociable is a choice. This characteristic is especially important in the area of marriage, as well as, in family relations.

Many people today will never meet the qualification to "bee" sociable. They excuse themselves by declaring they are too timid and shy. If this is the case for you, make a decision to "bee" sociable. Ask the Lord to help you become more sociable and friendly without being silly, blunt or foolish. It may take time to overcome your shyness, but if you persist, it will be very rewarding. At one time, I was extremely shy and timid, but being in the ministry, I knew I couldn't remain in that state of limitation. It wasn't easy to change, but it certainly did make life more enjoyable for myself, as well as others. Learn to "bee" sociable. This precious "bee" will indeed never leave a painful sting.

HUNG BY THE TONGUE

If you let bitter words
Come pouring from your tongue;
The moment that you do,
My brother, you are hung.

Bee Someone

If someone would help someone to become someone, that someone would "bee" someone that is someone. In that little play on words, I want you to know that everyone can "bee" someone. Instead of being a liability, be an asset. Instead of being late, be early. Turn your words of criticism into helpful words. Try to find the good in others. Turn your sadness into happiness. Instead of crying about all your troubles, start singing. Instead of hating, start to love. Instead of gossiping, be a peacemaker. Instead of being proud, be humble. Be what you always wanted to be deep down inside. You start by changing your thinking, *"Finally, brethren, whatsoever things are true, whatsoever things are honest, whatsoever things are just, whatsoever things are pure, whatsoever things are lovely, whatsoever things are of good report; if there be any virtue, and if there be any praise, think on these things"* (Philippians 4:8). Next, ask the Lord to help you make the changes in your life to "bee" someone He can use. Most people are hoping that someday they will become someone. "Bee" someone right now. You can begin right where you are to "bee" someone!

" The difference between a man of failure and a man of success—one brings failure to birth, the other births success. Train yourself to bring your visions and dreams to birth."

Bee Something

E very great man or woman in the world became great because they dared to "bee" something. They dared to try something others feared to try. They dared to "bee" something more than a failure. Many of them faced challenges that made them feel like quitting. They faced discouragements, backsets and some even faced failure. However, they chose to "bee" something, do something and to rise above their defeated contemporaries.

The angel of the Lord had to inform Gideon that he was something. He was identified as a mighty man of valor. After Gideon received that information, he chose to "bee" something for the Lord.

Jephthah chose to "bee" something and became another man mightily used of the Lord. Although he had been expelled from his father's house as an unsuitable person, the Lord was able to use him mightily to win the war for Israel: *"So Jephthah passed over unto the children of Ammon to fight against them; and the LORD delivered them into his hands."* (Judges 11:32) He relied on the Lord to help him win the battle.

The Lord is still looking for the inferior to make them superior to the ones who do not choose to "bee" something. Some associate this "bee" with ego, pride or a haughty spirit. This is not necessarily true. There are those who have chosen to "bee" something who were not proud, haughty nor filled with ego. They desired to be someone used by the Lord to help serve their fellowman. Go ahead, "bee" something, this "bee" will never leave a painful sting.

Bee Sound

Throughout the Scriptures, there are numerous verses instructing us to "bee" sound. Titus 1:13 tells us to *"be sound in the faith."* This is not fantasy, but the real thing—genuine faith. Faith that trusts God under all circumstances. Abraham had sound faith: *"He staggered not at the promise of God through unbelief; but was strong in faith, giving glory to God"* (Romans 4:20). Paul warns us to "bee" sound in doctrine. *"For the time will come,"* he says, *"when they will not endure sound doctrine"* (II Timothy 4:3). Sound doctrine is Biblical doctrine.

II Timothy 1:7 give the promise of a sound mind: *"For God hath not given us the spirit of fear; but of power, and of love, and of a sound mind."* You need to "bee" sound in your thinking. You need a sound mind to think right in this generation. When you think right, you will act right.

You need to "bee" sound in your words. II Timothy 1:13 instructs, *"Hold fast the form of sound words"* (II Timothy 1:13). Sound words are useful, meaningful and pleasant. Sound words are wholesome. They are safe. They are words that do not injure others. Sound words are free from slander and gossip. They are the kind of words spoken of in Colossians 4:6: *"Let your speech be alway with grace, seasoned with salt, that ye may know how ye ought to answer every man."* Sound words brings forth peace and blessing. "Bee" sound is flying everywhere, buzzing in the ears of all who will hear. So, "bee" sound in every area of life.

Bee Special

In the Old Testament, God chose a special group of people: *"For thou art an holy people unto the LORD thy God: the LORD thy God hath chosen thee to be a special people unto himself, above all people that are upon the face of the earth"* (Deuteronomy 7:6). These people were not just average, they were willing to go beyond the norm. Elijah was a man chosen to "bee" special. He was willing to pray for things that looked impossible because He trusted His God to answer. Look at King David. He was a special man. But not before he faced tests; not before God could prove him. Because of his total dependence on God, he was qualified to kill a fearsome giant who defied the armies of the living God. God proved him to be a mighty man even before he became king.

In preparation for the birth of the Messiah, God was looking for some special people. He found two individuals who were interceding for the redemption of Israel. He also found a man, full of the Holy Ghost, who would become the forerunner of the Lord Jesus Christ. Jesus later testified of this man, *"Verily I say unto you, Among them that are born of women there hath not risen a greater than John the Baptist"* (Matthew 11:11).

Today, God is looking for someone who will chose to "bee" special. A special person may need to prove himself to reach that position. God has given us a responsibility and duty in James 1:27: *"Pure religion and undefiled before God and the Father is this, To visit the fatherless and widows in their affliction, and to keep himself unspotted from the world."* Can you be trusted with that responsibility? Those who are chosen to "bee" special are true servants. Jesus spoke of these people in Matthew 25:35-36: *"For I was an hungred, and ye gave me meat: I was thirsty, and ye gave me drink: I was a stranger, and ye took me in: Naked, and ye clothed me: I was sick, and ye visited me: I was in prison, and ye came unto me."* These people did not even realize they had fulfilled such tasks. They were simply serving those around them. God has chosen us to "bee" special people. This "bee" will never leave a painful sting.

Bee Specific

W hen you pray, you should "bee" specific. Suppose someone went to a butcher shop and said to the meat cutter, "I need some meat."

"What kind of meat would you like to purchase?"

"Oh, I don't know. Just give me whatever you have."

"How much would you like?"

"It doesn't matter. Just give me some."

You would think that person was weird, wouldn't you? Yet, how many people pray in a similar manner? "Lord, I need a job."

"What kind of job do you want?"

"It doesn't matter."

You may end up with something you may not enjoy doing. Whatever you need from God, remember He is your Heavenly Father and desires you to "bee" specific. He says if you ask for bread, He will give you bread. If you ask for a fish, He'll give you a fish. If you ask for an egg, He'll give you an egg (Luke 11:11-12). In Mark 11:24, Jesus said to ask for what you desire. That means, "bee" specific. *"What things soever ye desire, when ye pray, believe that ye receive them, and ye shall have them."* To "bee" specific indicates you strongly desire for God to answer your request. Learn to "bee" specific. This "bee" will never leave a painful sting.

Bee Spiritual

Just how important is it to "bee" spiritual? Romans 8:6 explains, *"For to be carnally minded is death; but to be spiritually minded is life and peace."* The natural (carnal) mind cannot reach God. It cannot understand the things of God, *"Because the carnal mind is enmity against God"* (Romans 8:7). The carnal mind is hostile to the things of God and opposes them. The spiritual mind operates by faith while the carnal mind operates by reason. It is impossible for the carnal mind to fully understand the things of the Spirit.

We observe the carnal mind to the extreme when we see the evolutionist who tries to reason that the world came into being by a "big bang," even though the Bible clearly states, *"Through faith we understand that the worlds were framed by the word of God"* (Hebrews 11:3). A spiritually minded individual will not have a problem believing that God created heaven and earth. The spiritual man has the mind of Christ. He has been transformed by the blood of the Lord Jesus Christ. He has a relationship with God. He thinks God's thoughts. He meditates upon the Word of God instead of the latest television show or something that the carnal mind craves. The Psalmist said, *"As the hart panteth after the water brooks, so panteth my soul after thee, O God"* (Psalm 42:1). Listen to the gentle buzzing of "bee" spiritual. He will never leave a painful sting!

Bee Stable

In a world that is continually changing, it is easy to become unstable. If people do not chose to "bee" stable, they may change jobs as the seasons come and go. They live here a while and there a while. One time they are going to church and before long, they are offended and leave. One time they are testifying about what the Lord has done; the next time you meet them, they are mad at God. The Bible talks about people who are "*...carried about with every wind of doctrine...*" (Ephesians 4:14). They can't make up their minds what or who to believe.

Stable people are dependable. They can be trusted. That is why the Lord seeks for stable people to use in the ministry. They know what they believe and have a Biblical basis for that belief. Stable people help to stabilize others. They have stable lives, marriages and homes. They have well trained children. Stability is an important characteristic that you can possess. "Bee" stable. What a blessing!

"Worry and faith can't live in the same person. Worry drives out faith; faith drives out worry."

Bee Stayed

I n Isaiah 26:3, a wonderful promise is given to God's children: *"Thou wilt keep him in perfect peace, whose mind is stayed on thee: because he trusteth in thee."* Those who choose to "bee" stayed on the Lord are promised perfect peace. It would be good to rise from your bed in the morning and confess, "Today, my heart is stayed on the Lord. I will trust in Him whatever may come my way."

To "bee" stayed on the Lord gives stability. It keeps you from becoming disturbed when things go wrong. It keeps your eyes focused on the Lord instead of your problems. It keeps you from becoming double minded. When a person chooses to "bee" stayed on the Lord, he becomes strong in faith and strong in the ways of the Lord. He has power in prayer. He has reasons for having a joyful life. He is filled with praise. "Bee" stayed. What a wonderful "bee" to have operating in your life!

PRECIOUS MOMENTS

Remember, each minute is precious
For God alone has sent it.
The time you have wasted so foolish
Remember, it's you that spent it.

Bee Steadfast

In the world in which we find ourselves, it is important that we understand the value of steadfastness, to "bee" steadfast when things around are unstable. You need to "bee" steadfast in the things of God so you are not sidetracked by the strange doctrines that are among those who call themselves Christians. When you are steadfast, you are not changed from one thing to another quickly. You know where you are going and how to stand, even in times of tests and trials. *"Therefore, my beloved brethren, be ye stedfast, unmoveable, always abounding in the work of the Lord, forasmuch as ye know that your labour is not in vain in the Lord"* (I Corinthians 15:58). In this verse, notice the word *abounding*. Isn't it wonderful to abound in the work of the Lord? Isn't it wonderful to know that your labor is not in vain in the Lord? You have a glorious hope that helps you to "bee" steadfast and rejoice in the Lord, regardless of what takes place around you. You have the armor of God to "bee" steadfast and win every battle you face in life. Paul, in writing to the church of Ephesus, instructed them to put on the whole armor of God so they could "bee" steadfast in an evil time: *"Wherefore take unto you the whole armour of God, that ye may be able to withstand in the evil day, and having done all, to stand. Stand therefore..."* (Ephesians 6:13-14). What a declaration! What a comforting thought to "bee" steadfast knowing you are standing for something worthwhile. Beloved, it is time to make that important decision to "bee" steadfast all day, every day, until the end of your life. Hallelujah!

Bee Still

In the midst of the turmoil, confusion and pressures of life, it is good to set aside a time to relax and "bee" still. Too many people rush through life without listening to what the Lord has to say to them. "Bee" still and think about God. The Psalmist writes, *"Be still, and know that I am God"* (Psalm 46:10). "Bee" still and consider the greatness of God. He is sovereign. He is monarch and supreme above all. He is not one God among many, nor is He one among few. He is the one and only eternal, almighty, majestic God. He declares, *"I am the LORD, and there is none else, there is no God beside me"* (Isaiah 45:5). "Bee" still and let your whole spirit, soul and body rest in Him. He is your God. He cares about you!

Many of your problems in life would begin to fade from view if you would "bee" still and ponder the mighty acts of God. The Bible reminds us, *"Casting all your care upon him; for he careth for you"* (I Peter 5:7). "Bee" still and think on the precious promises of God. Constantly remind yourself that God is bigger than your problems. Here is a lovely scripture to meditate upon, *"But know that the LORD hath set apart him that is godly for himself: the LORD will hear when I call unto him. Stand in awe, and sin not: commune with your own heart upon your bed, and be still. Selah"* (Psalm 4:3-4). Sometimes, it is good to lay in bed and drink in the peaceful, sweet, quiet presence of God. "Bee" still and let Him commune with you. It is in those precious, quiet moments with the Master that you learn to know him better. You learn His likes and dislikes. You learn to be more like Him. You become closer to the heart of God. You understand where you have unintentionally said or did something that displeased Him. You find answers to your problems. What a blessing to experience the peace, rest and assurance that comes when you take time to "bee" still. Heaven becomes sweeter and earth becomes more heavenly. So, take time out of your busy schedule to "bee" still!

Bee Stopped

When I was a young boy, a flood destroyed a bridge. Someone standing nearby tried desperately to stop an oncoming car but to no avail. The driver didn't even slow down but plunged into the rushing waters. It remains a mystery why this driver didn't even slow down. He apparently didn't see the warning light that was trying to stop him. Because he couldn't "bee" stopped, it cost his life.

Another time, when we were away, floodwaters blocked us from returning home. Roads were closed at most places. I told my wife I knew of another road I believed we could take. We started down this back road and came to the brow of the hill. Suddenly, a dog ran out in front of us and began to bark frantically. When I turned to the right, the dog stood in front of the car. So I turned to the left, but he refused to let us pass. Then, the lights of the car showed something moving; there was several feet of water across the road in front of us. We often thanked the Lord for using that dog to stop us. After the incident, we never saw that dog again.

One time, Saul (Paul) set out on a mission that was against God's will. The Lord had to stop him as recorded in Acts 9:3-4: "*And as he journeyed, he came near Damascus: and suddenly there shined round about him a light from heaven: And he fell to the earth, and heard a voice saying unto him, Saul, Saul, why persecutest thou me?*" Balaam also had to "bee" stopped by the Lord. He saw the angel of the Lord standing with a drawn sword, "*And Balaam said unto the angel of the LORD, I have sinned; for I knew not that thou stoodest in the way against me: now therefore, if it displease thee, I will get me back again*" (Numbers 22:34). There are times along life's highway where the Lord may be trying to stop you from trouble, but unless you learn to heed "bee" stopped, you may have to suffer the sad consequences.

Bee Strengthened

It is one thing to desire to "bee" strengthened, but another to allow yourself to "bee" strengthened. It is hard for some to believe the Lord wants to strengthen them. From the pen of the Psalmist, we read, *"Be of good courage, and he shall strengthen your heart, all ye that hope in the LORD"* (Psalm 31:24). This is a promise to all who need the strength of the Lord in their lives.

Apparently, the Palmist experienced a sickness that bound him in bed because he wrote, *"The LORD will strengthen him upon the bed of languishing: thou wilt make all his bed in his sickness"* (Psalm 41:3). He knew he need to "bee" strengthened by the Lord. The strength of the Lord can keep you encouraged when you face a problem: *"My soul melteth for heaviness: strengthen thou me according unto thy word"* (Psalm 119:28). When I was a young man, I believed I was in a good state of health, but suddenly, my whole world changed. I had a major heart problem that kept me bedfast for many long months. When you are in a state of weakness, you are not capable of functioning properly. Regardless of why you may be in a weakened state, you are instructed to say, *"Let the weak say, I am strong"* (Joel 3:10). When the weak call themselves strong, they expect to "bee" strengthened. "Bee" strengthened; this is a wonderful "bee" to help you when the unexpected happens.

"To have faith in God is to have faith in yourself."

Bee Strong

W e are living in a time when the world needs to see strong men and women rise on the scene. Paul encouraged the Corinthians, *"quit you like men, be strong"* (I Corinthians 16:13). To live in these perilous times, we must "bee" strong. Men and women who choose to *"be strong in the Lord, and in the power of his might"* (Ephesians 6:10) will be victorious. They will overcome weakness. They will fight the battles of life and win. They will have the philosophy: "Why be weak when we can "bee" strong? Why lose when we can win? Why pout when we can shout?"

You can "bee" strong if you choose to "bee" strong. In Deuteronomy 31:6, Moses instructed the children of Israel, *"Be strong and of a good courage."* In verse 23 of that same chapter, he charged Joshua, *"Be strong and of a good courage: for thou shalt bring the children of Israel into the land which I sware unto them: and I will be with thee."* When Joshua was taking the place of Moses as commander over God's people, the Lord once again drilled the same message into him, *"Be strong and of a good courage"* (Joshua 1:6). In verse 9, the Lord asked, *"Have not I commanded thee? Be strong and of a good courage; be not afraid, neither be thou dismayed: for the LORD thy God is with thee whithersoever thou goest."* He knew Joshua had to "bee" strong as a leader over that vast group of people.

We need to "bee" strong and courageous as the people of God. The Lord expects us to "bee" strong. We need to stand up for the right. Our Heavenly Father needs leaders who refuse to compromise. That includes fathers, mothers, school teachers or anyone else in a leadership position. When Paul was writing to Timothy, he knew this church leader would have to exercise strong leadership qualities, so he wrote to him, *"Thou therefore, my son, be strong in the grace that is in Christ Jesus"* (II Timothy 2:1). We will never accomplish all we are to accomplish until we are ready to "bee" strong and empowered with the strength of the Lord. Therefore, "bee" strong.

Bee Subject

To "bee" subject is to be submissive. It remains a mystery to me why the average person finds it difficult to "bee" subject to those in authority. God ordained that everyone submit to law and order. The Bible says, *"Let every soul be subject unto the higher powers. For there is no power but of God: the powers that be are ordained of God"* (Romans 13:1). You are to "bee" subject to those in authority because they are ordained of God. In Paul's letter to Titus, he instructed him to teach the people, *"Put them in mind to be subject to principalities and powers, to obey magistrates, to be ready to every good work"* (Titus 3:1). Not only is it God's plan for you to "bee" subject to those over you, but it is the way of peace.

The Bible also commands to "bee" subject to your employer: *"Servants, be subject to your masters with all fear; not only to the good and gentle, but also to the froward"* (I Peter 2:18). You must not only "bee" subject to those who are easy to submit to, but also to those who may not treat you as desired. In I Peter 5:5, to "bee" subject to others the way God commands is an act of humility: *"Likewise, ye younger, submit yourselves unto the elder. Yea, all of you be subject one to another, and be clothed with humility: for God resisteth the proud, and giveth grace to the humble."* May the Lord help you to "bee" subject as outlined by the Scriptures. Thank God, He will give you grace to "bee" subject to this command

Bee Submissive

L earning to "bee" submissive is very important in the life of a Believer. You must first learn to submit to the authority of your parents. By submitting to them, it becomes much easier to submit to the Lord. When you learn to "bee" submissive, life is very rewarding. There is an exceeding great promise concerning submission found in James 4:7: *"Submit yourselves therefore to God. Resist the devil, and he will flee from you."* After you learn to submit to God, you have the authority to cause the devil to flee. Those who have never learned this vitally important lesson are missing out on the authority God has given against the powers of evil.

The Bible says in Colossians 3:18, *"Wives, submit yourselves unto your own husbands, as it is fit in the Lord."* The carnal mind may resist such a commandment, but it is still God's order in marriage. Although, the wife is instructed to submit, this doesn't mean a husband is never to submit to the desires of the wife. Years ago, my precious wife and I came across this scripture that has been such a blessing through the years: *"Submitting yourselves one to another in the fear of God"* (Ephesians 5:21).

Another verse that can prove to be a great blessing to those who choose to "bee" submissive is found in Hebrews 13:17: *"Obey them that have the rule over you, and submit yourselves: for they watch for your souls, as they that must give account, that they may do it with joy, and not with grief: for that is unprofitable for you."* Long before I became an overseer over numerous churches, I knew the importance of submitting to the authority over me. Now, as an overseer, our church leaders and I have learned to submit one to another. "Bee" submissive. This precious "bee" will never leave a painful sting!

Bee Successful

To "bee" successful starts in the mind. You begin to think success. That causes you to talk about success. Most people became successful in life because they refused to meditate, ponder and think about all that could cause them to become a failure. Every prosperous person had a desire to be successful. Every one of them had opportunities and situations that could have caused them to fail. They refused to ponder all the possibilities of failure. They began to see that nothing was impossible as long as they had faith. Jesus said, "...*For verily I say unto you, If ye have faith as a grain of mustard seed, ye shall say unto this mountain, Remove hence to yonder place; and it shall remove; and nothing shall be impossible unto you*" (Matthew 17:20).

To "bee" successful is a choice. Success comes in different ways to different people. The hymn writer, Fanny Crosby, was blind, but she was a very successful hymn writer. She refused to let her handicap destroy her usefulness. Millions of people have been blessed by her songs. Success comes to those who believe they can be successful, regardless of their weaknesses, handicaps and backsets. The Bible says, "*For a just man falleth seven times, and riseth up again*" (Proverbs 24:16). This just man did fall. In fact, he had seven backset experiences, but he was successful in overcoming. He rose up again.

Successful people have the same temptations, trials, tests, victories and defeats that all others have, but their attitude is different. They believe in success. They expect success to come their way. They befriend "bee" successful. This precious "bee" is still buzzing in the ears of those who are unsuccessful. If you failed and you failed and you failed, do like the just man—rise up again. "Bee" successful!

Bee Suitable

J esus gave the account of a wise man who found a suitable place to build his house: *"Therefore whosoever heareth these sayings of mine, and doeth them, I will liken him unto a wise man, which built his house upon a rock: And the rain descended, and the floods came, and the winds blew, and beat upon that house; and it fell not: for it was founded upon a rock"* (Matthew 7:24-25). In the next few verses, Jesus talks of another man who did not find a suitable place to build his house. Because this man chose to build his house upon the sand, *"the rain descended, and the floods came, and the winds blew, and beat upon that house; and it fell: and great was the fall of it"* (Verse 27).

If a farmer desires to grow certain crops, he must find a suitable tract of land. No matter how good the land, it would not "bee" suitable to raise oranges in Alaska. In your life, you may not "bee" suitable to be fruitful and productive. You may have chosen a route that was more pleasing to the flesh than to your Heavenly Father. You can change, today, and "bee" suitable and useful for your Heavenly Father: *"If a man therefore purge himself from these, he shall be a vessel unto honour, sanctified, and meet for the master's use, and prepared unto every good work"* (II Timothy 2:21). "Bee" suitable. This "bee" will never leave a painful sting!

Bee Sure

O ne thing is for sure, you need to "bee" sure! "Bee" sure to do the work you are called to do. "Bee" sure to keep your promises. Many have been disappointed because someone made a promise to them but never fulfilled it. "Bee" sure to keep your word. "Bee" sure you do what is right at all times.

Achan should have remembered and heeded the warning given by Moses years before, "*...be sure your sin will find you out*" (Numbers 32:23). He would not have fallen prey to the temptation to covet the "*...goodly Babylonish garment, and two hundred shekels of silver, and a wedge of gold of fifty shekels weight.*" When confronted for his sin, he confessed, "*...I coveted them, and took them*" (Joshua 7:21). When you are tempted to do wrong, listen to the warning buzz of "bee" sure. Heed his warning. Always "bee" sure to "bee" sure and you will avoid the painful sting of sin.

"I thought carefully what I should say and didn't say anything."

Bee Surrendered

B ee" surrendered! It will change your life. When you surrender to the Lord, you can be used by Him. The story of Saul (later called Paul) depicts a man of great determination, yet he was surrendered to the wrong lord. *"And Saul, yet breathing out threatenings and slaughter against the disciples of the Lord, went unto the high priest, And desired of him letters to Damascus to the synagogues, that if he found any of this way, whether they were men or women, he might bring them bound unto Jerusalem"* (Acts 9:1-2). Paul thought he was right. His zeal led him to destroy anything that was linked to Jesus. He desperately needed to "bee" surrendered to the Savior he was trying to destroy. With every intention to continue his mission, he travelled toward Damascus with authority in his hand. Soon—very soon—he was to come face to face with this Jesus he was fighting against. *"And as he journeyed, he came near Damascus: and suddenly there shined round about him a light from heaven: And he fell to the earth, and heard a voice saying unto him, Saul, Saul, why persecutest thou me? And he said, Who art thou, Lord? And the Lord said, I am Jesus whom thou persecutest: it is hard for thee to kick against the pricks. And he trembling and astonished said, Lord, what wilt thou have me to do? And the Lord said unto him, Arise, and go into the city, and it shall be told thee what thou must do"* (Verses 3-6). God, in His great mercy, looked beyond Saul and saw Paul. Who would have believed a man of this nature could be so mightily used of God? Saul had determined to end Christianity on the earth, but when he surrendered, he was forever changed. He began promoting the very gospel he had tried to destroy. Later, he was used by God to write much of the New Testament. When you choose to "bee" surrendered to what the Lord has called you to do, you can be useful in His kingdom.

Bee Swift

A long many of the main interstates in North America, you see signs directing you to fast food restaurants which focus on swift food preparation. This can be helpful when people are traveling and want a quick meal.

There are areas in life you need to "bee" swift. To "bee" swift is to be prompt or ready. Romans 12:11-13 counsels us to be *"Not slothful in business; fervent in spirit; serving the Lord; Rejoicing in hope; patient in tribulation; continuing instant in prayer; Distributing to the necessity of saints; given to hospitality."* You need to "bee" swift to do the work of the Lord. You should be ready at any moment to minister to others or pray for someone in need. Learn to "bee" swift when someone needs you. If you would learn to "bee" swift, you could accomplish much more in life. /*James 1:19 instructs, *"Wherefore, my beloved brethren, let every man be swift to hear, slow to speak, slow to wrath."* If you would "bee" swift to hear the voice of the Holy Spirit, you would be more considerate of others. "Bee" swift. This "bee" will never leave a painful sting.

"While some people are waiting for their ship to come in, their ship is leaving the dock."

Bee Sympathetic

J esus was moved with compassion and sympathy when he met Mary and Martha after the death of their brother, Lazarus. The Bible says, *"Jesus wept"* (John 11:35). Jesus was probably moved to tears because He realized that death could bring a great loss. He expressed much sympathy. There were others who came to comfort Martha and Mary, but only the Lord brought true comfort.

To "bee" sympathetic is very important in a Believer's life. Multitudes of people have suffered because of a sudden change in their lives. You need to "bee" sympathetic when tragedy strikes. You need to "bee" sympathetic when you hear someone has an incurable disease, a family is broken or a marriage is destroyed. To "bee" sympathetic is more than just showing pity. It is offering comfort and understanding to those who are affected by the tragedy. The Bible says, *"Rejoice with them that do rejoice, and weep with them that weep"* (Romans 12:15). Sometimes tears are necessary to help bring healing. "Bee" sympathetic. This "bee" will never leave a painful sting.

Bee Systematic

It is important to "bee" systematic. When you choose to "bee" systematic, your life will be more orderly. Paul said, "*Let all things be done decently and in order*" (I Corinthians 14:40). Systematic people keep things arranged properly in their mind and in their work place. To "bee" systematic is more than having a system. It is learning to work with the system, doing things properly and being organized. In the workplace, this is especially important.

I had a mechanic work on my car who, obviously, was not very systematic. He had a habit of forgetting where laid his tools. He would ask his employees to stop their work to help him find his tools before he could continue working on my car. If he had learned to "bee" systematic in returning each tool to its proper place, he would have completed his work faster. We all need to learn to "bee" systematic. It may save us from much wasted time.

"The unwise compromise."

Bee Tactful

The dictionary defines tactful as having a keen sense of what to do or say to keep good relations with others. "Bee" tactful is a very important "bee" in the area of relationship. Many relationships have been hindered or destroyed because someone failed to "bee" tactful. It is not often what you say, but how you say it, that causes trouble.

You need to "bee" tactful, even when someone comes against you. The book of Proverbs reminds us, *"A soft answer turneth away wrath: but grievous words stir up anger"* (Proverbs 15:1). Chosen words have a way of correcting wrong and bringing healing. "Bee" tactful is a very important "bee." Those who learn from this "bee" will understand that it will never leave a painful sting!

"A flattering tongue triggers caution in the wise."

Bee Tame

O ne of hardest things mankind has to manage is the tongue. James wrote some discouraging facts about the tongue: *"But the tongue can no man tame; it is an unruly evil, full of deadly poison"* (James 3:8). Many people live and die unable to tame their tongues. If they had listened to the familiar buzzing of "bee" tame, they could have learned to tame their tongue. It is true that no man can tame the tongue without determination and the help of the Lord. Many who were foul-mouthed victims of untamed tongues, later, had flaming testimonies how the Lord helped them tame their tongues. If you have been unsuccessful in taming your tongue, you can change now. The Lord is ready to help you as He has helped multitudes of others. Let "bee" tame gently warn you when you are on the verge of misusing your tongue. This "bee" will never leave a painful sting!

"A tongue is like a flame of fire;
if either warms or burns."

Bee Teachable

We are living among a society of people who are not teachable. They want to go their own way and are not willing to make changes. To "bee" teachable means you are open to be taught correctly. This does not mean you are gullible or open to all teaching. A teachable person is wise. He is ready to listen and learn but also wise enough not to be deceived or persuaded by unscriptural teaching.

When children enter school, they must be teachable. There are many valuable things in life they must learn. If they are not teachable, they won't learn them. Many frustrated teachers have testified that not all children are teachable or want to learn. Pastors have also found that not all church members are teachable. Some are more interested in fun than in learning the basic principles of life that will help them to become well established in the faith.

Even Jesus, the greatest Teacher who ever lived, was rejected by the high ranking church leaders in His day. They didn't like His message: *"And he taught daily in the temple. But the chief priests and the scribes and the chief of the people sought to destroy him"* (Luke 19:47). On the contrary, it was the followers of Christ who 1were open to learn. When they heard Jesus pray, they requested, *"Lord, teach us to pray,"* (Luke 11:1). They chose to "bee" teachable. You can gain much wisdom from others when you choose to "bee" teachable.

Bee Temperate

Y ou need to "bee" temperate in all things. I Corinthians 9:25 explains: *"And every man that striveth for the mastery is temperate in all things. Now they do it to obtain a corruptible crown; but we an incorruptible."* In the secular world, athletes exercise and discipline their bodies with the hopes of winning in their sport. You must learn to "bee" temperate and discipline your flesh in order to obtain spiritual goals. If you are not temperate, you will eventually miss out on the things of God and not reach the goal that is required.

To "bee" temperate is to have self restraint and stability. Paul instructed: *"That the aged men be sober, grave, temperate, sound in faith, in charity, in patience"* (Titus 2:2). Although Paul was directing this to the aged men, the same instruction applies to those who are young. People who do not have self control live in chaos and confusion.

Those who are temperate in all things are walking in victory with the Lord's blessing upon their lives. They are more confident and sound in their decisions. They keep their lives in line with the Word of God. A person who has learned this virtue will guard his whole life with temperance. "Bee" temperate is very precious and his buzz should be heeded by all people. This "bee" will never leave a painful sting.

Bee Tenderhearted

A tenderhearted person is a blessing. The harsh, snappy lifestyle that plagues the hardhearted is missing in the life of the tenderhearted. To "bee" tenderhearted, like any other characteristic, is a choice. "*And be ye kind one to another, tenderhearted, forgiving one another, even as God for Christ's sake hath forgiven you*" (Ephesians 4:32). In this verse, it is implied that a tenderhearted person is also one who is quick to forgive.

To "bee" tenderhearted is not only a characteristic you express toward others, but it is also something you show toward your animals. Proverbs 12:10 says, "*A righteous man regardeth the life of his beast: but the tender mercies of the wicked are cruel.*" A cruel person is cruel to both man and beast, but a tenderhearted person will be kind. When I was a young man, I visited a friend who owned livestock. When we went out to do the chores, he was so cruel to his livestock that I pitied them. When we came into the house, he gave his wife similar treatment. Perhaps, no one had ever taught him the value of being tenderhearted.

We need to "bee" tenderhearted to each other. Sometimes it is good to confess out loud with the mouth, "I will 'bee' tenderhearted toward those at home, at work, in my neighborhood and at church." That sweet "bee" will never leave a painful sting!

Bee Terrified

To "bee" terrified sounds like a ridiculous statement, but let me explain. We have a reason to "bee" terrified at the apostasy we see all around us. Recently, some university professors were trying to prove that the Bible was incorrect in what it says about Jesus. Although this was a secular university, I am terrified that some of our seminaries are training pastors and church leaders to question the integrity of the Word of God. Let's carry it just a little further. Even in some of the more fundamental churches, we hear such statements as, "The Lord didn't mean that," or, "That doesn't apply to us," or, "Since we are living in the dispensation of grace, we don't have to be subject to the laws and commandments."

I am terrified, deep within, when I see ministers of the gospel walking away from truth. The Bible says, *"And judgment is turned away backward, and justice standeth afar off: for truth is fallen in the street, and equity cannot enter"* (Isaiah 59:14). Beloved, it is time to "bee" terrified. I would like to encourage all my fellow pastors and church leaders, as well as all the laymen, to be sure we are listening to the right voices and hearing sound doctrine. To "bee" terrified has an important part in each of our lives.

"A dishonest preacher cannot preach the truth."

Bee Tested

B efore an invention is released, it must "bee" tested to make certain it will perform as planned. When the Lord wants some-one to do a special work for Him, He must test that person to prove they can be trusted with such a responsibility. After Abraham received the promised child he had waited so long for, he had to "bee" tested, *"And it came to pass after these things, that God did tempt Abraham, and said unto him, Abrham: and he said, Behold, here I am. And he said, Take now thy son, thine only son Isaac, whom thou lovest, and get thee into the land of Moriah; and offer him there for a burnt offering upon one of the mountains which I will tell thee of"*(Genesis 22:1-2). What a test! Yes, but what a man! Abraham's faith had reached such a dimension that he trusted the Lord through it all. We get a picture of this man's heart of faith from Hebrews 11:19: *"Accounting that God was able to raise him up, even from the dead; from whence also he received him in a fig-ure."* It may appear, at first sight, that no one can reach the place where they can "bee" tested as Abraham and remain faithful. Yet, we are promised in the Word, *"There hath no temptation taken you but such as is common to man: but God is faithful, who will not suf-fer you to be tempted above that ye are able; but will with the temp-tation also make a way to escape, that ye may be able to bear it"* (I Corinthians 10:13). The greater the work that God has called you to, the greater the tests you will face. Instead of becoming down-hearted, discouraged and depressed, exercise the same faith as Abraham. Determine that regardless of the testing and chastise-ment, you will learn your lessons and learn them well. You have that promise, *"Being confident of this very thing, that he which hath begun a good work in you will perform it until the day of Jesus Christ"* (Philippians 1:6). When you cleave to these promises, "bee" tested will never leave a painful sting.

Bee Thankful

To "bee" thankful is to be joyful. To be a thankful person, you must have a life of true "thanks living." Most people can write a list of things to "bee" thankful for on Thanksgiving Day, but "thanks living" is being thankful every day and in every way. I Thessalonians 5:18 says, *"In every thing give thanks: for this is the will of God in Christ Jesus concerning you."* You should give thanks to God in spite of bad things that happen. Even if you had nothing in this world and were destitute of food and clothing, you still should be thankful for salvation and that your name is written in the Lamb's Book of Life. If you are truly thankful and are willing to express that thanksgiving and gratitude to almighty God on a regular basis, you can expect Him to meet your every need.

To be truly thankful is to be free from murmuring and complaining and meditating upon lack and insecurity. True thanksgiving comes from the heart. Paul said, *"Rejoice in the Lord alway: and again I say, Rejoice"* (Philippians 4:4). You should "bee" thankful for all the blessings the Lord has bestowed upon you. Whether you sing, pray or do any other activity, you should be thankful. Psalm 100:4 says, *"Enter into his gates with thanksgiving, and into his courts with praise: be thankful unto him, and bless his name."*

I remember someone once saying he had nothing to "bee" thankful for. This man was asked if he had a wife. He said, "Yes."

"Does she love you?"

He answered, "Yes."

"Do you have children?"

"Yes."

"Do they love you?"

"Yes."

"Do you have friends?"

"Yes."

"Do they love you?"

"Yes." He then began to realize that he had more to "bee" thankful for than he had thought.

To "bee" thankful is a Christian attribute. To "bee" thankful is Scriptural. I believe if people would be more thankful for their spouse, they would have a better marriage. If people would "bee" thankful for their employer or employees, they would have a better relationship. If they would "bee" thankful for their church leaders, they would view them differently. They could pray for them more effectively. You should "bee" thankful for your neighbors, friends and fellowmen. "Bee" thankful for your food, raiment and shelter. "Bee" thankful for all the blessings God has given you. "Bee" thankful for the mercy, grace and goodness of God. Thanksgiving is a very important part of Christian living. Thanksgiving focuses your attention on the Lord instead of your troubles. It brings expectation. It gives hope and helps you develop a more meaningful and quality relationship with the Lord. By all means, "bee" thankful. This "bee" will never leave a painful sting.

Bee There

There are times when others need you to "bee" there for them. It may be your spouse or children need you to "bee" there to bring comfort or encouragement. There are people who desperately need your help. Someone may be dying who needs you to "bee" there. I remember being led by the Lord to visit a precious man. Little did I know the struggles he was facing. He said to me, "I'm dying, but I don't know if I'm saved." I had the blessed privilege of helping this man to understand what it means to be saved and prepared for Heaven. I don't know what would have happened to him if I had not chosen to "bee" there. When the Lord needs someone to "bee" there, could you say with Isaiah, *"Here am I; send me"* (Isaiah 6:8)?

In talking with a number of ministers across the United States, one of the concerns they have expressed to me was when it is time for services to start in their churches, most of the people are not there. Employers have complained, over the years, that their employees were often late for work. When people are late, they often become careless and unconcerned about other matters in life. You can get into a bad habit of being late everywhere you go, but you can change into the habit of arriving at your destination on time. Beloved, when it is time for you to be at church, "bee" there. When it is time for prayer meeting, "bee" there. When you have promised to meet someone at a certain time, "bee" there. When it is time to arrive at your job, "bee" there. As a Believer, you should put forth every effort to be on time. To "bee" there on time requires a plan. It's a choice. You can program yourself to be on time every day. It can be as easy to be early as it is to be late. Don't give up. If you fail, start over again until you can boldly say, "I'll 'bee' there," and mean it!

Bee Thirsty

Have you ever been so thirsty you longed for a cool, refreshing drink of water? As you thirst for refreshing water in the natural, you also need to thirst for the spiritual. To "bee" thirsty is to earnestly desire something to satisfy your deep longing. David wrote in Psalm 42:1, "*As the hart panteth after the water brooks, so panteth my soul after thee, O God.*" The word "*panteth*" indicates that he was extremely thirsty. In the next verse he adds, "*My soul thirsteth for God, for the living God: when shall I come and appear before God?*" (Verse 2). You must "bee" thirsty for the things of God before you will truly be satisfied. Jesus invites us to drink, "*If any man thirst, let him come unto me, and drink. He that believeth on me, as the scripture hath said, out of his belly shall flow rivers of living water*" (John 7:37-38). Earthly water only satisfies for a short time, but living waters satisfy the deep thirst of the soul. Like the woman at the well, you need to keep returning for natural water, but Jesus said the water He gives, "*shall be in him a well of water springing up into everlasting life*" (John 4:14). The more you drink from that water, the more it will flow out of you to bless others. Wouldn't it be great if everyone would be thirsty for the things of God and draw water from the presence of the Lord? Then, they could minister blessing and refreshment to those around them.

How do you obtain that thirst for God? By meditating upon His Word and praising and worshiping Him. Only when you choose to "bee" thirsty will you be satisfied with that wonderful water of life. What a precious "bee," to "bee" thirsty and seek after God.

Bee Thoughtful

Many are the injuries caused by a word or action by some thoughtless husband, wife, father, mother or friend. Before you say something jokingly about your spouse or children, "bee" thoughtful. Many husbands and wives injure each other in the public by some thoughtless word that never should have been uttered. Some people are not aware of how thoughtless they may be. The Bible warns that your words can bring life or death. Notice where the power is found: *"Death and life are in the power of the tongue: and they that love it shall eat the fruit thereof"* (Proverbs 18:21). It is good to examine your words before you utter them to see if they are thoughtless.

You need to "bee" thoughtful in the presence of someone who may be handicapped or unable to function like the average person. You should "bee" thoughtful to the elderly around you. Be considerate of how others may feel. A thoughtful act or deed can make a big difference in the life of someone. Analyze your behavior to see if you display thoughtfulness. Your friends appreciate those who are considerate and thoughtful. Choose to "bee" thoughtful at all times. This "bee" will never leave a painful sting.

"A pessimist is a pest."

Bee Tolerant

In your everyday life, you will meet people who may not agree with you. You need to "bee" tolerant toward them, even when you differ in opinions, beliefs or practices. Of course, there are some things which a child of God cannot tolerate. You must draw the line between right and wrong, good and evil.

Most of what causes trouble in the home, workplace and church is not a major ordeal but, *"the little foxes, that spoil the vines"* (Song of Solomon 2:15). Sometimes people have a tendency to become upset or irritated when something disturbs them, such as a child crying. Now, I'm not promoting children being out of control, but sometimes, you must learn to be more tolerant. I have known people who had major problems and were offended by things that should have only been minor because they had not learned to "bee" tolerant.

A husband and wife may have a difference of opinion concerning where to live or what kind of furniture to purchase for their home. This gives them an opportunity to "bee" tolerant toward each other while bringing their ideas together and discussing the matter to decide which way is best. When there is a lack of unity concerning a decision, praying together can often help the situation to be resolved quickly. Whenever possible, learn to "bee" tolerant! Then, this "bee" will never leave a painful sting.

Bee Total

To "bee" total is to be whole and complete. The Lord desires for you to be totally committed to Him. The church of the Laodiceans was not totally dedicated to the Lord. He was vexed by their lukewarm lifestyle. His response to such a state of "Christianity" revealed His displeasure: *"So then because thou art lukewarm, and neither cold nor hot, I will spue thee out of my mouth"* (Revelation 3:16). God desires for you to be complete in Him, to totally surrender to His will, plan and purpose. A partial commitment or partial Christianity won't pass the test. The Lord wants your total obedience. When you give Him your all, you will not object to the direction He leads. You must choose to "bee" total in every area of your life.

PERSEVERANCE

When the way is getting harder
And you are about to faint,
When you know you must press onward
but you feel you simply can't;
It is then you must take courage
Should the hour be getting late,
For it may be only moments
Till you enter heaven's gate.

Published by Christian Light Publications
© Copyright 1983 Daniel D. Rodes

Bee Touched

I t is important to "bee" touched. I am not talking about physical touch, but a sympathetic action toward others. You should "bee" touched with deep concern when someone is lost and not walking with the Lord. You should "bee" touched when others are suffering. Jesus is touched with our griefs and sorrows. The Hebrew writer informs us, *"For we have not an high priest which cannot be touched with the feeling of our infirmities; but was in all points tempted like as we are, yet without sin"* (Hebrews 4:15). "Bee" touched when others are going through hard tests in life. Job's friends were touched when they saw his misery, but they were not touched with the feelings of his infirmities. They ended up accusing Job of doing something wrong. You may not always understand what someone is facing, but if you will choose to "bee" touched with their problem, that "bee" will never leave a painful sting.

"What I can't do, the Lord can."

Bee Tough

To "bee" tough is to be strong, robust and hardy. Tough people stand in tough times. They are not weakened by opposition. When the going is rough, they choose to "bee" tough. You need to "bee" tough when facing temptation. You need to "bee" tough in your fight against wrong. Wrong is wrong and right is right. You need to be hard to influence when someone wants you to do evil. You should "bee" tough to convince to believe something wrong. I have told my fellow pastors on a number of occasions that they need the hide of a rhinoceros and the heart of a dove to pastor a church. In other words, when they face a tough situation, they must choose to "bee" tough enough to withstand that pressure and be victorious.

"Bee" tough on yourself when you feel like quitting. Make yourself get up and go! "Bee" tough when you feel like complaining. "Bee" tough when you are under pressure to make a decision too quickly. When a salesperson is trying to pressure you to buy his product, "bee" tough. To "bee" tough does not mean to be rude, difficult or stubborn. It simply means to stand your ground. A person can "bee" tough and still be gentle, kind, tenderhearted and easy to live with. To "bee" tough is a quality decision you should make. When you choose to "bee" tough, you will be hard to insult, injure or offend. Therefore, let us "bee" tough that we may be *"more than conquerors through him that loved us"* (Romans 8:37).

Bee Trained

Y ou need to "bee" trained what direction to take and what doctrines to believe. You need to "bee" trained in the Biblical way rather than the secular. One of my jobs here on this earth is to train people for the ministry as well as to train Christians how to fulfill their God-given calling upon this earth.

To "bee" trained may require retraining. You may need to train your thinking in a different direction than you once believed. Many Believers have been trained contrary to Biblical teaching. The traditional teaching in our seminaries and colleges has been the downfall in many churches. Pastors teach the traditions, doctrines and commandments of men based on their theological training and upbringing. For the most part, the congregations are unaware of the unscriptural bondage from this influence. Jesus warned this would make the Word of God of none effect. If you choose to "bee" trained according to the Word of God, this "bee" will never leave a painful sting.

"Learn to bring your ideas to birth."

Bee Transformed

To "bee" transformed means the form or appearance of something is completely changed. Romans 12:2 says, *"And be not conformed to this world: but be ye transformed by the renewing of your mind, that ye may prove what is that good, and acceptable, and perfect, will of God."* God desires for you to "bee" transformed by renewing your mind. You will not think or operate as before. To "bee" transformed will bring development and strength within your life. A person who is weak in an area can "bee" transformed and made strong.

You need to "bee" transformed to walk in the direction the Lord desires: *"Therefore it is no great thing if his ministers also be transformed as the ministers of righteousness; whose end shall be according to their works"* (II Corinthians 11:15). If you follow God's guidance, this "bee" will never leave a painful sting.

" Treat fear as you would a loaded gun."

Bee Translated

L ooking at a verse in Colossians brought to my remembrance the glorious translation the Lord performed in my life: *"Giving thanks unto the Father, which hath made us meet to be partakers of the inheritance of the saints in light: Who hath delivered us from the power of darkness, and hath translated us into the kingdom of his dear Son"* (Colossians 1:12-13). How wonderful it is to "bee" translated from the old life to the new. How much has changed since I have been delivered and set free.

When you fully surrender to the Lord, you will "bee" translated into the kingdom of God and set free from the old life. Everything will change: *"Therefore if any man be in Christ, he is a new creature: old things are passed away; behold, all things are become new"* (II Corinthians 5:17). You will act different, talk different and think different because you ARE different. You are translated from the hands of the enemy to the protection of heaven. There will be such a translation that others may think you are peculiar. Your hopelessness will "bee" translated to the glorious liberty of the children of God: *"Because the creature itself also shall be delivered from the bondage of corruption into the glorious liberty of the children of God"* (Romans 8:21). You will no longer yield to the pressure of temptations because you are led by the Spirit of God. Your weaknesses will become strengths. Fears will "bee" translated to faith, doubt to trust and tumult to peace. Your goals, visions and plans will change. Your focus will "bee" translated onto the Lord Jesus Christ instead of yourself. You will seek to win souls for the kingdom of God and bring them to the glorious liberty which you found. You will have a strong desire to help others instead of speaking against them. Through the grace of God, you will be able to forgive others more easily because God has cleansed, washed and forgiven your sins. If you have not been translated by the glorious power of the Lord Jesus Christ, then choose to "bee" translated by surrendering to the Lord. This "bee" will never leave a painful sting.

Bee Tried

When gold is tried in the fire, all the impurities are burned out and it becomes pure. Many of the patriarchs of yesteryear had to endure severe trials and affliction, but they realized great value laid in the time of testing and trying. The book of Hebrews gives a list of these champions of faith. Today, you also will "bee" tried. The Lord will sometimes put you through the furnace of fire to strengthen your faith or increase your usefulness. Although to "bee" tried is not desirable, it can be valuable in your life. *"If a man therefore purge himself from these, he shall be a vessel unto honour, sanctified, and meet for the master's use, and prepared unto every good work."* (II Timothy 2:21). If you could realize this time of proving is a benefit to your life in Christ, you would be less apt to object to such an experience. In I Peter 1:7, we are told why we must "bee" tried, *"That the trial of your faith, being much more precious than of gold that perisheth, though it be tried with fire, might be found unto praise and honour and glory at the appearing of Jesus Christ."* "Bee" tried. This "bee" will not leave a painful sting when you focus on the results.

"Constantly remind yourself God is bigger than your problems."

Bee Triumphant

To "bee" triumphant is to be successful and victorious. The difference between the average Believer and the triumphant Christian is choice. When you choose to "bee" triumphant, you enjoy victories over the enemy, whether that enemy is the devil or something tormenting you. There may be a weakness in your thinking, your behavior or your relationships. When you are triumphant, you overcome these weaknesses. Then, you have reason to celebrate and rejoice. You can shout victory at last.

I remember an individual who was overcome by drugs, alcohol and other addictions, but the Lord saved, redeemed and changed him. He became a new creature in Christ. This man was truly triumphant. He chose to "bee" triumphant instead of being defeated.

You can "bee" triumphant in every area of your life: "*Now thanks be unto God, which always causeth us to triumph in Christ, and maketh manifest the savour of his knowledge by us in every place*" (II Corinthians 2:14). This "bee" will never leave a painful sting.

"Hold your troubles to the promises of God's Word."

Bee Trusted

P aul was a man originally named Saul, but Saul had a bad reputation. He couldn't "bee" trusted. He had a zeal, but it was not
focused in the right direction. When God transformed this man, he
was changed from a murderer to a mighty man of God. Paul said of
himself: *"And I thank Christ Jesus our Lord, who hath enabled me,
for that he counted me faithful, putting me into the ministry; Who
was before a blasphemer, and a persecutor, and injurious: but I
obtained mercy, because I did it ignorantly in unbelief"* (I Timothy
1:12-13). This man, who later proved he could "bee" trusted, testified, *"For yourselves know how ye ought to follow us: for we behaved not ourselves disorderly among you; Neither did we eat any
man's bread for nought; but wrought with labour and travail night
and day, that we might not be chargeable to any of you: Not because we have not power, but to make ourselves an ensample unto
you to follow us"* (II Thessalonians 3:7-9). Paul could "bee" trusted
to bring the pure Gospel to the people. Oh, how we need ministers
who can "bee" trusted with the precious responsibility to preach the
true Gospel and be examples to the Believer.

Timothy was instructed, *"O Timothy, keep that which is committed
to thy trust, avoiding profane and vain babblings, and oppositions
of science falsely so called"* (I Timothy 6:20). I would like to encourage all my fellow ministers to handle the Word of God carefully and prayerfully. Not only ministers, but all people everywhere
should be trustworthy to spread the Gospel. Everyone should be
soul winners and carry the true, powerful, unadulterated Word of
God with them everywhere they go. We should hear the words spoken to Timothy ringing in our ears, *"O Timothy, keep that which is
committed to thy trust."* If everyone took that instruction to heart,
what a different world it would be in which we live! It's not too late
to change. You can "bee" trusted to be a witness of Jesus Christ
everywhere you go. Surely, "bee" trusted will never leave a painful
sting.

Bee Trustworthy

To "bee" trustworthy is to be dependable, reliable and worthy of trust. Many people have difficulty meeting this quality condition. One businessman said he couldn't find reliable, dependable employees. He could find people who wanted to work for him, but they were not trustworthy. They would show up to work late or not at all. To "bee" trustworthy is a choice. It is your responsibility, duty and privilege to "bee" trustworthy, whether you are the employee or employer.

The Lord said, *"For many are called, but few are chosen"* (Matthew 22:14). Why are they not chosen? Because they are not trustworthy. To "bee" trustworthy, you must meet certain conditions. You must not only be available, but able to fill every rank where you are placed in a trustworthy manner. Paul recognized that even a trustworthy person may have a tendency to lose some of that trustworthiness. Paul cautioned Timothy, *"O Timothy, keep that which is committed to thy trust, avoiding profane and vain babblings, and oppositions of science falsely so called"* (I Timothy 6:20).

"Bee" trustworthy is a wonderful bee. You will often hear his buzz—be dependable, be reliable, do what is right.

" Be the kind of employee you would like to hire if you were the employer."

Bee Understanding

How many times have you heard someone say, "I don't understand," or, "You don't understand?" A lack of understanding can be frustrating to both parties. Solomon prayed, *"Give therefore thy servant an understanding heart to judge thy people, that I may discern between good and bad: for who is able to judge this thy so great a people?"* (I Kings 3:9). His prayer pleased God and the Lord replied, *"Behold, I have done according to thy words: lo, I have given thee a wise and an understanding heart; so that there was none like thee before thee, neither after thee shall any arise like unto thee"* (I Kings 3:12). Solomon chose to "bee" understanding. When you have understanding, you have the necessary knowledge for the occasion. A builder may understand how to build a house or structure, but his knowledge may be limited for other construction projects.

A pastor needs to "bee" understanding with his people. This is especially true in times of tragedy or when someone has lost a loved one. Such loss is real. The right use of words and expressions of kindness and understanding is of utmost importance.

If husbands and wives could be more understanding with each other, there would be less marriage problems. An understanding heart has a listening ear toward those who are facing difficulties in life and have lost hope. "Bee" understanding toward others. This precious "bee" will never leave a painful sting.

Bee Undisturbed

Many things happen that can be disturbing and cause your faith to be shaken. You must learn in those areas to "bee" undisturbed. The writer of Proverbs said, "*In the fear of the LORD is strong confidence: and his children shall have a place of refuge*" (Proverbs 14:26). You can dwell in a safe, secure, peaceable habitation where you are undisturbed by the trouble around you: "*And my people shall dwell in a peaceable habitation, and in sure dwellings, and in quiet resting places*" (Isaiah 32:18). What a precious place to abide. Here, you can "bee" undisturbed when the storms of life are raging and you face an unknown future.

The apostles were great examples of those who chose to "bee" undisturbed. Notice how they responded to threats from the religious leaders of the day: "*And now, Lord, behold their threatenings: and grant unto thy servants, that with all boldness they may speak thy word*"(Acts 4:29). What peace and confidence they had in the Lord. That undisturbed nature did not change, even after they were beaten, "*And when they had called the apostles, and beaten them, they commanded that they should not speak in the name of Jesus, and let them go. And they departed from the presence of the council, rejoicing that they were counted worthy to suffer shame for his name*" (Acts 5:40-41). Even when Peter was scheduled to be executed, an angel had to wake him out of a deep sleep the night prior to his execution.

You can choose to "bee" undisturbed. With the help of the Lord, you can stand unshaken until the storms pass by. What a precious "bee" is "bee" undisturbed!

Bee Unified

T here is a verse in I Corinthians that describes unity: *"Now I beseech you, brethren, by the name of our Lord Jesus Christ, that ye all speak the same thing, and that there be no divisions among you; but that ye be perfectly joined together in the same mind and in the same judgment"* (I Corinthians 1:10). The secret to unity is having the same mind. Unity of this type will work in a home, business, church, organization or nation. The book of Psalms says: *"Behold, how good and how pleasant it is for brethren to dwell together in unity!"* (Psalm 133:1). I have watched our affiliate churches work together in unity for years. When our leaders meet together, along with their wives, there is beautiful unity. Although we had different upbringings and have different likes and dislikes, when it comes to spiritual matters, we are in unity.

Unity is pleasant and creates a joyful atmosphere. Unity brings power and victory that division can never produce. If there is less than 100% unity, it can cause a blight that will destroy the work. No matter how beautiful a field of vegetables appears, if blight invades them, they are soon destroyed. People who are unified do not allow division to enter. They are strong and accomplish things that would otherwise have been impossible.

A perfect example of how to "bee" unified is illustrated by the Father, Son and Holy Ghost. There is never division between the Trinity. There is never division between the angels and other ministering spirits. They are perfectly joined together. By observing these examples, you will understand the value of true unity and learn how to "bee" unified. "Bee" unified. This "bee" will never leave a painful sting!

Bee Unique

To "bee" unique means to be highly unusual, extraordinary and rare; however, it does not mean you must be an oddball. To "bee" unique means you are different from the average, downtrodden, defeated person. The reason you are highly unusual is because you are not sitting around in self-pity nor bearing a chip on your shoulder. Instead, you are zealous to accomplish great things for the Lord. Titus 2:14 says, *"Who gave himself for us, that he might redeem us from all iniquity, and purify unto himself a peculiar people, zealous of good works."*

Those who choose to "bee" unique are extraordinary because they have high moral standards. Unclean jokes, vulgar talking and wickedness are not a part of their lives. They have clean minds and pure hearts. They have parted ways with their old buddies because they have become new creatures in Christ Jesus. Their hearts are no longer perverted but are now right with God.

Don't be ashamed if you are identified as unique. When my old buddies saw a change in me, they called me "preacher." They were actually accusing me of a "better-than-thou" attitude, but I was not offended for I knew I was called to be a preacher one day. The Lord is seeking for people who are willing to "bee" unique, so don't be offended if you are classified as unique. It is better to "bee" unique than to be a part of this sin-cursed world.

Bee Unmovable

I Corinthians 15:58 stresses the importance of being unmovable, *"Therefore, my beloved brethren, be ye stedfast, unmoveable, always abounding in the work of the Lord, forasmuch as ye know that your labour is not in vain in the Lord."* When you are unmovable, you are unchanging. You are firmly fixed in your decisions. You are serving the Lord with no intention to fall. You are not stubborn, but stable.

An employer can trust workers who are unmovable because they keep their minds focused on the job before them. Those who are unmovable in marriage will remain firm in the decision to stay faithful to their spouse. They will not allow anything to separate their marriage.

The Psalmist made a firm decision to "bee" unmovable. He said, *"I have set the LORD always before me: because he is at my right hand, I shall not be moved"* (Psalm 16:8). Make a similar declaration that you will not allow anything to sidetrack you from serving the Lord. "Bee" unmovable. This "bee" will never leave a painful sting if you use it correctly.

"Fear is afraid of faith.
If you don't weaken fear with faith, fear will weaken you."

Bee Unstoppable

What would it take to stop you? What would it take for you to give up and quit? We all face situations in life when it appears disaster is inevitable. It looks like the end. It looks like we are complete failures. Then, "bee" unstoppable begins to buzz in our ears telling us not to quit. Paul was a man who chose to "bee" unstoppable. After he was stoned and left for dead, he rose up and continued his ministry. He rejoiced in the midst of persecution and declared, *"Great is my boldness of speech toward you, great is my glorying of you: I am filled with comfort, I am exceeding joyful in all our tribulation"* (II Corinthians 7:4). He was unstoppable.

There is a winning side to every test, every trial, every circumstance. A winner motivates himself during difficult situations because he has learned to heed "bee" unstoppable. This "bee" reminds him that no matter how rough and tough life has become, there is always a solution. You should "bee" unstoppable. There should be no thought of backsliding in your heart. When you choose to "bee" unstoppable in obeying the commandments of the Lord, this "bee" will never leave a painful sting.

Bee Upright

When you study the Scriptures, you will notice people in the Bible were upright. In I Samuel 29:6, Achish recognized David as being an upright man. Job 1:1 says that Job was an upright man. These men did not automatically become upright; they chose to "bee" upright. God expects you to be downright, upright! To "bee" upright means to be just, straight, doing things right. This world needs more people who will choose to "bee" upright. Leaders need to "bee" upright, displaying true righteousness and holiness. Our churches need more upright people in them. The Heavenly Father is looking for upright people, so, "bee" upright. This "bee" will never leave a painful sting.

WALKING AND TALKING WITH JESUS

How would you feel some morning
If you walked along the way
With a special friend or neighbor
With not a thing to say?

Some people claim they love the Lord
It must be rather slim
For if they love Him from the heart
They seldom talk with Him.

Bee Useable

To "bee" useable, you must be trustworthy and responsible. You must be dependable to accomplish the work assigned to you. To "bee" useable, you need a determination not to quit when the way is hard.

David became one of the greatest kings ever to reign over a dominion because he was useable. He trusted in the Lord and not his position. God could use David because He was a man after His own heart.

To "bee" useable requires preparation. Before a woodsman uses his ax, he sharpens it to make it useable. A logger makes sure his chainsaw blade is sharp and ready to "bee" useable. Corporations are looking for useable personnel who are dedicated to the work ahead of them. God is looking for those who will "bee" useable in His work. If you desire to "bee" useable in the work of the Lord, you must be committed. Surrender and dedicate your life completely to the Lord. "Bee" useable. This "bee" will never leave a painful sting.

Bee Useful

Paul wanted to "bee" useful to the Lord. At times, he was gripped with fear of not being useful as he explained to the Corinthians, *"But I keep under my body, and bring it into subjection: lest that by any means, when I have preached to others, I myself should be a castaway"* (I Corinthians 9:27). What a disaster if he would have become an outcast or a castaway because he was no longer useful to the Lord. He disciplined himself to help him remain useful. He took control of his mind, will and emotions. Although he faced some of the most difficult trials in life, he overcame every obstacle and hindrance with a shout of victory.

If you are struggling (as many are), wanting to know why the Lord does not use you, ask the Lord plainly to reveal the cause. Pray and seek his face with an honest heart. Tell Him that you want to "bee" useful in His Kingdom. Make the necessary changes to "bee" useful to the Lord. This "bee" will never leave a painful sting.

"A job that is not well done is not done."

Bee Valiant

With faith and confidence, the Psalmist proclaimed, "*Through God we shall do valiantly: for he it is that shall tread down our enemies*" (Psalm 108:13). Notice, the Psalmist didn't say we can "bee" valiant in our own strength nor our own power and might; but through our awesome, mighty, sovereign God, we can bring down our enemies. We must let the Lord fight our battles. It is our great God who will cause us to "bee" valiant.

Jehoshaphat chose to "bee" valiant when he was facing a great multitude in battle. He felt helpless, but the Lord answered his prayer for help, "*Thus saith the LORD unto you, Be not afraid nor dismayed by reason of this great multitude; for the battle is not yours, but God's*" (II Chronicles 20:15). What a timely message! Jehoshaphat could "bee" valiant, know that God would fight for him.

David chose to "bee" valiant when he faced Goliath. He shouted, "*for the battle is the LORD'S, and he will give you into our hands*" (I Samuel 17:47). When you face your Goliath, "bee" valiant as a soldier marching to the battle, "*And having done all, to stand. Stand therefore*" (Ephesians 6:13-14). Beloved, you will face battles in life, but remember, your Captain will fight for you. He will give you the valor, strength, and might "*to quench all the fiery darts of the wicked*" (Ephesians 6:16). He promised, "*Resist the devil, and he will flee from you*" (James 4:7). "Bee" valiant—the Lord is on your side. When He is fighting for you, you will be a winner! "Bee" valiant will never leave a painful sting.

Bee Vexed

There are times in life when you should "bee" vexed, especially when you see the sin and evil in this world. II Peter 2:7 reveals that Lot was vexed by the sin within his own hometown of Sodom and Gomorrha. Peter says God *"delivered just Lot, vexed with the filthy conversation of the wicked."* Verse eight records why he was vexed, *"For that righteous man dwelling among them, in seeing and hearing, vexed his righteous soul from day to day with their unlawful deeds."* Only the righteous will "bee" vexed with the unrighteous and evil deeds of the wicked.

You should "bee" vexed by the apostasy that is prevalent on every hand. You should "bee" vexed by the deception that is accepted as Christianity. Paul warned, *"Let no man deceive you by any means: for that day shall not come, except there come a falling away first, and that man of sin be revealed, the son of perdition"* (II Thessalonians 2:3). When you are vexed by unrighteousness, this "bee" will never leave a painful sting.

"Even the devil believes there is a God. Watch out fools!"

Bee Victorious

N o matter how rough and tough life may seem, you can "bee" victorious. Obstacles won't stop a victorious person. Failure won't stop him. Defeat won't stop him. He will declare with Paul, *"Nay, in all these things we are more than conquerors through him that loved us"* (Romans 8:37). In Jesus, there is no failure or permanent defeat. Setbacks will only be temporary if you are determined to *"Fight the good fight of faith"* (I Timothy 6:12). If you keep on keeping on when it appears all hope is lost, you can "bee" victorious.

Some of the greatest Christian businessmen in the world, at one time, were on the verge of failure but they wouldn't quit. Some of the greatest ministers of the gospel experienced backsets and failures, but they refused to quit. Some of the great patriarchs in the Bible made mistakes but rose up to "bee" victorious. You may not be intellectual or highly educated, but you can "bee" victorious, both in the natural and in the spiritual. Keep your eye on the goal and your heart fixed on God. Say with Paul, *"I press toward the mark for the prize of the high calling of God in Christ Jesus"* (Philippians 3:14). Nothing could stop Paul, so don't let anything stop you. "Bee" victorious. This "bee" will never leave a painful sting.

Bee Vigilant

To "bee" vigilant is to be awake and watchful lest you be caught off guard. If you choose to "bee" vigilant, it will help protect you when the devil sends out his forces. *"Be sober, be vigilant,"* writes Peter, *"because your adversary the devil, as a roaring lion, walketh about, seeking whom he may devour"* (I Peter 5:8). That's a good reason to "bee" vigilant, isn't it? The enemy may appear as a roaring lion, but he can never stand before the Lion of Judah (Revelation 5:5).

To "bee" vigilant, you need to be armed with the whole armor of God, *"Wherefore take unto you the whole armour of God, that ye may be able to withstand in the evil day, and having done all, to stand"* (Ephesians 6:13). You should "bee" vigilant. You must "bee" vigilant. You can "bee" vigilant because you are on the winning side! What victories can be won when you chose to "bee" vigilant and become a part of the mighty army of the Lord! If everyone works together to "bee" vigilant, this "bee" will never leave a painful sting.

"Never keep company with fear."

Bee Violent

O ne day, Jesus told His followers, *"And from the days of John the Baptist until now the kingdom of heaven suffereth violence, and the violent take it by force"* (Matthew 11:12). When Jesus said, *"the violent take it by force,"* He wasn't thinking of timid, childish cowards. He was talking about men—real men, strong men, able men, uncompromising men, daring men. Men who chose to "bee" violent when the cowards fled. Men who were determined to "bee" violent and stay in the battle until victory was won. It is time for the people of God to "bee" violent and militant. War is raging. The devil must know you are not on his side and never will be. Only those who decide to "bee" violent in the battles of life will triumph in the end.

There may be times in life when you need to "bee" violent in prayer. King David prayed, *"Plead my cause, O LORD, with them that strive with me: fight against them that fight against me"* (Psalm 35:1). Those who are violent will press on in the midst of hardship and trying times. Have a goal in mind to "bee" violent until the kingdom of heaven no longer suffers violence. If there was ever a time the church needs to "bee" violent, it is now. What a powerful "bee" is "bee" violent. You must "bee" violent lest the evil "bees" leave a painful sting!

Bee Wanted

O ne of the definitions for wanted is to be needed. Someone may need you. The Lord wants well-mannered, godly, stable people to do work for Him. He is not looking for someone with intellect or special gifts as much as He wants a dependable, reliable worker. In Isaiah 59:16, He wanted an intercessor: *"And he saw that there was no man, and wondered that there was no intercessor...."* Would you be available if the Lord wanted you to be an intercessor?

I know of nothing more exciting than to "bee" wanted by the Lord to do something. As a young boy, I knew I had a call on my life to preach the gospel, yet I continually wondered, "Why would the Lord want me? After all, I'm just a farm boy. I'm not the kind of Christian that would 'bee' wanted." If you feel unable to fulfill the work assigned to you, the Lord can help to change you. He can bring you into a position where you are wanted and useable. "Bee" wanted. This "bee" will never leave a painful sting.

"If you don't pursue it you won't do it."

Bee Wary

To "bee" wary means to exercise caution; to guard what you see and hear. You need to "bee" wary of the person who is critical of other races, nations or people. "Bee" wary of a person who is quick to judge another or who justifies himself for his own wrongdoing. "Bee" wary when someone tries to make you suspicious of a Christian brother or sister. Their gossip may appear to be true, but upon investigation you may find it isn't all truth. Proverbs 18:8 warns, *"The words of a talebearer are as wounds, and they go down into the innermost parts of the belly."* Many have been misinformed by tattlers who spread gossip and questionable tales.

Let's befriend, "bee" wary but not "bee" suspicious. There is a difference between these two "bees." "Bee" wary helps you to be cautious while "bee" suspicious causes you to become judgmental. If you learn to heed the buzzing of "bee" wary, you can save yourself from many future problems. Then, "bee" wary will never leave a painful sting.

" Out of the water deep
Jonah went to sleep
Became dinner for a fish
Which vomited up his dish."

Bee Watchful

I t is extremely important to "bee" watchful because we are living in a dangerous time. If you are not watchful, you may lose some of the things you hold dear in this life. You must "bee" watchful that you do not lose your faith in God, your desire to study God's Word or your desire to be in fellowship with the saints. In God's message to the church of Sardis, He said, "*Be watchful, and strengthen the things which remain, that are ready to die: for I have not found thy works perfect before God*" (Revelation 3:2). The church in Sardis needed to "bee" watchful and alert because some things were ready to die. There may be some things in your life that are ready to die. That is why you must "bee" watchful and defend yourself against any attack of the devil.

Jesus said, "*Watch and pray, that ye enter not into temptation: the spirit indeed is willing, but the flesh is weak*" (Matthew 26:41). If you are not watchful, you may fall in the hour of temptation. In I Corinthians 16:13, Paul admonished the people, "*Watch ye, stand fast in the faith, quit you like men, be strong.*" Another time, he said, "*Continue in prayer, and watch in the same with thanksgiving*" (Colossians 4:2). If you are not watchful, you may lose your desire to pray. Many well-meaning people thought they could stand but could not endure under pressure because they had not chosen to "bee" watchful.

Those who are married need to "bee" watchful lest satan should attack their homes. Fathers and mothers need to "bee" watchful to protect their children from the evil in this generation. To "bee" watchful can keep you from a lot of trouble. "Bee" watchful every day. In fact, there are three days in a year you should "bee" watchful: yesterday, today and tomorrow. This "bee" will never leave a painful sting.

Bee Wise

Y ears ago, an elderly man was sitting in a city park when he saw two teenage boys walking toward each other. When they met, the older boy rolled up his fist and shouted, "I dare you to hit me." The younger boy refused to respond and started to walk away. The oldest began to accuse, "You're a chicken."

The only reply he received was, "Well, whatever I am, I plan to stay that way."

At this, the elderly man called to the young fellow, "Come here. Why didn't you fight that boy when he challenged you?"

The young man replied, "I made a decision, one day, that I will never fight anyone."

Looking at him with a smile, the elderly gentleman said, "Young man, you made a wise decision. Hold to your commitment."

Job 32:9 says, *"Great men are not always wise."* That is why you must choose to "bee" wise. The book of Proverbs tells the sluggard to learn to "bee" wise from the ant, *"Go to the ant, thou sluggard; consider her ways, and be wise"* (Proverbs 6:6). What did this fee- ble little creature teach the sluggard? I think anyone could have un- derstood his lesson as he watched the hardworking ant busily carry- ing on his duties of life. Sometimes nature can teach certain lessons of wisdom that otherwise would be missed.

In Proverbs 19:20, Solomon described the importance of instruction to make one wise, *"Hear counsel, and receive instruction, that thou mayest be wise in thy latter end"* (Proverbs 19:20). Why did Solo- mon ask the Lord for wisdom? What motivated him to request a heart of understanding? The answer is rather simple—he made a choice. Not only did he choose to "bee" wise, but he also instructed others: "*He that walketh with wise men shall be wise*" (Proverbs 13:20). Any wise person will be careful of his associates and those who counsel and instruct him. Rehoboam rejected the counsel of the wise old men and turned to his peers for advice. Later, he suffered the consequences of that choice. Remember, Rehoboam was the son of Solomon, a man whom God empowered with supernatural wisdom. If Rehoboam would have chosen wisdom as his father, his life could have ended with success instead of failure. To "bee" wise and receive wise counsel is the right choice for everyone. "Bee" wise. This "bee" will never leave a painful sting.

LEARNING THE LESSON

I dare not sit and mourn the past
Nor would I seek to borrow,
From trouble's past, and fail the test
That I may meet tomorrow

Although I know that past is past,
It is not wrong to borrow
From yesterday what I have learned
To fit me for tomorrow.

Bee Withdrawn

O ften, when people become mentally distressed, they want to withdraw and be alone. This is dangerous and only makes matters worse. By stressing the importance to "bee" withdrawn, I am talking about a completely different subject. You need to learn to "bee" withdrawn from those who do not have Biblical standards in life. Evil days are upon us and you need to "bee" withdrawn from those who are not dedicated Believers. At the same time, you need to be respectful and not present yourself as superior to others. It is by the grace of God you are what you are.

It is good to "bee" withdrawn from those who have a slandering tongue, who talebear or separate friends. Proverbs 16:28 says, "*A froward man soweth strife: and a whisperer separateth chief friends.*" You need to "bee" withdrawn from those who mock and scorn the way of righteousness. It seems rather normal to hear people criticize and condemn those who stand for the Lord. They blame them for being in bondage, legalism or part of a cult. They may use some other degrading remarks to make them feel intimidated. You also need to "bee" withdrawn from people who are disrespectful and critical toward leadership. This is a weakness in many circles. People are not afraid to speak disrespectfully of national or church leaders. "Bee" withdrawn will spare you many heartaches and bad influences in the days ahead when you use this "bee" correctly. Then, this "bee" will never leave a painful sting.

Bee Witnesses

We need to "bee" witnesses for the Lord Jesus Christ. A witness is a person who has experienced true salvation. We are to represent the life, death and resurrection of the Lord to the world. Acts 2:32 instructs: *"This Jesus hath God raised up, whereof we all are witnesses."* Just before returning to the Father, Jesus assigned His followers a job of utmost importance, *"But ye shall receive power, after that the Holy Ghost is come upon you: and ye shall be witnesses unto me both in Jerusalem, and in all Judaea, and in Samaria, and unto the uttermost part of the earth"* (Acts 1:8). We cannot truly "bee" witnesses until we are filled with the Holy Spirit. The assignment is urgent: *"And this gospel of the kingdom shall be preached in all the world for a witness unto all nations; and then shall the end come"* (Matthew 24:14). So, lets "bee" witnesses on a continual basis. When we choose to "bee" witnesses for the Lord, this "bee" will never leave a painful sting.

"Truth does not need to defend itself."

Bee Worshipful

Perhaps one of the weaknesses in churches today is an understanding of how to "bee" worshipful. Many believe they know how to worship, but is it Biblical? Jesus spoke to the scribes and Pharisees, "*This people draweth nigh unto me with their mouth, and honoureth me with their lips; but their heart is far from me*" (Matthew 15:8). Are you truly worshipping the Lord from the heart? Are you worshipping in spirit and in truth? Jesus said, "*God is a Spirit: and they that worship him must worship him in spirit and in truth*" (John 4:24). Only an honest heart can truly "bee" worshipful.

Worshipful people are distinctly different from the average Believer. Their hearts are full of adoration and their lips are full of praise to the Lord for His awesome greatness. A body of Believers can be taught to "bee" worshipful. Through training, even young people can understand the value of true worship. Train yourself to "bee" worshipful. Surely, this "bee" will never leave a painful sting.

HOLY GROUND

Like old Moses, I have found
That I was treading Holy Ground;
Not by a burning bush, as such,
But where I walked was just as much
A hollowed spot; for where I trod
Was on the mountain top with God.

Bee Worthy

When the prodigal son returned to his father, he said, "*And am no more worthy to be called thy son: make me as one of thy hired servants*" (Luke 15:19). Because of his repentant heart, the father restored him as a son.

Without the Lord, we are all unworthy: "*For all have sinned, and come short of the glory of God*" (Romans 3:23). Through the cross of Calvary, the blood-washed saints of God become worthy. Revelation 3:4 reveals, "*Thou hast a few names even in Sardis which have not defiled their garments; and they shall walk with me in white: for they are worthy.*" What a precious promise—the Lord will clothe you with His righteous and cause you to "bee" worthy when you follow His ways and keep yourself from the filth of the world. It is not because of your greatness, but through His righteousness you can "bee" worthy.

Colossians 1:10 reveals how to "bee" worthy: "*That ye might walk worthy of the Lord unto all pleasing, being fruitful in every good work, and increasing in the knowledge of God.*" When you bring forth fruit in your life and increase in the knowledge of God, it causes you to "bee" worthy. "Bee" worthy to fulfill the calling God has placed on your life. "Bee" worthy as an employee in your workplace. "Bee" worthy of honor. This "bee" will never leave a painful sting

Bee Yoked

Years ago, I was preaching at a crusade in Honduras when a storm emerged. We were in a remote area and the only access was a bumpy dirt road. Due to the storm, the road turned to mud and was very slick and treacherous. On the way home, our driver tried to navigate through a mud hole. Unfortunately, the vehicle sunk into the mud. While we were contemplating what to do next, someone brought a yoke of oxen to pull us out. I marveled as I watched those oxen standing on their hind legs pulling with all their strength. What perfect harmony as those two oxen worked side by side to do a job. How they worked in unity still astounds me today. Wouldn't it be great if we, who love the Lord, would "bee" yoked together? We would be able to work with our brothers and sisters in great unity and help each other pull the load of life.

To "bee" yoked together in marriage is wonderful. I had the privilege of living with my wife for over 50 years before her decease. It was a pleasure to "bee" yoked with such a wonderful person; but it is even more precious to "bee" yoked together with the Lord Jesus Christ. Jesus invited his followers: *"Come unto me, all ye that labour and are heavy laden, and I will give you rest. Take my yoke upon you, and learn of me; for I am meek and lowly in heart: and ye shall find rest unto your souls. For my yoke is easy, and my burden is light"* (Matthew 11:28-30). He is inviting you to "bee" yoked to Him. He is your Leader. He is your Guide. Most importantly, He is your Heavenly Father who lovingly cares for you in every area of life. "Bee" yoked with the Lord Jesus Christ. This "bee" will, indeed, never leave a painful sting.

Bee Yourself

Everyone is different. We all have different interests, different likes and dislikes. Our maturity levels may differ, as well as our abilities and talents. Someone may supersede you in one area, but you supersede them in another. Don't try to be like someone else. Your talents, abilities and interests should be valuable to you. If you try to attract attention by mimicking someone else's abilities, it will not be genuine. Imitating them is unnatural to you because your gifts and callings may be altogether different. Paul warned against this in I Corinthians 12:15-18, *"If the foot shall say, Because I am not the hand, I am not of the body; is it therefore not of the body? And if the ear shall say, Because I am not the eye, I am not of the body; is it therefore not of the body? If the whole body were an eye, where were the hearing? If the whole were hearing, where were the smelling? But now hath God set the members every one of them in the body, as it hath pleased him."* If you try to be someone else, you will become frustrated and discouraged. You are not someone else; "bee" yourself. This "bee" will never leave a painful sting.

" God is not your problem;
He is your solution."

Bee Zealous

The Lord wants you to "bee" zealous to raise above the norm; to be remarkable; to be different. To "bee" zealous is to be devoted to a purpose and to have a fervent, enthusiastic outlook in life. Those who are zealous are not satisfied until they put forth the best. They are weaned from the mediocre, casual way of life. They have a plan, a purpose and a drive to accomplish something great for the Lord and mankind.

Apostle Paul was a zealous man. Nothing could stop him. Put him in prison and he writes the Gospel to the churches. Beat him with rods and he responds, *"I am filled with comfort, I am exceeding joyful in all our tribulation"* (II Corinthians 7:4).

The Lord is raising up a generation who will fulfill His plan and purpose for man. We need to "bee" zealous and become vessels God can use. Titus 2:14 tells us, *"Who gave himself for us, that he might redeem us from all iniquity, and purify unto himself a peculiar people, zealous of good works."* The Lord desires all of us to "bee" zealous of good works. To be a people who are ministering to the needs of others. A people who are different in the way they serve the Lord. Those who are zealous are not hypocrites, but real men and women of God. Those who choose to "bee" zealous can leave this world with a shout of victory, *"I have fought a good fight, I have finished my course, I have kept the faith."* Surely this "bee" will never leave a painful sting!

I'm A Victim Of His Grace

Daniel D. Rodes

Daniel D. Rodes
Harm. by Edith S. Witmer

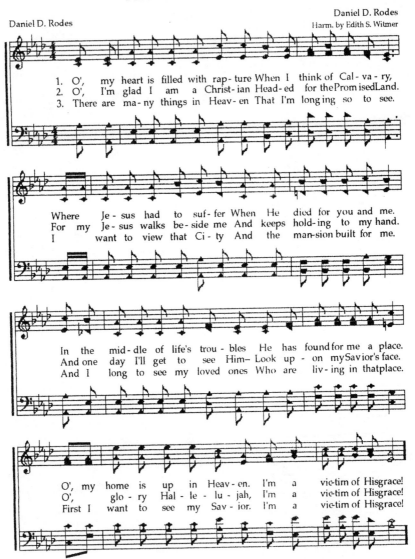

1. O', my heart is filled with rap-ture When I think of Cal-va-ry,
2. O', I'm glad I am a Christ-ian Head-ed for the Promised Land.
3. There are ma-ny things in Heav-en That I'm long ing so to see.

Where Je-sus had to suf-fer When He died for you and me.
For my Je-sus walks be-side me And keeps hold-ing to my hand.
I want to view that Ci-ty And the man-sion built for me.

In the mid-dle of life's trou-bles He has found for me a place.
And one day I'll get to see Him— Look up-on my Savior's face.
And I long to see my loved ones Who are liv-ing in that place.

O', my home is up in Heav-en. I'm a vic-tim of His grace!
O', glo-ry Hal-le-lu-jah, I'm a vic-tim of His grace!
First I want to see my Sav-ior. I'm a vic-tim of His grace!

O', glo - ry hal - le - lu - jah, I'm a vic - tim of His grace!

I'm re- deemed by His pow - er. He is now my hid - ing place.

Some - day I'm going to Heav - en And I'll see Him face to face.

O', glo - ry hal - le - lu - jah, I'm a vic - tim of His grace!

Our Friends All Wish We Were There

Daniel Rodes

Daniel Rodes

1. When loved ones are called to go ov - er Home To the glo - ri - ous land of the bliss,
2. So of - ten we sing what glo - ry will be When Je - sus our Sav - ior we see;
3. What fel - low-ship sweet when we all get up there With fam'lies u - nit - ed once more.

All sor - row shall cease, for all will be peace In a land that's far bet - ter than this.
When our voic - es raise, in an - thems of praise With such love and sweet har - mo - ny.
Sweet home com - ing day, all tears gone a - way That meet - ing we've all wait - ed for.

I'm home-sick for Heav - en where loved ones have gone, Who are safe in His won - der-ful care.

If we could but hear from our loved ones so dear, They'd all say they wish we were there.

Harmony by Edith S. Whitmer

Additional songs by Daniel Rodes are available upon request.

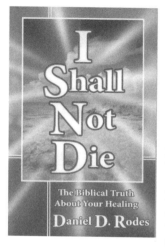

Whom should we believe? The doctors who say we only have days or weeks or months to live? Or God, Who has promised health and healing to all of those who love and serve Him?

Whom should we believe? The people around us who have given up hope for us and speak negatively about our condition and our prospects for recovery? Or should we believe the unchanging and ever present God Who promises us that we can live, whatever others may say?

In this book, *I Shall Not Die*, Daniel D. Rodes lays out God's plan of healing for His people and helps those who are sick to know how to find their way to health in God. He has been healed himself and firmly believes that you don't have to die!

Softcover 130 pages—Available for a donation of $8.00

- *Why is it that, no matter what we do, some of us never seem to get victory over sickness or personal problems?*

- *Is it possible that there could be a very simple key to having the kind of victory we all desire in our lives?*

Brother Daniel D. Rodes believes that if we obey the simple commands of the Bible to worship God in the ways He desires, victory will be ours. He declares: "I personally believe that you will not have nearly as many problems in life if your lifestyle is one of rejoicing. Praise and rejoicing can head off a lot of troubles that we otherwise mighty face.... Our focus has shifted from the difficulty to the Lord, and we are looking to Him who is able to hold us and carry us through the most difficult of times."

Softcover 192 pages—Available for a donation of $10.00

If you would like to order either of these books or obtain a list of other books available by Brother Daniel Rodes, contact:

Truth, Light & Life Ministries International
PO Box 70
Mt. Crawford, VA 22841
1-800-311-1277